The City Staged

The City Staged

Jacobean Comedy, 1603–1613

Theodore B. Leinwand

THE UNIVERSITY OF WISCONSIN PRESS

Published 1986

The University of Wisconsin Press
114 North Murray Street
Madison, Wisconsin 53715

The University of Wisconsin Press, Ltd.
1 Gower Street
London WC1E 6HA, England

First printing

Printed in the United States of America

For LC CIP information see the colophon

ISBN 0-299-10670-5

Contents

Acknowledgments

The University of Maryland General Research Board has supported my research with a grant in 1982, and a Book Subsidy Award in 1985. Librarians at the Folger Library and the Library of Congress, Washington, D.C. have been most kind and helpful to me. I am also grateful to Wendy Martin for her permission to reprint in Chapter 5 material which appeared originally in *Women's Studies*.

When I first began to work on this book, I was fortunate to have the counsel of Leo Braudy and Stephen Orgel. At that time, I was also able to turn to Jeffrey Skoblow for support and encouragement. At a later stage, I benefited from the advice of colleagues at the University of Maryland: Gary Hamilton, Sam Schoenbaum, and Joseph Wittreich read versions of the manuscript and shared with me their comments. Throughout this period, and throughout my professional career, I have turned to Annabel Patterson for encouragement and penetrating criticism that no one else could so readily muster. For generous doses of both, I am deeply grateful to her. During the past year, I have incurred a large debt to my superb copyeditor, Susan Tarcov, and to Peter Givler, formerly of the University of Wisconsin Press. I have also profited from the comments of Leah S. Marcus as well as two anonymous readers for the Press. It is a pleasure to add that this was also a year during which I could count on the friendship of John Auchard, Rose Ann and Neil Fraistat, and Beth and Bill Loiseaux.

Acknowledgments

Finally, I want to thank my parents, who have always been generous and timely supporters of my work. And I want to thank my wife, Joan Rachel Goldberg. Her love and understanding sustain me each day that we are together.

The City Staged

I

City Comedy and City Types

In a letter dated 28 March 1605, Samuel Calvert wrote that the plays of the day did not "forbear to present upon their Stage the whole Course of this present Time."[1] Although Calvert was not an advocate of the theater—he goes on to note the liberties and the "Absurdity" of contemporary productions—he points us in an important direction. The plays that I examine in the pages that follow are informed by the social and economic reality in which playwrights found themselves. Now this does not mean that we turn to these dramatizations for a mirror image of the time. London is not reflected on the stages and scaffolds. The merchants and usurers on the boards are not perfect indices to the merchants and moneylenders in the City. Surely the relationship between the theater and extratheatrical reality, at any moment in history, is more subtle than this. The theater adopts, and relies on, the same attitudes, traditions, and discourses that organize and articulate men's day-to-day lives. It stages contemporary perceptions and, frequently, interprets the beliefs that underpin these perceptions. But, as Jeffrey Sammons has written, "society . . . is likely to be far less coherent, less clearly patterned, and more centrifugal than any aesthetic representation it generates."[2] The theater articulates human hopes and fears, the same hopes and fears that grow out of men's and women's perceptions of their place in society and of their relations to others in that society. The plays considered here dramatize not the way things are in the City, or some objectively arrived at zeitgeist, so much as the ways Londoners typed one another. In contemporary pamphlets, proclamations, sermons, and ballads, prejudices and stereotypes serving particular interests were formulated and then repeated. Plays enacted, exaggerated, parodied, questioned, or endorsed what was already common coin.

What arrives on any stage has already passed through the filters of tradition. It will not do simply to argue that the gentry represent idleness or that a stage merchant symbolizes avarice or materialism. The stage merchant embodies one or another version of what the gentry, merchants' wives, preachers, and merchants themselves said he embodied. We cannot therefore limit our study to moral issues. By staging men's perceptions of one another, the theater locates its morality within a social or political context. Similarly, I do not want to make a case for a theater of convention, if this were to mean that clever gallants and tightfisted merchant fathers are mere reworkings of their New Comedy forbears. If the gallant is a source of sexual energy or wit, it is not simply because he is comedy's young hero. He is a gallant, he has (or has had) money, and it is said that he stalks merchants' wives and daughters; therefore he enters into a very specific and historical social economy. He is society's heir, as well as drama's. The conventions that give rise to him are constituted by a society "in order to sustain the shared typifications of relevant realities essential to ordered social life."[3] But the sharing is never universal, the typifications are always bound to desire, and one's idea of an ordered life is rarely disinterested.

Neither a reading of city comedies based purely on literary conventions, nor a reading whose touchstone is the satirical quality (and so the morality) of city comedy, is adequate. We must construct an analysis that takes seriously the denomination "city comedy." This is a book about comedy, about Jacobean comedy, and about a particular variety of Jacobean comedy which depends very obviously on its setting, the City. Although a literary form establishes the focus of this study, it turns out that once interpretation begins, it is not possible to give absolute priority to either the form or its extraliterary context. The City at once interprets and constitutes the comedy as the comedy represents and fashions the City. More specifically, the role of the merchant in London in the early 1600s and the role of the merchant in Jacobean city comedy inform one another. For the sake of analysis, we must begin with one or the other; however, it soon becomes clear that Londoners borrowed conventional dramatic types to characterize contemporary merchants, and that playwrights availed themselves of familiar stereotypes to shape their play merchants.[4]

The problems with an interpretation that neglects the social context of a genre like city comedy become clear when we examine a theoretical argument such as the one posed by Richard Levin in *New Readings vs. Old Plays.* Levin divides what he calls "ideas-of-the-time" readings into two varieties.[5] "In one of them the critic tries to ascertain how the ideas or attitudes which he finds in the plays are related to the mental climate of the period" (p. 148). There are, in effect, two airtight elements (for this variety of critic, at least): on one side is the already interpreted play; on the other, the mental climate which it reflects or modifies. This critic's reading of the contemporary intellectual climate does not influence his or her interpretation of the play because he has already interpreted the play. What Levin misses here is a sensitivity to the ways the play itself is a part of the intellectual movement(s) of the time, and the ways these ideas limit or put stresses on the working dramatist. The dramatist does not merely engage linguistic or dramatic forms; rather he turns to them because of the evaluations that such forms imply. Moreover, Levin fears that we tend to dethrone the artist, turning him into a "conduit" through which the ideas of the time pass "regardless of what he may do or not do in the play itself" (p. 161). Of course, to a considerable extent, the artist *is* a prisoner of his times, its vocabularies and its points of view. This does not mean that we can "deduce his meaning from the ideas of his time," but neither should we be asked to isolate a play, as "art," in some inviolable space.

Levin's second variety "does not treat the plays as independent data to be related to the ideas, but starts with the ideas and uses them to interpret the plays" (p. 148). He warns us against reading *King Lear* as an exemplum of a threatened Renaissance world picture, against judging Desdemona on the basis of her filial disobedience, and so on. These examples of foolish, purely deductive ideas-of-the-time readings deserve Levin's criticism. But behind Levin's censure we find a belief in a "felt experience of the play" that is the basis of his discussions. This experience is understood to be a category free of interpretation, unmediated and directly in touch with the reified art object—the play itself. He claims we are guilty as readers if we establish a Renaissance attitude "toward some aspect of life, and then [censure] the character for failing to measure up to it" (p. 161). Levin does not consider that the play may be participating in the establishment of attitudes or that the play interprets and is interpreted by them. According to Levin, the play, already interpreted (or engaged) through our direct experience of it, tells us about the ideas of the time. But such ideas and the plays are mutually constituting; we do not start with a definitive idea of the time any more than we start with a complete understanding of a play.

And so we come back to the felicity of the denomination "city comedy."[6] Social context informs genre, and genre, or dramatic form, impinges on history, thus organizing, ordering, and plotting the social conflict that is a constant outside the theater. Most city comedies take shape as romantic comedies subservient to intrigue. The romantic comedy moves toward the adjudication of struggle, but the intrigue, which stages conflict in order to reveal its sources and structure, is predominant. Whatever transcendence we may look toward will occur not on the stage, but in the audience. The theater enacts the roles in which we cast one another, and we, as spectators, may see our typecasting for what it is. We may even turn to the work of liberation: not the impossible release from role playing, but an increased sensitivity to the ways others see themselves, and to the ways they react because imprisoned by our gaze. When a spectator comes to see a stage gallant as a stage merchant can never see him (both are types, and at any one moment either may be typecasting the other, or both may be simultaneously victims and victimizers), he awakens to the tyranny of stereotyping. And when the exaggerated types that populate a city comedy's intrigues suggest the discrepancy between merchant-as-type and merchant as a bundle of flesh-and-blood particulars, the play challenges its audience's self-serving prejudices.

City comedies, plays staging the relations among merchants, gentry, and women in their various roles, flourished between 1603 and 1613. While I take note of nondramatic writings composed prior to and after these years to indicate the context for city comedy, I concentrate on the decade that witnessed the greatest concentration of city comedies on London's stages. City comedies of this period share more than a London setting, complete with shops, halls, and familiar streets. The plays I examine are intrigues and romances in which a particular configuration of the dramatic triangle formed by citizens, gallants, and wives, whores, widows, and maids is plotted. Most of these plays look critically at this triangular social formation: the playwrights do not unthinkingly champion one status group over another. Consequently, the jingoism that motivates the tedious plot of what is probably the earliest city comedy, William Haughton's *Englishmen for my Money* (1598), exempts it from remark in this volume. Haughton's uncritical endorsement of the careers of three thriftless English gallants, and his wearisome mockery of their rivals—three wealthy, foreign merchants—suggest that he is uninterested in either the conflict, or the sources of the conflict, that pitted one status group against another. It is considerably more rewarding to probe a play like *Michaelmas Term.* When Middleton takes up the prodigal-merchant-daughter triangle mechanically scripted by Haughton, the social origins of a conventional dramatic conflict are set in the foreground. I have also passed over a play that the Admiral's Men performed shortly after Haughton's play, *The Shoemaker's Holiday*, although Simon Eyre will be used as a basis of comparison. Glorification of citizen life in Dekker's play generates a fantasy that suppresses precisely the social tensions that characterize mature city comedies.

Status-group rivalry is also silenced in the anonymous play *The London Prodigal* (1603–5). At first glance, it would seem that a clever rethinking of city comedy's stereotypical characters is at work in this play. The superintending, benevolent figure here is not a member of the gentry but instead a disguised merchant and father. The prodigal gallant has been replaced by the prodigal son of the merchant. And the multiple marriage that ought to conclude the play is qualified when the remaining daughter opts for a virgin's life, leaving both the "gallant knight" and the Devonshire clothier to bachelorhood. Yet although it contains these provocative reversals, and does adumbrate the genre's paradigmatic social triangle, *The London Prodigal* eschews city comedy's acknowledgment of social conflict. This is but a prodigal-son tale which borrows city comedy's familiar characters. Because the playwright is concerned more with morality than with the polity, it makes no difference to him whether it is a young gallant or a merchant's young son who must reform. The play's competing suitors represent disparate social groups but their rivalry is based artificially on moral probity divorced from social status. The long-suffering Luce is the daughter of a gentleman with an estate in Kent; but her role as a patient Griselda has nothing to do with her class. In sum, *The London Prodigal* does not encourage the linkage between moral roles (prodigal, Griselda, benevolent disguised father) and social roles (gallant, maid, merchant) that characterizes mature city comedy.

Plays that unfold in and around London but are not marked by a self-conscious concern with status groups fall beyond the purview of this study. I include plays that are not neatly structured by the usual social triangle if they nonetheless render critically one or another particular type caught up in the urban social economy. Plays like *Epicoene, A Mad World, My Masters,* and *Your Five Gallants* are of this sort. I also include plays, such as *Ram Alley* and *The Dutch Courtesan,* in which instances of uncritical characterization call our attention to city comedy's customary exposure of conventional aspects of the genre's types. But plays like *The Shoemaker's Holiday,* the sentimental, moralizing *Green's Tu Quoque* (1611), or the much more complex *Bartholomew Fair* must await a further study of "London plays"—tragedies as well as comedies—that moves beyond the otherwise coherent genre "city comedy." The division of this book into chapters based on social and gender differences fits the genre's characters and plots well. That a play like *Bartholomew Fair* cannot be contained by this frame suggests that it is best read in another context.

My reading of Jacobean city comedy is in fact organized along lines which seem at first glance to have nothing to do with the theater. Merchant-citizens, gentleman-gallants, and wives, whores, widows, and maids represent gender or status groups. Furthermore, organizing a study on the basis of such groups splinters the readings of individual plays. I discuss historical merchants and their productions in the second chapter; in the third chapter, I turn to the draper Quomodo, in Middleton's *Michaelmas Term,* and his version of citizenship. By the fourth chapter, I arrive at Quomodo's gentle gull (Easy); and finally, in the fifth chapter, I reach Quomodo's wife. City comedy's dramatic triangle has its origin, perhaps, in the familiar plots of New Comedy; but the substance of city comedy, and its pertinence to its audience, are to be found in Jacobean London's interdependent gender and status groups. Merchants, gentry, citizens' wives and daughters were continually playing out roles, and conceiving of roles for others, in the streets and meeting places of London. It was only a short step to adapt formulations of contemporary roles, to emphasize or distort their contours, and then to "put them on" before their real authors, on the public and private stages of the city.

Perhaps the key word that allows us to bring together the social and dramatic dimensions is "role." The drama, pamphlets, letters and proclamations of the late sixteenth and early seventeenth centuries constitute an unceasing discussion of social roles: the role of the sovereign and that of the gentry as gentlemen or as gallants, the role (and so the status) of the newly wealthy merchant and that of the usurer, and every other conceivable role, from city wife to courtier. The actor playing out his scripted part on the boards was an epitome of multifarious role players improvising their performances and appearances in the *theatrum mundi*. The playbook was analogous to the plethora of instruction and advice manuals available to interested Elizabethans and Jacobeans. John Hoskyns' *Directions for Speech and Style* was a style book for young Inns of Court men, similar in its acknowledgment of self-conscious role playing to Hamlet's speech to the players; the mirrors for magistrates instructed the king in a part not unlike the role elaborated in the Tudor plays of political advice.[7] William Perkins' *A Treatise of the Vocations* insisted on the unwavering performance of a single social function, while humour theory distended role awareness to caricature; so too, Scott's *An Essay of Drapery* analyzed the merchant's part and Cleaver's *A Godlie Forme of Householde Government* mapped out courses in bourgeois domestic economy. City comedy may be thought of as the staging area upon which these already self-conscious urban roles are brought into sharp relief—but in neither arena (stage or city) can we ascertain an invariable definition of a particular role. The performance on the street, self-aware though it was and must always be, is too protean and too often compromised by unexpected pressure to reveal a clear and reliable shape or substance. The performance on the stage both parodies and refracts the actual social role: it develops a contemporary version of a role through stage conventions (the *senex* turns usurer, the *adolescens* or witty slave turns gallant) while it animates the dialectic between art and history, between stage usurer and Jacobean moneylender.[8]

This discourse of social roles both on and off the stage suggests a variety of relations between an often unspecifiable self and the enacted role of a given moment. At times, we want to ask whether a role or a repertory of roles has altogether replaced the self: when identity reifies, "a total identification of the individual with his socially assigned typifications" may result.[9] In *Discoveries*, Jonson notes that our lives are like plays, "wherein every man, forgetfull of himselfe, is in travaile with expression of another. Nay, wee so insist in imitating others, as wee cannot (when it is necessary) returne to our selves."[10] The articulation of a social role is also in the service of authority. The contours and potentialities of a given role indicate what the poet and preacher omits, as well as what he requires. By silencing a potentiality or nuance, the playwright both assumes and bows to authority. His decision to satirize or ignore the expected features of a role bespeaks a power that is in its turn limited by a perhaps greater authority, one that establishes terms for what the playwright himself may perceive or admit. Thus it is not wise to enshrine the author of this or that comical satire in the all-powerful role of a controlling moralist or ironist. The decision to punish Volpone but to spare Face indicates considerably more than increasing cynicism on the part of Jonson; both choices point also to *available* modes of characterization. Lovewit returns and Face immediately snaps to attention as Jeremy—another role, of course, but a role within the traditional, if currently debased, Jacobean hierarchy. Jonson and his stage surrogates offer their allegiance to Jacobean London's conservative status system. Playwrights often function as unconscious conduits for sentiments too "obvious" to be noticed explicitly by them or their contemporaries.

Perez Zagorin is one among many historians who have argued that Jacobean England was a status-conscious society: "it was status that conditioned men's social awareness; equally, it was status that provided the frame of political action."[11] A gentleman may have had close relations with a merchant, but each stood in a distinct place within the hierarchy of social orders. No matter how "secure and authoritative the merchant's position was among his fellow townsmen . . . his status in the general body politic was much lower and even somewhat contemptible to those above him."[12] And the "status ideology"[13] of the day is staged in city comedies. We see merchants as the gentry thought of merchants, we see gallants as citizens thought of gallants, and we see women as men depicted women. Citizens, gentry, and women are represented as obvious types. They are exaggerated, comic figures that call attention to the stereotypes that constitute "a merchant" or "a wife" outside the theater. They are not symbols for lechery or wantonness so much as social integers that gather to themselves contemporary prejudice. And they do not represent realistically the city merchant or gentleman nearly so much as they "mime the imprisonment of the public in its multiple social parts."[14]

Members of Jacobean London's various status groups expected their contemporaries to fill the roles specified by their status. Each role bespeaks a set of functions for individuals or classes, and the value of these functions in a particular community. "Value" in this instance is not intrinsic, or, as Hobbes writes, "absolute"; rather, it is a "thing dependant on the need and judgement of another."[15] And "community" is best understood in terms set out recently by Harry Berger, Jr.: "[community] refers to the more or less corporate, more or less institutional, structure of roles and relationships into which individual characters are cast and which they try to manipulate. That is, the community is a group of speakers placed in relation to each other by differences in gender and generation, of social rank and political status. . . . Their interactions are mediated by these roles, their attitudes and projects heavily influenced by the assumptions and expectations, the constraints and opportunities, that adhere to the roles."[16] The status groups in Perez Zagorin's account of Jacobean London resemble those Erving Goffman has identified in our time. Indeed, Goffman's work looks back to Hobbes, and it relies on the vocabulary that was later to inform Berger's understanding of "community." Goffman has written that a social role is "the enactment of rights and duties attached to a given status." He adds that "Society is organized on the principle that any individual who possesses certain social characteristics has a moral right to expect that others will value and treat him in an appropriate way. . . . In consequence, when an individual projects a definition of the situation and thereby makes an implicit or explicit claim to be a person of a particular kind, he automatically exerts a moral demand upon others, obliging them to value and treat him in the manner that persons of his kind have a right to expect." [17] Jacobean London was the scene of many failures to meet such demands and obligations. Confusion and willfulness marked the encounters of rising and falling gentry, greater and lesser merchants, newly apprenticed sons of landed gentry, and overconfident courtiers.

City comedy's comic staging of social roles permits audiences to question their adequacy. The plays reveal the points at which self-interest determines the demands made on a role. They conjure up a society that has no more obvious roots than contemporary prejudice. Writing of "Shakespearian performance," Harry Berger, Jr., argues that Shakespeare's plays "accommodate" prejudice, but "nevertheless [invest their] charismatic representation of a world with verbal traces of the hidden processes by which the communities of the play and the theater join in producing the world. These traces tease us by suggesting the presence of a loophole, or peephole, through which we may target the triumphant fiction our applause ratified." [18] City comedies depend less on verbal traces than on exaggerated characterizations to suggest the presence of loopholes. But like Shakespeare's plays, city comedies are produced in a theater that is shaped by the city and that, in its turn, crystallizes the attitudes *of* city dwellers *for* city dwellers. These plays embody men's attitudes, not merely their vices. Better still, these plays do not mirror attitudes; they participate in them, and in men's imaginations. They remind us that "there is no literature . . . that is not, in some measure, the joint production of author and public."[19] To laugh at the foolishness figured in one of city comedy's merchants, gallants, or wives would have been to laugh at attitudes that were already stale and inadequate. Louis Adrian Montrose writes of Shakespeare that "the practical effect of performing his plays may have been to encourage the expansion and evaluation of options. Plays are provocations to thought and patterns for action."[20] Similarly, citizen and gallant might recognize the citizens and gallants of city comedy as their very own productions.

Although there have been a number of bases for discussing city comedy, we encounter only rare or unsystematic attention to the ways the period and its audience produced its drama. In part, this is because negotiating between city comedy and social history raises familiar and vexing questions about the relationship between art and history. Conventional Jacobean discourse itself affirms the notion of the world as a theater, the *theatrum mundi;* on the other hand, we hear Hamlet saying that actors are "the abstract and brief chronicles of the time." In Act 3, he says that the end of playing is "to hold, as 'twere, the mirror up to nature, to show virtue her own feature, scorn her own image, and the very age and body of the time his form and pressure."[21] Of course, Shakespeare's notion of drama as a mirror held up to nature is not original. In what is reputed to be Cicero's definition, comedy must consist of *imitatio vitae, speculum consuetudinis,* and *imago veritatis.* That this is not a call for photographic realism has been argued most eloquently by Madeleine Doran.[22] Verisimilitude was meant to include universal truth and decorum, means or aims that quickly reveal the mirror to be more refractive than reflective. Comedy's angled mirror catches the seams and edges of accepted truths. It sets prejudices and authorized accounts in the foreground, allowing us to see that these are imperfect fits, that traditional narratives are interpretations of everyday events. Or comedy may stage old truisms as all-too-perfect fits, as social analyses tailored to a special interest and a particular point of view.[23] Jacobean theater did not stand in relation to reality only as a comment on, or abstraction of, an event; it too was inscribed within reality, and it could fasten only onto already available cultural terms (even when the vocabulary was borrowed from the theater). The process was truly dialectical, not hierarchical: art, and especially the theater, did not stand above the community as some uncontaminated distillation of its essence.[24] The bond between theater and what we may call actuality (actual only insofar as it is an already organized perception) is their shared discourse of types and conventions. Most critics have either broken or ignored this bond.

Thus L. C. Knights believes that none of the plays written in "the age of Jonson" "is a dramatization of an economic problem or consciously intended as propaganda for this or that form of economic organization, and only a few of them . . . are meant to make the audience think about questions of social morality." But he believes also that the dramatists drew their material from "the movements, the significant figures of contemporary life."[25] If Knights's second remark is true, it is hard to see how these plays will not be dramatizations of economic problems, propaganda, and moments in the debate over social morality. If we are literalistic, and limit the dramatization of an economic problem to the figuration of the Miseries of Monopoly, then Knights is right. But surely all these plays pitting merchants against gentry, set firmly within an urban topography of shops, brothels, and prisons, and directed at identifiable public and coterie audiences, constitute a very explicit and effective discussion of contemporary "propaganda" itself. At the root of Knights's analysis lies a belief that the Elizabethan, unlike twentieth-century man, has no "hazy medium" (or "veil to pierce") which "interposes between him and things as they are" (pp. 11–12). There is no ideology in this world picture; the possibility that the Elizabethans were caught in a contemporary discourse is ever so slight. But by Knights's own account, there was considerable haze on the horizon. The Elizabethan "web of beliefs and prejudices" included an insistence on degree, the subordination of private profit to public good, and a desire for ordered trade. Knights makes these important points but cannot see that they are very close to the center of the plays he discusses. Thus Middleton's comedies are exclusively comedies of intrigue; "they do not embody the thought and opinion of the time, since that is irrelevant to the intrigue" (p. 261). It is not suggested that these same thoughts and opinions give rise to, or make possible, a dramatization of the City as the scene of intrigue. Nor does Knights allow that Middleton, like Jonson, was exposing and examining, rather than accepting and reflecting, "a world of thriving citizens, needy gallants . . . and fortune-hunters of all kinds" (p. 261).

Knights would have had an easier time had he argued, as has Anthony Covatta, that there is little about the period that is unusual, that times were changing, but they were changing for all.[26] Covatta grants that "conditions were changing in England under the last Tudor and first Stuarts, in ways that had not obtained previously," and he proceeds to enumerate the standard list of economically motivated disruptions that paralleled, if they did not engender, social dislocation. But Covatta's argument becomes unreliable when Tawney and Weber are set up as straw men whose overly dramatic and "simplistic" stress is on class warfare and emergent capitalism: "Images of class warfare do not do justice to the social reality" (p. 30). Covatta writes that class divisions were "duly recognized, with little fuss from any quarter," but he ignores the fact that "while little structural change took place," a very significant and heated discussion about the definitions of roles within that structure was going on. When he writes that heredity "was not a radically determinant factor in social status," he ignores the extent to which it remained a subject for debate (as the usage "radically" suggests). When he argues that "no great gulf was fixed between merchant turned squire and squire turned merchant," he ignores the pamphlet literature which illustrates the difference between an economic truth and a social uncertainty. And when Covatta rightly minimizes the number of men who moved out of their class, he once again ignores the discrepancy between statistics and the way men perceive social change. Covatta is wrong when he asserts that "on the whole the middle class was docile." Puritan righteousness and financial success lie behind an especially proud citizenry, even if they were still engaged in fashioning an acceptable role for themselves. So too, Covatta (and his source, J. H. Hexter) is wrong in thinking that the merchants were standing by, "cash in hand . . . trying to buy their way in" to the aristocracy (although this was certainly what many thought was happening). The research of Frank Freeman Foster and R. G. Lang demonstrates that, no matter what the moralists were saying, most London merchants were not clambering for landed estates and that they had established a meaningful and viable urban service system to meet their own class needs.[27]

In part, Covatta appears to be reacting to the first book devoted solely to city comedies, Brian Gibbons' *Jacobean City Comedy*, where the stress is on their didactic and satiric aspects. While prefiguring Covatta in his interest in conventional and formal elements, Gibbons traces the origins of city comedy to Roman comedy, to the moralities, and to Donne and the tradition of verse satire. The satire evolves into the early presenter plays of Jonson, Marston, and Middleton, and matures into a full-blown didacticism. Thus Gibbons believes that city comedy offers us a "keen analysis in moral terms first and last."[28] Further developing a version of Knights's argument that no city comedy dramatizes the Miseries of Monopoly, Gibbons writes that these plays must not be "rashly cited as evidence of actual conditions at the time" (p. 29). The conventional city-comedy characters and their neat ethical debates (greed vs. generosity, etc.) have only a tenuous historical specificity. The moneylender is not a moneylender so much as a symbol of avarice and of anarchy (p. 30). In sum, Gibbons' argument follows a trajectory opposite to the one found in Covatta's work: there, the comedy began with conventions and came to intimate the real world; here, *"typical* elements of city life [are transformed] into meaningful *patterns"* (p. 17; my emphasis). But city comedy's plots are not built with elements that proclaim themselves to be typical of city life. These comedies remind their audience that it alone is responsible for determining what men and women may call typical of city life in Jacobean London. City comedy characterizations become meaningful precisely when they permit us to see that so-called typical elements fail to do justice to the contemporary City and its inhabitants. When city comedies function as "interrogative texts," disrupting "the unity of the [spectator] by discouraging identification with a unified subject of enunciation," they permit spectators "to construct from within the text a critique of [its] ideology."[29] The "radical critique" of the age that Gibbons finds in city comedies consists not in their satire of, or even their ambivalence toward, greedy merchants and idle gentry, but in their self-conscious staging of the clearly inadequate roles and types which Londoners tolerated for the purposes of identifying one another.

It is Alexander Leggatt's recognition of the social roles embodied in these plays that makes his reading seem especially promising.[30] Unlike Gibbons, who stresses the nondramatic antecedents to city comedy, Leggatt points to the influence of New Comedy plotting as well as native moralities and Italian comedy. But Leggatt tells us that his overriding concern is with "social relations in their most material form" (p. 151). This focus allows him to discuss the ways city comedy's urban communities constitute an image of the City. Leggatt is indeed alert to "social situations" on the stage; however he is less interested in the ways that social, political, and theatrical factors produce these very situations. Relations in their "most material form" are to be found outside the theater; or perhaps this is where the men who thought they were *finding* these relations were in fact generating them. Missing in Leggatt's book is a consistent awareness of the artificiality of the social relations he examines. Leggatt sees this artificiality in *Eastward Ho*, but he does not extend this perception to city comedies in general, nor does he allow that conventional stage relations are shaped by equally conventional extratheatrical relations.

Others have worked to uncover the relationship between city comedy and its sociohistorical context. Anne Barton offers a number of suggestive insights into the bonds between the City and its comedy. The City offers drama a permanent home, a full house in a specialized building. Its middle-class citizens are closer to the figures of comedy than to the exalted types of tragedy. For Barton, "the realistic London background established a tension between the ordinary experience of the theatre audience, and the comedy plot."[31] This understanding leads to many helpful comments on the ways in which the characters of various city comedies express the "ethos" of the City. More recently, in *Puritanism and Theatre*, Margot Heinemann has made an important contribution to our understanding of two forces often thought to be exclusively antagonistic. We learn that Parliamentary Puritans were at one with playwrights who censured the court and sectaries; that Stubbes and Gosson, champions among the antitheatricalists, were not doctrinal Puritans; and that, with the exception of their desire to observe the Sabbath, the City fathers' objections to the theater were a practical (the plague, traffic jams), not a theological, matter.[32] Heinemann recognizes that a playwright like Middleton cannot accurately be seen as "merely 'anti-citizen.'" She situates Middleton within his society and, more specifically, within London, where the humanity of citizens as well as the gentry was distorted. As a result, we see that Middleton's city comedies (and, as I will suggest, those of his contemporaries) are not directed against status groups so much as they examine the effects of a status society itself under pressure.

To criticize Knights or Gibbons or Covatta is not to suggest that their arguments would have been more effective had they found (or fashioned) one-to-one correspondences between contemporary history and the theater. Rather it is to remark just how seldom drama criticism is informed by the historical account. Whether city comedy is read as didactic and satiric, as ironic, or as comedy of intrigue, few have asked why the City should be the target of satire and the seat of gulling. To argue that city comedy evolves out of verse satire is simply to push the problem a few years further back. To argue that city comedy reworks, or even subverts, New Comedy conventions is to fail to explain such questions as Why now?, and, Why this way? We may begin to account for the plots and character types in city comedy by locating the entire genre within the discussions and disagreements Londoners were having about the way they perceived their city and those who populated it. These discussions gave rise to regular types with regular social roles and protocols, and city comedy could borrow these (already dramatic) characters for its own needs.

2

The Merchant-Citizen in History

Late-sixteenth- and early-seventeenth-century pamphlets
devoted to matters of trade, shopkeeping, apprenticeship,
and business ethics responded to the forceful presence of
the London merchant-citizen. However, this figure was not
clearly defined. Because both city comedy and pamphlets
are variously specific and indeterminate in their identifica-
tions of city dwellers, the term "merchant-citizen" (or
simply "merchant") is but a convenient rubric for more
pointed designations, like freeman, shopkeeper, or tradesman. Contemporaries might have described a merchant as
one involved in overseas trade; he was not a "tradesman" (a
skilled craftsman) or a "retailer" (one who resold goods for
others). But even for a citizen, such distinctions were inex-
act. Richard Grassby argues that "merchant and craft functions overlapped in the urban trades." And David Cressy
reminds us that a "tanner, for example, could be an artisan
or a guildmaster." Even the common distinction between
"marchandize" and "manuarie" is "indicative rather than
exhaustive." Thus to use the term "merchant-citizen" is to
collapse several notions under one heading. We know that
seventeenth-century economic "divisions between entre-
preneur and artisan, between industrial and commercial
capitalist, were deep"; however, more than one term was
used metonymically with "citizen" or "merchant."[1]

Even if the merchant-citizen were a man with an identifiable economic role, for the community that included nobility, gentry, and professional men he was a man with an uncertain "social place." For the merchant-citizen to whom we refer, and thus the merchant-citizen of city comedy, was not a gentleman who had turned to large-scale overseas trade. This latter figure could pursue trade throughout the Elizabethan and Jacobean period with little concern for the taint that commercial dealings would have had for the merchant-citizen. In *The Merchant of Venice*, Antonio's social status is secure and taken for granted by the gallants who surround him, although Shakespeare makes it clear that "business" occupies a good deal of Antonio's time. It was not the gentleman merchant but the many merchant-citizens who needed defenders, provoked detractors, and required an explanation of just what in fact they represented. Contemporary pamphlets suggest the various tactics that were deployed—some argue that the merchant represents greed and ambition, others protest that he is the backbone of an increasingly commercial nation (thus John Browne writes: "When marchants trade proceedes in peace, / And labours prosper well: / Then common weales in wealth increase . . .").[2] Each pamphlet implies a discoverable social role: in one instance the merchant is a dignified member of the commonwealth, in another, he is directed not to meddle in national affairs. He is confined to the City and its already corrupt values, and he is depicted as a world traveler, the lifeblood among nations. But in an era whose values were defined predominantly by the aristocracy, these pamphlets constituted a struggle to bolster, suppress, or reformulate the traditional story, the time-honored derogation of the merchant. Even in the *late* seventeenth century, when wealth had become more significant than "traditional hierarchy and tenurial status, . . . for Gregory King, the great political arithmetician, 'esteem still overrides wealth.'"[3] Tudor and Stuart pamphleteers thus were waging either a rearguard, critical attack on conservative opinion, or a progressive, constitutive campaign to refashion "the merchant" and a social discourse suitable to him.

On the stage, in the plots and characterizations of Jacobean city comedies, the merchant-citizen has at once fewer faces (or roles) and greater complexity. Looking to the competing models that were being shaped for the merchant outside of the theaters, the playwrights fastened onto the conservative account: the greedy or ambitious, deceitful or foolish merchant-citizen.[4] Setting merchants in relation to gallants, city comedies could examine precisely *why* the merchant had come to signify avarice, precisely how he menaced the City, just what assumptions such characterization presumed, and for whom these presumptions were valid. Just as savagery and deformity are seen to be the arbitrary if dramatically necessary qualities of Caliban's role as slave, so too avarice or guile could be seen as arbitrary (and here too, dramatically necessary) characteristics of merchant-citizens. City comedy filled the role of New Comedy's conventional blocking figure with the merchant in part because such comedy thrives when it can vanquish just such a blocking figure. But once this solution is staged, unexpected results follow. The artificiality of the conjunction of merchants and deceit is exposed. More precisely, city comedy centers the responsibility for judgment in its audience: the spectator may accept the total identification of the merchant with the conservative version of him, or may come to a new understanding of the inadequacy of such a characterization. While there is always ample room for complicity and acquiescence, the opportunity to rethink assumptions is rarely absent.

The playwrights of city comedy give the merchant the conventional villain's role and then strain and exaggerate this characterization—often, as in the case of Middleton's Quomodo, to the point of parody. The playwrights simultaneously reinforce prejudice (they portray the merchant as a figure for greed) and undermine the very same prejudice by exposing its social function (they suggest that avarice is one response to aristocratic profligacy, and they remind us that gentlemen too can be greedy). The plays do not challenge audience assumptions by ridiculing avarice or guile: they challenge the conventional ways members of the audience personify these vices. And they challenge too the ways citizen spectators equate lust and idleness with the gentry.

City comedy is consistently prepared to present a nasty merchant formed along the lines of humours conventions; but to emphasize conventional elements is also to destabilize stage conventions, and to call into question the assumptions that shape social roles. To talk about Quomodo as a conventional (merchant-) villain is also to talk about elements of the authorized version of the merchant of the streets. City comedies reveal the foolishness of constructing actual social roles according to the requirements of the theater. In fact, they show that gentlemen borrowed the features, if not the substance, of their formulas from the theater, that when the theater chose the gentleman's version of the merchant, it chose one of its own types. Finally, if the image of the theater looms large in this analysis, it is because successful city comedy indicates that both its own characters and its spectators are actors. The play's the thing that unmasks both spectator and type, that reveals them casting one another's roles. Again and again, merchants or gentry, playwrights, and stage merchants or stage gentry produce and act in variations of an urban drama on their respective city stages. The folly and danger that are part of each drama point to the need for new, more generous roles in a new, more unified city.

Fashioning the Merchant

Elizabethan and Jacobean London brought strong and observable pressure to bear on the entire country. Goods which had passed through Venice and Florence on their way to England were now carried directly to London. By the end of the sixteenth century, the financial centers at Antwerp and Lyons were in shambles. In England, with London in command, textiles and mining were showing a steady rate of growth. Joint-stock companies were flourishing, and a proper money market was established in the capital. In the words of one modern historian, "London, as the fountainhead of privileges, the centre of government, the site of the principal law courts, the seat of the great trading companies, the crux of the land market, the main repository of trading capital, and the primary source of credit, was the inevitable controller of much economic activity in other parts of the land, and . . . the narrow bottleneck through which . . . textiles produced in the remotest areas passed for shipment abroad." In the words of yet another historian, London "supplied the machinery for financing the exports of wool staplers and merchant adventurers, did an extensive insurance business among shipowners, took up government loans, met the demands of the landed gentry for advances on their estates, provided the credits needed by the clothiers, and even found capital to invest in tin mining . . . and coal mining."[5] And yet, despite this advanced mercantile setting, the pamphlets that appeared in London were not a congeries of comment and countercomment on an already understood phenomenon. They were, among other things, a purposeful, sometimes strained attempt to fashion "the merchant" and to find a vocabulary adequate to him.

Now it may be objected that by this late date the merchant had come into his own, that he was already an indisputable presence in the community. The work of many medievalists has certainly established the economic reality within which we may locate the merchant, and it has been argued that the Merchant adventurers comprised one of the most powerful bodies in Tudor England; but it remains true that the very commentators who acknowledged the economic reality of the merchant class were still struggling to define *homo mercans.* Indeed, it has been argued persuasively that "Elizabethans who wanted to appeal to merchant consciousness" and citizen pride, had for many years to make this "appeal in the language (and the social ideology) of the elite."[6] In Italy and the Low Countries the merchant had found his way to dignity by the fourteenth or fifteenth century, but not in England. Lord Mayors' shows represent an attempt to confirm the honor and probity of "the merchant," but the merchant elite's message was relayed almost exclusively to its own kind.

Those sympathetic to the merchant class, or those with a vested interest in it, tend to adopt a defensive rhetoric, hoping to soothe the worries of the larger community. It is argued that merchants are not a threat to the gentry, that they are the means to national economic health. Others argue more assertively that trade is the basis for all societies and that the merchant is both founder and protector of his nation. The arguments unsympathetic to the merchants are more predictable: they are concerned less with the fashioning of "the merchant" than with reiterating a conservative cry in defense of all levels of society that were not merchant—all levels that the merchants are said to be devouring. The excerpts that follow are offered as representative voices marshaling a sometimes new language in an oftentimes acrimonious debate.

A most canny move made in defense of the merchant may be found in the opening pages of *A Treatise of Commerce* (1601), where John Wheeler presents the merchant as an Everyman figure. He demurely suggests that

there is nothing in the world so ordinarie, and naturall unto men, as to contract, truck, merchandise, and traffike one with an other, so that it is almost unpossible for three persons to conuerse together two houres, but they wil fal into talk of one bargaine or another, chopping, changing, or some other kinde of contract. Children, assone as euer their tongues are at libertie, doe season their sportes with some merchandise, or other: and when they goe to schoole, nothing is so common among them as to change, and rechange, buy and sell of that, which they bring from home with them. The Prince with his subjects, the Maister with his servants, one friend and acquaintance with another, the Captaine with his souldiers, the Husband with his wife, Women with and among themselues, and in a word, all the world choppeth and changeth, runneth & raueth after Marts, Markets and Merchandising, so that

all things come into Commerce, and passe into traffique (in a man-
er) in all times, and in all places:

Wheeler is not yet done. He is sufficiently confident to acknowledge the merchant's more aggressive "Merchandise."
The secretary of the Merchant Adventures Society is merely
building toward a climax:

Not onely that, which nature bringeth forth, . . . but further also,
this man maketh merchandise of the workes of his owne handes,
this man of another mans labour, one selleth words, another maketh traffike of the skins & bloud of other men, yea there are some
found so subtill and cunning merchants, that they perswade and
induce men to suffer themselues to bee bought and sold, and we
haue seene in our time enow, and too many which haue made merchandise of mens soules. To conclude, all that a man worketh with
his hand, or discourseth in his spirit, is nothing els but merchandise . . .[7]

What sounds like part of a radical argument (all men are
traders) in prose, is enacted regularly in the theaters. There
we see gallants, as well as merchants, running after marts
and trafficking in the "skins and bloud" of other men (more
often, of women). Ideologies best served by separating merchants from gentry are subverted on the stage as one status
group starts to look more and more like another. But John
Wheeler was interested in writing a defense of the society
and of regulated trade. He would have his readers understand
that he is willing to enter into the free-trade debate, but he
has little patience with the larger discussion, the social and
political examination of the status of the merchant. Nevertheless even he is not completely free of the compulsion to
defend the merchant, and so he prefaces his short merchant
pedigree from Solon forward with just one reminder:

Now albeit this affectation [to trade] bee in all persons generally
both high and low, yet there are of the notablest, and principallest
Traffiquers which are ashamed, and thinke scorne to be called Merchants: whereas indeed merchandise . . . is honorable, & may be

exercised not only of those of the third estate (as we term thē) but also by the Nobles, and the chiefest men of this Realme with commendable profit, and without any derogation to their states, honour, and enriching of themselues and their Countries, the Venetians, Florentines, Genoueses, and our neighbours the Hollanders haue used this trade of life, who knoweth not?

Wheeler's last point—profit to the state—is a favorite of many of the merchants' advocates. The more emotional point—the shame felt by some merchants—is developed at great length by Edward Bolton in *The Cities Advocate* (1629).[8] The subtitle of this pamphlet, *In This Case or Question of Honor, and Armes; Whether Apprentiship extinguisheth Gentry . . .*, establishes the point of contention. Bolton, "an indigent gentleman . . . who was in the Marshalsea prison for debt in the year that he published *The Cities Advocate*," brings Roman precedent as well as contemporary contract law into his rather windy defense of the City.[9] Bolton would refute those who lay *"upon the hopefull, and honest estate of Apprentiship in London, the odious note of bondage, and the barbarous penaltie of losse of Gentry . . ."* (p. 2). He adopts an indignant, almost disbelieving tone when he refers to those who "through vanity, or other sicknesse of the wit, or iudgement, disdaine to seeme either Citie-borne, or Citie-bred, or to owe any thing of their worship, or estate, either to the City, or to Citizens . . ." (p. 5).

Bolton's stance is defensive but his tone works at being assertive. Not unlike Wheeler, he would have us think the trader, or would-be trader, on equal terms with the nation's other status groups (Bolton speaks of the *"questio status"*— p. 4). However, Bolton follows a rather obvious detour that permits him to bypass a head-to-head confrontation with one of the most significant changes of the day. While in men's minds England continued to be a status society dominated by the gentry, that which in fact increasingly distinguished among men was not rank but wealth and property.

This was an uncertain moment: at the same time that ac-
quisitiveness was gaining in respectability, "the merchant's
profit remained suspect."[10] So too, men were often unwilling to acknowledge the connection between the recent increase in social mobility and signs of a new commercial
theory based on exchange, not production. The allegiance
of the gentry to primogeniture made necessary the possibility of a career in trade for younger sons. "The absence of
legal prohibitions did not make a business career universally
popular with the gentry, particularly when trade was identified with republicanism and Puritanism, land taxes and
usury, utilitarianism, pretension, and moral regression."
However, "the growth of cities and an urban gentry, the in-
stitutionalization of business in undying corporations, and
the self-confidence engendered by the obvious utility of
trade, all helped to increase the prestige of business."[11]

So Bolton addresses the fact that many younger sons
among the gentry were apprenticing themselves in the City;
but with only occasional exceptions, he is evasive about the
wider implications of what he writes. Apprenticeship is said
to be a title of "politicke or ciuill discipline," and apprentices are compared to "souldiers in armies, or schollers in
rigorous schooles, or nouices in nouiceships: each of whom
in their kind usually do, and suffer things as base and vile
in their owne quality, simply, and in themselues considered,
without respect to the finall scope, or aime of the first institution" (p. 14). Bolton asserts that the duties and details
of apprenticeship are of little consequence ("the end denom-
inates the meanes and actions tending to it") while at the
same time he elevates the concept of apprenticeship, reminding his reader that it is regulated by civil contract. Apprenticeship "is a degree, or order of good regular subjects,
out of whose as it were Nouiceships, or Colledges, Citizens
are supplied" (p. 37). Whereas Wheeler argued that all men
are in effect merchants, Bolton's "good regular subjects"
prove that merchants (here, apprentices) are like all other
men. But the equivocating "as it were" mitigates the force

of the assertion and opens the door for an unexpected caveat: even for Bolton, "Citizens, as Citizens, are not Gentlemen, but Citizens; To holde otherwise were to take one order, or degree of men out of the Realm" (p. 45).

Bolton's subject, the effect of apprenticeship on gentry, had already found its way to the stage in *Eastward Ho*. The goldsmith Touchstone has two apprentices, each "a gentleman born." If there were a moral to this highly ironic play, it would be that apprenticed gentry succeed when they dismiss their gentle origins and concentrate on becoming good citizens. And such a moral might well have been drawn from the fact that gentlemen were less likely to prosper in business (because they lacked the requisite skills, start-up capital, contacts, luck, and time) than on their family estates. Quicksilver, the prodigal apprentice, swears by his pedigree and suffers for it; Golding, the sober apprentice, refuses to "be like a gentleman," and therefore he thrives. Chapman, Jonson, and Marston poke fun at citizen self-righteousness and at the merchant's disdain for the gentry. Less subtle men attacked the merchants for precisely the opposite reason, arguing that all merchants were in fact would-be gentlemen, or, less generously, thieves, usurers, and what Henry Brinklow referred to as "rich jolly crackers and braggers."[12] Of course this is an old story; around 1550, Robert Crowley wrote wittily of merchants as "Members unprofitable."[13] In "The Last Trumpet," Crowley spelled out "The Merchant's Lesson":

> Let it suffice to mary
> Thy daughter to one of the trade:
> Why shouldest thou make hir a lady,
> Or bye for her a noble warde?
>   And let thy sonnes, every chone,
> Be bounde prentise yeres nine or ten,
> To learne some art to lyve upon:
> For why should they be gentlemen?
>   There be already men inowe
> That beare the name of gentil bloud;

Tell thou me then, what nede haste thou
So vainly to bestow thy good?
(ll. 1125–36)[14]

In 1583, Philip Stubbes repeated Crowley's lesson, complaining that "now a daies euery Butcher, Shoomaker, Tayler, Coller and Husbandman, yea, euery Tinker, Pedler, and Swineherd, euery Artificer and other, gregarii ordinis, of the vilest sorte of men that bee, muste be called by the vaine name of Maisters at euery woorde. But it is certaine, that no wise man, will intitle them, with any of these names, worshipful and Maister (for thei are names and titles of dignitie, proper to the goodlie wise)."[15] Under the guise of a traditional claim for order and hierarchy, the antibourgeois literature evoked images of a predatory merchant class set on devouring a defenseless gentry. A widespread incomprehension of credit mechanisms and a willful distortion of the difficulties faced by the gentry in a period of unprecedented inflation permitted the defenders of the "old order" to fashion an ideologically motivated merchant type. The stingy Roman *senex* and the medieval version of the merchant offered these commentators rough contours for their new men, but far more powerful material was culled from their perceptions of the contemporary social and economic scene.

As men grappled to invent a new vocabulary for a new (or changing) economy, the merchant's defender was in the uneasy position of having to substitute instant dignity for generations of socialization. Sylvia Thrupp has written that William Scott's *An Essay of Drapery* (1635) "is the first substantial piece of writing known in English that exalts business as a career."[16] The novelty of this pamphlet suggests something of the era's temporary failure of vocabulary, of conceptualization, and of imagination. Just how remarkable Scott's essay is becomes clear when we notice that he is not defending trade simply for the profit it brings to the commonwealth. Scott is quite willing to speak of the profit it brings to the trader—and the pleasure too! Self-interest is not, a priori, an evil. Scott has an unashamed respect for money, a youthful sense that borders on awe and that reminds us how easily we are taken in by those who categorically decry capital. For Scott, "the moneyed man is the mighty man: Honour, Liberty, and Royalty attend on Riches; Logick faileth, Rhetorick fainteth, when Gold pleads the Cause" (p. 31). Financial success is equated with power, and such power is expressed in a social and political setting: "Wealth is a pledge of their [the aldermen's] care of the Commonwealth: it is likely, he that hath done well for himselfe, will know how to doe well for the publicke good, being put to it" (p. 32).

The *Essay of Drapery* is an example of the fashioning of "the merchant" out of both old and new cloth. Scott has a deep religious concern and an equally profound interest in money; his wonderful master trope—*sancta avaritia*—offers us a sample of his originality. Boldly appropriating one of the most threatening of the seven deadly sins, Scott advises that the merchant "never be satisfied with doing good to his better part" (p. 36). Sylvia Thrupp is right to note the way Scott's "holy covetousnesse" leads to some rather "nice casuistry" (p. 4); but in the context of more predictable and defensive claims made for trade, Scott's toleration of flattery and a little deceit is surely welcome. We are brought to attention when Scott bends the Scripture ("as the Apostle said; *Be angry but sin not:* So I say, Flatter, but sin not, if that be possible . . . amiable lookes and faire speeches will goe farre enough . . ."—p. 20) and when he hedges on matters of truth ("Lying then is to be banisht: but this rule must be observed; as we may not lie, so we need not speake all the truth"—p. 21).

Moreover, Scott's thinking is not quite so simple as these apothegms may sound. Professor Thrupp isolates "the problem of individual success" as Scott's central dilemma (p. 7). His need to justify gain, as well as his fear of death and the encroaching movement of time, brings him into line with a solid tradition of Puritan thinking. Invoking medieval and Puritan arguments, Scott grounds his remarks on man's duty to work and the necessary coincidence of "wealth on one hand, Christ and immortality on the other," as Thrupp points out (p. 7). In this light, there is little new in his assertion that "Hee cannot be a good Draper which is not first a good man," or "honesty without wisdome is unprofitable" (p. 17). And there is both an elegiac and (as Thrupp has remarked) a stoic voice behind such statements as, "I thinke there is no Citizen can say hee hath had no losse," or "God makes men his Balls; and of these Balls, who is most tost up and downe then the Citizen? . . . but he is a man, that can endure violent Tides, and still swim aloft" (pp. 25 and 24). Scott calls for *sancta avaritia* but balances this with "festina lentè"; he would have his Citizen "diligent, but not passionate" (p. 31). He moves his arguments beyond the person-to-person debate on the status of merchants by simultaneously asserting his strong confidence in trade and turning his argument directly toward God, away from the conservative moralists who would act as His surrogates.

These tactics, while indicative of a new self-assurance, help to define a social role that still lacks the larger community's assent. The entire seventeenth-century Puritan elaboration of economic virtues seems merely to justify the merchant before his God, not before his fellow men. Puritan casuistry enters this debate obliquely; what Tawney has called Calvin's "whole-hearted *imprimatur* to the life of business enterprise"[17] both predates Scott's respectable trader and shares with it what we must see as a failure to socialize the merchant. And on the stage, the (Puritan) merchant stood out as an antisocial figure; even if Mulligrub, in Marston's *The Dutch Courtesan*, were a truly righteous vintner, Cocledemoy would still be ready to taunt him. Malvolio, though not a merchant, enjoys the conventional merchant's "sobriety." As "a man of business, and . . . a hard one," he might be less puritanical, but would still be unwelcome in Illyrian society.[18] Perhaps we are dealing less with a failure than with yet another moment in the effort to implant mercantile values in the everyday discourse of Englishmen. Tawney argues that the pre–Civil War "business classes, as a power in the State, were still sufficiently young to be *conscious* of themselves as something like a separate order, with an outlook on religion and politics peculiarly their own, distinguished, not merely by birth and breeding, but by their social habits, their business discipline, the whole bracing atmosphere of their moral life" (p. 173; my emphasis).[19] That this consciousness had to be articulated is the unwritten corollary to Tawney's reasoning and the genesis of the debate that we have been sampling. The merchant had to fight for his place in the polis, and then he had to fight for his place in the minds of the men of the polis. Tawney reminds us of this when he writes that the idea that "'business is business,' . . . if more ancient than is often supposed, did not win so painless a triumph as is sometimes suggested" (p. 187).

For some, lofty strains of argument were out of reach. Thomas Mun shared Scott's confidence in trade, but he was content to enumerate its more practical benefits. Mun was the son of a London mercer; he engaged in trade in Italy and the Levant, came to direct the East India Company, and became fabulously rich.[20] His *England's Treasure by Forraign Trade* (1664; probably written c. 1630) entered him in the heady discussion among contemporary mercantilists by detailing his belief in the need to keep exports running at a higher rate than imports.[21] Writing in the form of a letter to his son, Mun pauses in the first chapter to speak of "the merchant": "[he] is worthily called The Steward of the Kingdoms Stock, by way of Commerce with other Nations; a work of no less reputation than Trust, which out to be performed with great skill and conscience, that so the private gain may ever accompany the publique good." Because this sort of defense must have been rather predictable by the 1630s, Mun is more interesting when he enumerates the skills and knowledge required of a trader. In a long catalogue, he sketches in detail the lineaments of what Scott's subtitle, *The Compleate Citizen*, might have led us to expect. A merchant ought to be a good penman and accountant; he ought to know measures, weights, and monies of all countries. He would have to familiarize himself with the customs and impositions of foreign lands, and he ought to know what commodity was abundant and what scarce in each of these lands. He ought to observe rates of exchange, to know of prohibited export and import items, to consider freight costs and insurance rates at home and abroad, as well as the costs of shipbuilding, repair, provisions, and mariners' wages. In addition, Mun would have his merchant-trader speak in several languages, including Latin, and know the "customs, strengths, laws, politics, arts and religions of foreign lands." Mun's two-chapter rehearsal is more than a practical guide; the overwhelming effect of such rhetorical heaping (what Puttenham called *sinathrismus*) is to give substance to the merchant. Removing "the merchant" from the nexus of cold cash, Mun fashions a Renaissance man, conversant with everything from foreign customs to the minutiae of navigation. Were London traders to approximate this ideal, Mun believed that merchants would cease "finding less encouragement given to their profession [in England] than in other Countreys, and seeing themselves not so well esteemed as their Noble Vocation requireth." For the first time, Englishmen would have reason to nurture multigenerational merchant families, thus putting an end to the sad habit wherein "the memory of our richest Merchants is suddenly extinguished." (In *Michaelmas Term*, merchant-citizen Quomodo's son is a fool, not unlike Yellowhammer's dolt of a son in *A Chaste Maid in Cheapside*—it was convenient to think of the merchant as a potent breeder of gold.)

Mun was answering the need for a merchant of spiritual and intellectual substance. From the fourteenth century to Mun's own day, while the discourse appropriate to the gentry and nobility *might* deteriorate into what was appropriate to gallants and prodigal sons, the semantic universe of the merchant seemed always and only to be governed by capital. In 1593, Thomas Nashe described satirically "the course nowe-a-dayes":

euery one taketh to be ritch: being a young Trader, and hauing old Mumpsimus (his auaritious Maister) learned to bee hys Crafts-maister, for a yeere or two he is very thrifty, and husbandly he pays & takes as dulie as the Clock strikes, he seemeth very sober and precise, and bringeth all men in love with him. When he thinketh he hath thorowlie wrunge himselfe into the Worlds good opinion, & that his credite is as much as hee will demaund, hee goes and tryes it, and on the Tenter-hookes stretches it. No man he knoweth but he will scrape a little Booke curtesie of, two or three thousand pound (perhaps) makes up his month. When he hath it all in his hands, for a month or two he reuels it, and cuts it out in whole cloth. Hee falls acquainted with Gentlemen, frequents Ordinaries and Dicing-houses daily, where when some of them (in play) haue lost all theyr money, he is very diligent at hand, on their Checques, or Bracelets, or Iewels, to lend them halfe the value: . . . When thus this young Usurer hath thrust all his pedlary into the hands of nouice heyres, & that he hath made of his three thousand, nine thousand in Bonds and Recognizances . . . he breakes, and cryes out amongst his neighbors, that he is undone by trusting Gentlemen; his kinde hart hath made him a beggar: . . . For a quarter of a yeere or there-abouts, he flyps his necke out of the coller . . . in his ab-sence all is satisfied for eyght hundred. All matter thus underhand discharged, my young Merchant returnes, and settes uppe fresher than euer he did. In three Tearmes, of a banqrout he wexeth a great landed man, and may compare with the best of his Company.[22]

Now this is a far cry from the legendary Dick Whittington who seems to have held outright no land outside of London, who founded schools and almshouses, and who sat briefly on the king's council.[23] Nevertheless, it is Nashe's young Trader and not Dekker's Simon Eyre whom we read about so often in the sermons and plays of the day.

The attempt to fashion a positive image and social role for the merchant was inhibited by the conventional vocab-ularies of avarice and greed. The last pamphlet I will con-sider may be seen to pull up short even as it would pro-nounce a sure endorsement of the merchant-citizen. Because he (like his age) seems to be of two minds about the merchant, Thomas Gainsford brings together many of the arguments that we have heard already. Gainsford has every intention of declaring his admiration for "the merchant," and yet he seems constrained to take away with one hand what he proffers with the other.[24]

Merchant is a worthy common-wealthes man, *for how euer priuate commoditie may transport him beyond his owne bounds:* yet the publicke good is many ways augmented by mutuall commerce, forren trading, exploration of countries, knowledge of languages, encrease of nauigation, instruction and mustering of seamen, ... Merchant *is onely traduced in this*, that the hope of wealth is his principall obiect whereby profite may arise, which is not usually attained without corruption of heart, deceitful protestations. ... .[25]

Merchant continuing his estate, may settle his fortune, and augment his credit: *but if once turne Gentleman before his time*, he is like a gamester ... he now is counted but an intruder, and purchaseth only vanities. (sig. 90^{r-v})

A Citizen is a professor of ciuilitie ... *and how-euer he is condemned for too much ease*, yet cannot the souldier repulse the enemy ... except the Merchant adde fuell to the fire. (sig. 27)

The nervous double motion that we find in *The Rich Cabinet* (and again, in 1622, in Gainsford's *The Glory of England*) indicates the dilemma faced by anyone who attempted to articulate the role of the merchant. If the imaginative creations of the Lord Mayor's pageantry met with a degree of success in fashioning a merchant-citizen ideology *within* the ranks of the group, the larger debate from which we have been drawing examples suggests that there was still considerable work to be done beyond these boundaries.

The Modern Historian's Merchant-Citizen

Sylvia Thrupp believes that the medieval Englishman came to "associate the merchant and gentry together as significant middle strata, with certain similar functions."[26] There was a blurring of distinctions that took pressure off a social theory that was ill equipped to deal with social mobility (pp.

229 and 313). This does not seem to have been the case in the late sixteenth and early seventeenth centuries. The London merchant's income and net worth appear to have risen considerably throughout this period—the income of nobles and courtiers was falling sharply.[27] This economic leveling among merchants, landed gentry, and nobility paradoxically produced a desire in each group to differentiate itself as clearly as it could from the others. It is not by chance that Middleton reminds us that Lucre and Hoard (in *A Trick to Catch the Old One*), who live like comfortable, landowning aristocrats, have only one foot out of the City. According to Thrupp, the medieval merchant with a country estate "might gain the reputation in that neighborhood of being a gentleman mainly from his way of living when he visited the place" (p. 272). But in the fifteenth century, less than ten percent of the City merchants would have been in a position even to contemplate a "move to the country on a social level about that of a yeoman" (p. 284). By the early seventeenth century, merchant holdings in the counties and their ability to make the move to country estates had been greatly augmented. This is not to suggest that there was a vast migration of citizens to the country; rather it points to a new *recognition* on the part of Englishmen that merchants had this potential. And this awareness coincided with the much-talked-about sale of estates by landed aristocracy.

The importance of what men perceived as opposed to what account books might have revealed is crucial to an understanding of this period. Lawrence Stone argues that "the most fundamental dichotomy within the society was between gentlemen and non-gentlemen, a division that was based essentially upon the distinction between those who did, and those who did not, have to work with their hands" (p. 17). Such an analysis is more successful when applied to the extremes than to the middling ranks. Stone offers us no precise explanation of how and when merchants were seen on an equal footing with the country elite and lesser gentry, and when they were thought of as merely glorified traders. Merchants' aspirations, whether real or merely assumed, suggest more than a desire for prestige. They point also (as in the case of Tim Yellowhammer, on his way to the Inns of Court after graduating Cambridge [*A Chaste Maid*]) to a desire "for a place close to the sacred center of the common values of the society."[28] Their wealth pulled them in one direction; the fact that it was money that was used as a criterion pulled in the other. The gentry were caught in a similar bind: by birth and sometimes by breeding they were gentlemen, but their capital value might be well below that of a successful shopkeeper. The picture of unprecedented social mobility that Professor Stone presents for the period between 1540 and 1640 suggests what is perhaps the most coherent explanation of the flowering of city comedy and the debate over social roles that it refracts, analyzes, and satirizes. Where social change is occurring at an excited pace, the demand for role definition will be high; and as both Stone and Charles Wilson have argued, social flux works to strengthen degree by putting it up for auction.[29] By 1641, the aristocracy had regained its wealth (if not its prestige); but during the decade of city comedy that we are examining, land sales were nearing their peak.[30] More than half of the Lord Mayors of London between 1591 and 1640 were born in the country.[31] City deaths due to the plague (approximately fifteen percent of the greater London population in 1603) were made up for by extensive horizontal mobility from the country to the City.[32] And between the 1590s and the 1630s, the number of men called to the bar increased by more than forty percent.[33]

Since at the end of the seventeenth century some four out of every five Englishmen were still rural and poor, the activity that these figures document was necessarily confined to a minority of the people (just as it was most apparent in towns and in London). While the social contours of the countryside, even allowing for merchants' purchases, remained essentially stable, London was fast increasing in size and importance. It was the "nodal point where the main stream of domestic trade intersected the main stream of English foreign trade."[34] It was a haven for vagabonds and prostitutes, and it was a growing center of conspicuous consumption. London, as we have noted, was also the central money market. According to Tawney, gentlemen came to London to borrow money "to meet the current expenses of their establishments, to stave off creditors, or to renew debts."[35] They joined the crown in mortgaging their land to the same city merchants who provided raw materials, a market, and working capital for small masters and cottagers (pp. 35 and 38). The Elizabethan bourgeoisie had discovered profit in moneylending equal to profit in agriculture, industry, and commerce (p. 104). *Anyone* with money at hand knew how to put it out at interest; but the London merchants had more fluid, uncommitted capital than anyone else, and "they were all at one time or another moneylenders."[36] The fact that production would have come to a standstill without credit was unfortunately not universally acknowledged. All classes of men "dreaded the professional 'money master' because it was so easy to slip into dependence on the fatal luxury of loans." The moneylender, or usurer, was seen as a victimizer: "The riches of the cytie of London, and in effect all of this realme, shalbe . . . in the handes of a fewe men havinge unmercifull hartes."[37] Usury had been and continued to be a subject for ecclesiastical casuistry, but by the end of the sixteenth century, the burden of proof (as to unfair practices, extortion, etc.) had been transferred from the usurer to his critic. Economic expediency had supplemented traditional morality in the marketplace—but on the stage and in the minds of Londoners, the change was far from complete.

The very extent of the debate over usury was a significant factor in its domestication and secularization. Years of hairsplitting forced the critic to pick over the varieties of moneylending while the principle itself met with fewer and fewer objections. It was argued that any form of interest constituted usury, that moderate interest was tolerable, that circumstances were determinative, and that the class of people involved could change the designation. Some argued the spirit, others the letter, of the law. In 1577, there was a move to distinguish usury from interest taking: one was a threat to the nation; the other was equitable and good for the nation. Many argued that England was fast becoming a credit-barren island surrounded by trade competitors with an unfair advantage. If rent and profit from trade were acceptable, why not interest? The debate continued, but by the end of the sixteenth century, the church's position lagged well behind the state's, and ten percent interest was recognized as a tolerable standard.[38] Moreover, whatever the laments of stage and pulpit moralists, the "average" London merchant was not operating solely as a moneylender, and he was not the only one lending money.

Part of the problem we face when interpreting the role men thought Jacobean merchants were playing arises from our approach to the surviving records. Robert Lang has focused on the way Jacobean aldermen established their fortunes. He argues that many employed their capital domestically and "made their fortunes conservatively in long-established trade which permitted the employment of large sums of capital with good assurance of a return on investment."[39] Such men would have been perceived as highly successful traders and potential, if not actual, contributors to the health and wealth of the nation. Lawrence Stone concentrates on what these men did with their fortunes, noting that they "first made their money in overseas or retail trading and . . . then turned to the moneylending business."[40] Not surprisingly, such men were perceived in an unflattering light: "generally all merchants, when they have gotten any great wealth, leave trading and fall to usury, the gain thereof being so easy, certain, and great."[41] To take a specific example, Lang writes that the real source of wealth of Sir Baptist Hicks, "England's greatest shopkeeper," was his retail mercery. Lang makes no mention of Hicks's moneylending; instead, he tells us that "between Michaelmas 1608 and 17 August 1609, [Hicks] was paid £14,083 for 'wares, etc' sold to the crown."[42] Stone concedes that "To the end [Hicks] continued to vend his wares, but he got increasingly drawn into money-lending, which from being a convenient sideline must eventually have become his major preoccupation."[43] Hicks appears in Stone's volume as one of the Sir Avarice Goldenfleeces who were extorting land and blood, the sixteen goldsmiths and more than forty aldermen who are known to have made loans to peers between 1580 and 1620.[44]

Comparing Stone with Lang allows us to see once again just how easily the perception of a merchant's activities determines our estimation of his role. Since merchants were visibly involved in moneylending, it was not difficult to associate all city merchants with usury. Stone concludes his section on creditors by reminding us that "After 1600 the supremacy of the great city merchant in this aristocratic money market was undermined by diversion to speculation in government contracts and farms, and by competition from the thriving world of royal financial officials with government surpluses to play with, from the scriveners acting as brokers mobilizing the resources of small men in town and country, and from wealthy knights and squires operating on their own.[45] Bureaucrats, scriveners, and the gentry were busy lending money, but it would have been an anomalous definition of their social roles that included this activity. It would also have been unusual to find an analysis of England's high rate of interest that fixed on the demand for ready money instead of on usurers' greed. And although even we are accustomed to thinking of Jacobean clouds darkening the glorious days of Elizabethan sunshine, the last years under Elizabeth were in fact particularly sluggish, while the period from 1604 to the beginning of the Cockayne project in 1614 was alive with economic expansion and national prosperity.[46]

London had the best vantage from which to take in the shifting dynamics of late-sixteenth- and early-seventeenth-century England. Merchants, gentry, clergy, courtiers, and prostitutes, all were to be found in London. The stage, the pulpit, and the pamphlet were at one in treating London as either the cynosure or the canker of the realm. In 1598, Stow wrote that "Men by this nearness of conversation are with-

drawn from barbarous feritie and force, to certain mildness
of manners, & to humanity & justice, whereby they are
contented to give and take right, to and from their equals &
inferiors, and to hear & obey their heads & superiors."[47] In
The Customer's Alphabet (1608), Thomas Milles mimics
his anatomy of the City with his paratactic constructions
and leads us from the circumference of the nation to its
Babel-like center:

> Our trades do meet in Companies, our Companies at halls, and our
> halls become monopolies of freedom, tied to London: where all our
> Crafts and Mysteries are so laid up together, that outrunning all
> the wisdom and prudence of the land, men live by trades they never
> learned, nor seek to understand. By means whereof, all our creeks
> seek to one river, all our rivers run to one port, all our ports join to
> one town, all our towns make but one city, and all our cities but
> suburbs to one vast, unwieldy and disorderly Babel of buildings,
> which the world calls London.[48]

City comedy moved onto the London stages when Londoners were beginning to reflect on their own discussions of
social roles and their urban setting. It is a self-conscious
genre whose historical specificity enters it into an ongoing
debate. Without some sense of this context, we would be
unable to explain why so many city comedies were produced
between the years 1603 and 1613 alone.

3

The Merchant-Citizen
in City Comedy

Between 1603 and 1613, a Londoner could have attended
city comedies at the song school near St. Paul's, at Blackfriars and at Whitefriars, at the Fortune, the Globe, the Red
Bull, the Swan, and at court. Clearly, city comedies were not
unique to the private theaters: what many see as Middleton's finest city comedy, *A Chaste Maid in Cheapside*, was
performed at the Swan; *The Alchemist* was performed at the
Globe, at Blackfriars, and later at court (in 1612). Playwrights associated with the public theater collaborated with
playwrights associated with the private theaters. Plays performed at public theaters moved to the court or to private
theaters, and plays performed at one private theater were
later mounted at another private theater. Such theatrical
crosscurrents may be seen in the frequent allusions made in
one play to characters, intrigues, or even the audience of
another play. The boys who acted on stages at the private
theaters were often recruited into the ranks of the adult
companies. The King's Men, after 1609, were playing pub-
licly at the Globe and privately at Blackfriars. The City was
small: a theatergoer could leave St. Paul's and be in time for
the induction at Whitefriars fifteen minutes later. The
wealthy residents along the Strand were not far from the

private theaters—neither were the young men at the Inns of Court, nor the Alsatians, the debtors and prostitutes within the Whitefriars precinct.

The high price of admission (at least 6d) at the private theaters resulted in a monied audience; but we must not imagine that it meant an audience made up exclusively of the "Lords, Knights, and Squires" referred to in the prologue to *Epicoene*. The same prologue refers to "your waiting-wench, and city-wires; / . . . your men, and daughters of Whitefriars." In his commendatory verse to John Fletcher's *The Faithful Shepherdess*, Jonson wrote that the coterie audience that had rejected Fletcher's play was "Compos'd of gamester, captain, knight, knight's man, / Lady or pusill, that wears mask or fan, / Velvet or taffata-cap, rank'd in the dark / With the shop's foreman, or some such brave spark." Ann Jennalie Cook has argued recently that "most of the extant evidence made no distinction among the audiences of the various playhouses but simply associated the favored groups in society with playgoing in general." Still, Cook's "favored" or "privileged" few, while they shared an ability to pay for admission, do not represent a homogeneous social group. Wealth was not the equivalent or guarantee of status. Merchants and successful retailers, military officers and clerics, lawyers and gentry (from the city and the country), as well as nobility and teachers all find their way into the "privileged minority." Audience models based on available cash tell us only so much. The playwrights themselves were known to praise their audience in one play and damn it in the next. As we begin to examine the city comedies produced during the first decade of Jacobean rule, we may rest easily with the knowledge that if anything beyond a ready 6d unified audiences, it was their well-developed sense of the theater and its conventions.[1]

The Private Theaters

Westward Ho, the play with which Thomas Dekker and John Webster began a trilogy that would eventually take

45

their audience north and east as well, is thought to have been staged for the first time in 1604.[2] The burghers in the play include Justiniano, an Italian merchant residing in London, and the apparently prosperous citizens Honeysuckle, Tenterhook, and Wafer. The two plots of *Westward Ho* come together in the person of the Italian merchant. Believing that his wife, Moll, is involved in an affair with an earl, Justiniano disguises himself as a pedant/pander to add the three citizens to his fraternity of cuckolds. In the course of the intrigue, Justiniano discovers that his wife has in fact been faithful to him all along. Justiniano takes his revenge on Moll's suitor by bringing him to repent for attempting to seduce her. Meanwhile, in his citizen plot, Justiniano arranges an assignation at a "Brainford" inn for the wives and their suitors, Monopoly (nephew to the Earl), Linstock (son and heir of a London alderman), and Captain Whirlpool. As it turns out, the wives remain faithful to their husbands. And the frantic husbands, who set out westward hoping to catch their wives in flagrante delicto, close the fifth act properly chastened. In sum, Justiniano enters a suspicious merchant husband and exits happily married once again, the would-be lovers are cony-caught, the citizens are made to look foolish, and the wives remain uncompromised.

Like Thomas Middleton, Dekker and Webster prompt laughter at the expense of both citizens and their antagonists. However, unlike Middleton, who usually keeps his characters' social status clear, Dekker and Webster unsettle social hierarchy and disrupt expected alliances among *Westward Ho*'s husbands and paramours. The Italian merchant Justiniano is at home in the City as a merchant, but he does not line up naturally next to citizens like Honeysuckle, Tenterhook, and Wafer. In fact, it was common for lesser traders to join with the gentry and nobility in a mutual dislike of the successful international merchant. Furthermore Justiniano's Italian background is suited to the playwrights' rather Italianate plot centering on the Earl, Moll, and the latter's supposed death and return. Monopoly, though nephew to the melodramatic Earl, nonetheless seems by name and desire (he pursues a citizen's wife) a thorough-going English gallant. Or perhaps we are to think of him as a monopoly-holding courtier who dallies in the City. In either case, he consorts with a captain—who is more of a buffoon than a social type—and with Linstock, another figure who crosses social lines. As son and heir to an alderman, Linstock is related to the three citizens. As an idle youth, living off his father's money and knocking about with an earl's nephew, Linstock seems bent on putting his city affiliation behind him.

One result of such blurred social configurations is that the audience must quickly rethink traditional stereotypes. All members of the gentry are not alike, and all members of the "nongentry" are not alike either. Also, citizens as well as gentlemen can be lechers and they can be dupes. Criticism of familiar contemporary types—the hypocritical citizen husband, the idle urban gallant—is spread evenly throughout *Westward Ho.* However, limits are respected and certain distinctions persist. The cry "westward ho!" inaugurates a departure from the City. It signals release from civic ordinance and from the ward's close watch over the morality of city inhabitants. The journey westward along the Thames marks the distance between the City and a suburban inn, between town and country. The passage generates a sexual-social topography: citizens sleep with their wives and their whores in the City, but citizen wives sleep with their lovers in the country. As in *Northward Ho* and *The Roaring Girl,* the gallant or would-be gallant plans his rendezvous on ex-urban turf. He retreats to a non-*bürgerlich* world that threatens the citizen's freedom—a "freedom" that is overdetermined, at once economic, political, and religious.[3] Like the theaters themselves, located beyond the reach of the town fathers, the inn at Brainford reminds the merchant-citizen that his base of power is both circumscribed and vulnerable.

When *Westward Ho* requires a merchant figure with effective power, the playwrights turn to Justiniano and imbue him with capabilities remarkably similar to their own art. The Italian merchant responds to the threat to his self-respect represented in the Earl by putting aside his role as trader for that of a master intriguer. Justiniano turns to gulling to compensate for his financial and marital distress. In Act 1, scene 1, he elaborates his "comical business": "they say for one Cuckolde to knowe that his friend is in the like head-ake, and to giue him counsell, is as if there were two partners, . . . Haue amongst you Citty dames? You that are indeede the fittest, the most proper for a Comedy . . ." (ll. 221–26). A theatrical venture affords Justiniano powers that are normally beyond the reach of a merchant.

The guller who engineers intrigue and plays upon his "audience" is a version of the playwright. In city comedy, this role is adopted variously by young gallants and older merchants. The argument that coterie playwrights "identified their interests with those of the straitened aristocracy"[4] fails to account for this identification of the playwright with the merchant-as-playwright. Indeed it is probably no accident that Dekker and Webster's Justiniano proclaims his *business* to be Comedy—Dekker, in *The Gull's Horn-Book*, writes that "The theatre is your poets' Royal Exchange, upon which their muses, that are now turned to merchants, meeting, barter away that light commodity of words for a lighter ware than words; *plaudites* . . ." And the association between poet/intriguer and businessman is not confined to "popular" playwrights like Dekker: Quomodo, in *Michaelmas Term*, is just one of Middleton's playwright figures.[5] The playwright writes for the acting companies, the merchant must merchandize his wares, and like John Wheeler's Everyman, he "choppeth and changeth, runneth & raueth after Marts."

The city-comedy playwright puts capitalism to dramatic use, and he allows the stage capitalist, in his turn, to function as a dramatist. The playwright, as his audience's deputy, manipulates the merchant, and the play merchant manipulates the gentry. In Act 4, Justiniano disguises himself as a hag, tells the Earl that Moll is dead, then reveals himself and, finally, his "resurrected" wife. His response to his own bit of clever staging is but a version of Dekker and Webster's own aspiration—the whole affair would make an excellent best-seller: "the booke of the siedge of *Ostend,* writ by one that dropt in the action, will neuer sell so well, as a report of the siedge between this *Graue,* this wicked elder [the Earl] and thy selfe [Moll], an impression of you two, wold away in a May-morning . . ." (4.2.186–89). But this is just a chapter leading to the climax on the final stage at "Brainford." Justiniano leads the three husbands to the inn where their wives are coyly avoiding the advances of Monopoly, Linstock, and Whirlpool. He wants to be there when the citizens catch their wives with the gallants, but his plans break down and it is the wives who catch both the gallants and their husbands. The gallants never get into the wives' chamber, and Birdlime (the bawd) arrives in time to prove that the husbands are regulars at her "Chamber."

The citizen husbands appear to be the target of the satire that Justiniano escapes from. But we miss Dekker and Webster's larger design if we limit the satire to Honeysuckle, Tenterhook, and Wafer. Monopoly flirts with Tenterhook's wife just as soon as the citizen's back is turned, but we know that the young man is merely a conventional gallant—he is in debt to Tenterhook. Honeysuckle wastes no time setting himself up for Justiniano's horn jokes, but then Justiniano believes that he himself has been cuckolded. And when we learn that Mistress Wafer is pregnant annually, any suspicions of the conventional citizen's impotence are dispelled. Indeed, the rather tiresome farce in Act 4, scene 1, in which all three husbands are tricked by their whore and her bawd, is merely a rehearsal for the last act, in which all three paramours are tricked by the citizen wives. Dekker and Webster are generous mockers, turning now to the gallants, now to the citizens. Nearly everyone verges on infidelity, but no one is guilty of it, as we are presented with an "ambiguous tribute to virtue."[6] *Westward Ho* leaves only one thing certain: city comedy's and the City's stereotypical roles are malleable, they do not reveal essential traits. Once a citizen or an earl or a gallant is viewed in a social setting, we find that each aspect of his role is bound to another's interests. Playwrights as well as citizens and gentry will cast those they deal with in roles that bring them profit.

The choristers performed their sequel to *Westward Ho*, Dekker and Webster's *Northward Ho*, in late 1605. The overall structure of this play is more disjointed than that of its predecessor. Subplots and extended practical jokes borrowed from popular jest books fragment the main plot and divide our attention.[7] In the central action, the tradesman Master Mayberry is led to believe that his wife has had an affair with the gallant Luke Greenshield. Mayberry confronts his wife and quickly believes her spirited denial. From the second act to the end, we watch patiently as Mayberry plots and takes his revenge. As in *Westward Ho*, the merchant role in *Northward Ho* is partially split: Mayberry is momentarily the gulled husband and predominantly the manipulator, but he has the aid of a real intriguer in the person of would-be poet-playwright Bellamont. The only innovation to be found in this play is Kate, Luke Greenshield's wife. It is unusual to find a married gallant in a city comedy, and in *Northward Ho* it is Kate's affair with Luke's companion Featherstone that leads to Luke's embarrassment. In fact, not only is she consorting with Featherstone, but Mayberry and Bellamont's intrigue leads Greenshield to procure his own wife for Mayberry.

It has been argued that the important issue in this play is marital relations (the testing of a solid marriage and the unmasking of a bad one) and not class animosity.[8] Yet the careful pitting of citizen against gallant does reinforce status distinctions. Mayberry begins his revenge by inviting Greenshield and Featherstone to dinner; he tells his wife, "I will haue thee beare thy selfe, as if thou madest a feast vpon *Simon* and *Iudes* day, to country Gentlewomen, that came to see the Pageant, bid them extremely welcome, though thou wish their throats cut . . ." (2.2.3–6). Indeed, Greenshield had come to gaze upon a city wife, and now her husband would love to slit his throat. Later, when the gallants have arrived, Mayberry points repeatedly to their status and his own; they are always "gentlemen," and he has merely "the poore ability of a citizen" (2.2.36, 87, and 108–10). This same theme is a topic of conversation for Mayberry's man Squirrel and Greenshield's man Frog: "there's neare a Gentleman of them all shall gull a citizen, and thinke to goe scot-free . . ." (3.2.126–28).

When city-comedy playwrights plot status-group rivalries, they assert the very conventionality of social structure. City comedy sees through the convention of the virtuous or dissipated gentleman, the upstanding or upstart citizen, to the bases of urban existence in sexuality and capital. The humiliated merchant-citizen is not merely a scapegoat who draws off the pent-up resentments of the gentle members of the audience; he is also an embodiment of the social premises that make such a figure available. When a gallant captures (or attempts to capture) a city wife, he adopts the surest method of undermining the citizen's social stability, and he strips the citizen of all but his gold. By focusing on sexual and financial potency as forces whose origins are to be found in social conflict, the playwright allows us to concentrate on men and women who perceive their neighbors in conventional terms. We are not presented with static representations of lust or greed; rather we witness a social interaction, a staging of men's motivations for casting one another in traditional, antipathetic roles. Our gaze is directed away from the greedy merchant-citizen toward the gallant who thinks of merchant-citizens solely in terms of greed or impotence. Furthermore, by thus focusing on the sexual and monetary economies at the foundations of all city roles, city comedy allows its audience a glimpse of their own prejudices and assumptions.

In the same year that the Paul's boys performed the last of the *Ho* plays, they began their run of *Michaelmas Term*, one of Thomas Middleton's finest city comedies.[9] Before we turn to Quomodo, the play's infamous merchant-citizen, it is necessary to return our attention to the London milieu. A recent study of Middleton's comedies takes the depiction of the City in *Michaelmas Term* in deadly earnest.[10] The play's London is said to be "full of dark shops," it is sterile, deathly, and corrupt: "Chaos, confusion, and instability dominate this fallen and hellish environment." It is curious that a study so sensitive to the ways Middleton subverts and finally rejects New Comedy's values and conventions should miss the conventionality of the London scene. The gross exaggeration of the City as a sink of iniquity is at once self-conscious and self-serving. When Middleton became the City's chronologer, he quickly knew to change the tune. Thus we know, and the audience knew, that London was not the capital of hell—but we also know that it is just this sort of city that makes for good comedy of intrigue. Again, generic demands impinge on mimesis.

London is sterile for the play's purposes, but it hatches ingenious plotters like Quomodo, and Middleton too. Indeed, only by depicting such a nasty city can Middleton present a Quomodo as its representative man; and this, finally, is one of the seminal points of the play. If we accept the ideologies that separate country and city, gentry and citizens, then we will continue to define roles in the most conventional manner. By concentrating on these divisions and antique role models, *Michaelmas Term* does its utmost to permit an audience to question convenient assumptions. The spectator may simply confirm his opinions of a citizen or a gallant. However, the discrepancy between the play's London and the spectator's, or the play's scheming merchant and a city alderman, is large enough to suggest that the play is not merely a reflection of contemporary London. The gentleman who equates Middleton's London with the city beyond the theater reveals the magnitude of his fears and the degree to which he relies on tired accounts of the City. Moreover, he misses the parodic element of city comedy. He fails to recognize that the play is a staging of its own dismal ideology.

Much of the ideological basis of city comedy is expressed in the gulling that is such a regular feature in these plays. To gull, or to operate a commodities scheme (as does

Quomodo), is to establish yet another model for social relations. Because gulling is predicated on a hierarchy of sophistication or cleverness, it offers a structure within which the competing members of disparate status groups (old and young, merchants and gentry) can arrange themselves. It is a pliable model that can suggest chicanery as an ethos for the City and intrigue as a structure for drama. At a more suppressed level, gulling is an analogue for the relationship between the theater and its audience. Spectators who follow *Michaelmas Term*'s Easy, who accept the stage's caricature of city relations as an authoritative representation, allow themselves temporarily to be duped, and therefore they bear some of the responsibility for the ensuing drama.

The resonance of this feature of city comedy tempts us to think of gulling as the genre's master structure (the structure that organizes the sexual and financial relations which we noted in *Northward Ho*). But as we take delight in the action, we may begin to recognize that gulling, or intrigue, is but a vain instance of self-assertion and the will to mastery. Gulling and the guller are exposed as power play and powermonger. City comedy illustrates both how foolish and how dangerous gulling (and models of social interaction predicated on gulling) can be. Such drama might challenge its audience's complacency by delineating the power relations that animate society's sense of itself.

Quomodo is a rich London draper whom we see, not in the role of a trader, but as a usurer and a swindler. As a paradigmatic city-comedy merchant-scoundrel, Quomodo does not merely "stand for" greed; he also "stands for" the fact that both playwright and audience still identify the usurer with the cunning citizen, at a time when everyone from knights to scriveners was lending at interest. He satirizes his own type as much as he comments on the City. By presenting Quomodo as "a most mercilous devourer" in the "man devouring city" (2.2.21), Middleton both confirms the moralists' worst fears about predatory capitalists and directly subverts these fears. For although comedic form demands that the usurer be a devilish, cruel master and a

foolish figure available for humiliation—an accurate definition of an actual social role cannot have it both ways: the
merchant-usurer cannot be the terror of London and also its
gull. The play points to this discrepancy; it presents the
mythic usurer and then proceeds to demythologize him.

Middleton overdetermines the character of Quomodo in
much the same way that we have seen him present London.
Quomodo's principal project is to ensnare the young gallant
Easy in a commodities loan that will end with the merchant's confiscating the cony's estate. "Gentry," says Quomodo, "is the fish we tradesmen catch" (1.1.132). He wants
money and land, he educates his son at Cambridge in prep-
aration for the law, and he hopes to marry his daughter to
someone attached to the court. The unrelieved ambitiousness that characterizes Quomodo's every desire calls attention to itself before pointing to the City outside the song
school. Such ambitiousness has its origins in contemporary
perceptions of the activity of merchants. It is a caricature
that mirrors the way the audience thinks, pointing up the
crudeness of its antibourgeois formulations at the same moment that, at one level, it rearticulates them. The audience
might recognize the merchant on stage as a pastiche of conventional elements; it might not, however, have been ready
to admit that it shared some responsibility for such a figure.
So we find Dekker, in the prologue to *The Roaring Girl*,
lamenting that "each one comes / And brings a play in's
head with him: . . . / If that he finds not here, he mewes
at it."

The effort to satirize not the merchant but the conventional merchant motivates the outrageousness of the draper's mottoes. He lives in a black-or-white, all-or-nothing
world where "They're [the gentry] busy 'bout our wives, we
'bout their lands" (1.1.107). Shortyard, one of Quomodo's
"spirits," argues that "to get riches and children too, 'tis
more than one man can do" (4.1.34). Quomodo wishes there
were more gentry with short yards: he tells Shortyard that
"There are too few of thy name gentlemen, / And that we
feel, but citizens [in] abundance" (1.1.88–89). This leads to

what we might call the Allwit syndrome (after the wittol in *A Chaste Maid in Cheapside*): "To be a cuckold is but for one life, / When land remains to you, your heir, or wife" (1.1.109–10). The culmination is to be found in Quomodo's famous fantasies; in Act 4, scene 1, he makes plans for his (Easy's) estate:

A fine journey in the Whitsun holiday, i'faith, to ride down with a number of citizens and their wives, some upon pillions, some upon sidesaddles, I and little Thomasine i'th' middle, our son and heir Sir Quomodo, in a peach-color taffeta jacket, some horse-length or a long yard before us—there will be a fine show on's I can tell you—where we citizens laugh and lie down, get all our wives with child against a bank, and get up again. (4.1.70–77)

This is the "compleat citizen," and instead of evoking a shudder, he fills us with laughter. But we laugh less at an audience's propensity to perceive the world as Quomodo perceives it, and still less again at its willingness to believe in a world populated by such people.

By the end of *Michaelmas Term*, Quomodo has lost his dreamed-of riches, his daughter has married into the despised gentry, his son has shown himself an ungrateful fool, and he has temporarily lost his wife (to Easy!). As with the presentation of the City and the depiction of the usurer in action, when it is time for retribution, every last stop is pulled. If we feel just a little sorry for Quomodo, at wits' end and thoroughly embarrassed, it is not because we have so enjoyed his craft. We pity him because he is caught in a role that has allowed him no breathing space. He is at once a Bergsonian comic figure and a warning to those who define social roles in narrow and mechanical terms. The conservative voice in Jacobean London may have found it convenient to define the merchant-citizen as a bogeyman, but such reactionary and unimaginative social formulations could be turned back at their sources. Quomodo threatens to overwhelm Easy more as a remarkable presence than as a guller; he fills his lungs, struggling to escape his conventional limits. The inhumanity that Middleton intentionally invests him with confirms the contemporary gentleman's version of the merchant-usurer. If the private-theater audience leaves the song school pleased with the fall of the draper Quomodo, it perpetuates the simplistic prevailing ideology. But if, as I suspect they did, the choristers acted the conventions into high relief, then at this new distance the audience would have had a chance to consider its assumptions. In either case, with a noddy like Easy as our alternative to Quomodo, we can be sure that the theater-wise London audience was not overidentifying with anyone on the choristers' stage.[11]

The merchant-citizen reappears on the song-school stage in 1605–6, in Middleton's *A Mad World, My Masters* and *A Trick to Catch the Old One*.[12] In the former play, the citizen Master Harebrain is limited to a peripheral part. He is presented as a jealous husband before he is a citizen, and he is humiliated in one of the more audacious scenes in city comedy. In *A Mad World*, the merchant-citizen has been deprived of his power as playwright and is reduced to actor/pawn in the minidramas staged by Master Penitent Brothel and courtesan Frank Gullman (the guller returns). Several critics have argued that this play is "about" problems of reality and appearance, the theater and illusion, and blindness. Harebrain's lack of insight in his few scenes is analogous to that of Sir Bounteous Progress as it is seen most clearly in the fifth-act play within the play.[13] But like Dekker and Webster, Middleton is also interested in blurring the distinctions that were said to set gentlemen above citizens. Here, the gentleman makes a fool of himself by keeping a lavish open house in town, and the citizen is a fool for locking himself into his own austere tenement. Neither life is adequate and, unwittingly, Harebrain pays dearly for his narrowness.

In the subplot, Penitent Brothel, with the aid of Frank Gullman, draws Mistress Harebrain away from her jealous husband. In Act 4, Penitent imagines that he is visited by a succubus in the form of his lover, he repents, urges the same to Mistress Harebrain, and he joins hands with both the husband and the wife in a scene of reconciliation that concludes their story (4.4). Harebrain, like Quomodo, is a caricature citizen, but there is no celebration of the citizen's cunning that we can set against his humiliation. He is ill suited to both the comic and the real world because he must play out a specific formulation of a social role. When he first comes on stage, he invokes the world that he fears is threatening his household: "He-cats and courtesans stroll most i'th' night; her [Mistress Harebrain's] friend may be receiv'd and convey'd forth nightly. I'll be at charge for watch and ward, for watch and ward, i'faith" (1.2.1–4). Within minutes, he is entertaining the very person whom he had hoped to lock out. He accepts the courtesan as *Lady* Gullman, a "sweet virgin" and the "only companion" he wishes for his wife (1.2.36). And he hopes that Frank will "terrify" his wife by reading to her "the horrible punishments for itching wantonness, the pains allotted for adultery" (1.2.49–51). Of course, the courtesan has other lessons in mind. She counsels Mistress Harebrain that "The way to daunt is to outlive suspect" (1.2.93) and proves her lesson by successfully deluding the foolish husband.

Harebrain is one of the masters (and mastered) of the title; as Mistress Harebrain explains, his jealousy "masters him as he doth me" (1.2.105). Thus Harebrain finds his place within the sexual motifs of city comedy. His jealousy and Penitent Brothel's intriguing (carried on by the courtesan) are two contesting sides in a struggle for control of Mistress Harebrain's body. As was the case with gulling, this arrangement becomes a model for urban interpersonal relations. But it is an amphibolic structure that suggests at once the ways men deal with one another, and the remarkable insufficiency of their solutions. Both men treat the body as an object, a sexual site, or a piece of property which is entered into a game of domination. Sexuality offers a pretext for the display of power, and as with gulling, this display takes the form of intrigue because it is so effective on the stage. And the playwright has a stake in this skewed sexual battleground at the same time that he parodies it. Middleton too is locked into the ideological presumptions that he ridicules in that only by staging them can he hope to expose them. It bears repeating that the playwright does not stand free and uncontaminated by the prejudices of the society that finances the theater. City comedy offered no revolutionary models for city relations or roles. It could caricature and suggest the tenuousness of prevailing ideologies only by implicating itself. In Theodor Adorno's terms, art both dissents and concedes; it is "a force of protest against the pressure of domineering institutions . . . no less than it reflects their objective substance."[14] At the same moment that city comedy staged the narrowness and the imperfection of the "Harebrain = citizen" equation, it joined those who were humiliating the Harebrain type that they themselves had created.

Harebrain's will to mastery is a parody of the analogous fears and desires of the theater audience. The obsessive *need* for control generally characterizes the stage citizen's relations with his wife and daughter; the *game* of domination characterizes the gallant's connection with these women. This is not merely another way of phrasing the New Comedy configuration of blocking old man, unhappy wife or daughter, and romantically inclined youth. The will to mastery refracts conventional aspects of capitalism when it is seen as a dangerous game played for control over others as well as their resources. Sexual enslavement (in *The Family of Love* and *The Phoenix*, father figures covet their wives and daughter figures) and objectification of the body present us with yet another commodities game that, once again, serves as a structure for both the comedy and the society that comedy depicts.

Comic requirements naturally call for a total reversal of Harebrain's tyranny. In Act 3, scene 2, Harebrain attends down below while his wife goes up to visit the "ailing" courtesan. While Mistress Harebrain retires for lovemaking with Penitent Brothel, Frank Gullman feigns a conversation with her and times her coughs and sobs to the lovers' activity offstage. Harebrain's unwitting mortification is made complete for us as he interjects his foolish comments on the "conversation" up above. Once again it is the patent outrageousness of Middleton's plotting and characterization that directs the audience's attention away from such moral issues as jealousy and adultery and turns us instead to social and political issues figured in hyperconventional types. As is the case with the more subtly developed Shylock, we are interested less in the sin that Harebrain enacts than in the insecure society that needs to create scapegoats. The citizen embodies contradictory fantasies of domination and fears of being duped, but these are the projections of a complacent, or perhaps vindictive, society. City comedy leaves it to its audience either to accept the play's intrigue and characterizations as valid, if exaggerated, versions of the community and its business, or to recognize that the community's own stereotyping is responsible for the fantastic conclusions worked out on stage.

Those who are alert to Middleton's use of social types on the stage will see the social origins of his plays. To them it will be obvious that citizens are not, essentially, good or evil in city comedy. What is parodied, satirized, or caricatured is not the evil citizen, or the evil usurer, but the type of the evil citizen, the conventional usurer, the authorized version of the merchant. A literate city audience sees in a play like *A Trick to Catch the Old One*, not simply one more play about avarice (and, according to one reader, its disturbing pervasiveness—according to another, its comic defeat), but a play about traditional "power of money" plays. The traditional play is brought back to life to be seen for what it is. The foolishness, combined with the tired, old-news quality, of city comedy's characters and plots invites us to pause and notice the ways we imprison one another in inflexible social roles. The patterned, artificial business on stage suggests forcibly the plotted character of the ways men and women typecast one another on the streets. Thus Middleton's moneymen in *A Trick* are not part of a "disarmingly 'realistic' and deadpan presentation of a completely venal world [which] enables him to insinuate that vice is normal."[15] These figures are a presentation of types already precast beyond the theater walls, now set in a context which enables Middleton to examine what Londoners would have vice be. The play's bogeymen—Lucre, Hoard, and Dampit—are caricatures of anticomic types. What turns out to be foolish is not only these characters but the fact that these characters might be allowed by an audience as adequate models for actual citizens.

Middleton takes prejudice, embodies it, makes it look ludicrous, and so stages its shallowness. He presents the provenance of usury (not its morality). When we discover that the men in debt to Dampit are named Sir Lancelot, Lamprey, and Spichcock, we realize that the familiar usurer is related to familiar debtor types. In an economy in which money has made a victim of gallants as well as the usurer, we find that both types look to wit for still another medium of one-upmanship. But nothing changes. The gallants who come to "sport with" Dampit find that the sick old man can still muster his own display of verbal pyrotechnics (4.5.53–54). With the gallants crowding around the bed to abuse Dampit, with Gulf (his partner) cursing him, and with Hoard suggesting his own affinity with the usurer, it is difficult to separate their respective degrees of fatuousness and sordidness. The provenance of usury turns out to be a wide, class-crossing territory. The predominantly social and economic function of usury is seen to determine its morality.

City comedies like *A Trick to Catch the Old One* unfolded before gentlemen who would have been pleased to forget that Robert Cecil and Francis Bacon were greatgrandsons of London aldermen (or that Queen Elizabeth was the granddaughter of a Lord Mayor), and before gentlemen who used this information to explain their distaste for both these men. In the audience, too, were successful citizens who distrusted the court, its courtiers, and gentleman-gallants who had nothing better to do with themselves than to exercise their wit in the City. Simon Eyre was comprehensible to this audience because he was passed through the filters of legend and because he was a jolly old fellow. He would have challenged established prejudices had he been depicted as a thoughtful or meditative city father. And a Lucre or a Hoard fits easily into a barebones social analysis because he lacks complexity. But city comedy's predictable plots might dramatize the meagerness of these configurations. City comedy could suggest that the relations it made so perfectly clear were in fact poorly understood. To stage contemporary estimations of merchants and gallants was not to confirm the meaningfulness of these assessments; rather it was to intimate their impoverishment and to remind the spectator just how well his prejudice served his interests. *A Trick* balances delicately its complicity and its challenge.

The Children of the Revels at the Blackfriars theater seem to have produced *A Trick to Catch the Old One* not long after the choristers. They followed this with Middleton's *Your Five Gallants*, another city comedy that appears to have been mounted first at the song school, and with *The Knight of the Burning Pestle.* Also offered in this genre between 1603 and 1605 were John Marston's *The Dutch Courtesan* and the collaborative work of Chapman, Jonson, and Marston, *Eastward Ho.* The date of the first performance of *The Dutch Courtesan* is not agreed upon; however, because a precise dating is not crucial to our concerns, we may settle for a date between very late in 1603 and soon after *Eastward Ho* in 1605.[16] Marston's citizen, the vintner Mulligrub, seems to owe his presence in the play to the city wit Cocledemoy's need for a victim. Cocledemoy testifies to this when he tells us that "whats'er he has done has been only . . . for wit's sake. . . . All has been done for emphasis of wit" (5.3.134–36). First Cocledemoy steals a nest of Mulligrub's goblets; next, disguised as a barber, he lathers the vintner and runs off with his money; he then inveigles the Mulligrubs out of a salmon dinner and a new standing cup. In Act 4, Cocledemoy accuses Mulligrub of robbery, sees him put in the stocks and then imprisoned, and at the last minute appears to vindicate the vintner as the latter is being carted off to his execution. While Freevill arranges his scheme to shame his friend Malheureux and so teach him a lesson, Cocledemoy's humiliation of the Puritan citizen initiates a full-scale attack on bourgeois "preciseness." Like Malvolio, Mulligrub suffers enough gulling to cause him to worry about his sanity (3.3.96 and 144–50). He is undoubtedly a hypocrite (2.3.12) and a suitable mate for his even less pleasant wife; but the feeling persists that he is merely clay to be worked with. Though certainly a conventional enough citizen, Mulligrub never becomes the dramatist's own self-conscious comment on the type he has created. Marston, himself an Inns of Court man, is prepared to analyze the role of the gallant in ways that do not extend to his treatment of the often-duped vintner.

This point may be clarified by comparing Mulligrub with Harebrain. Both characters are confined to subplots (although both reappear in the fifth-act resolutions), and both are easily identified with conventional city vices: Harebrain is a jealous husband, and Mulligrub is a puritanical tradesman. Unlike Mulligrub, however, Harebrain is never aware that he has been had. The responsibility for any satisfaction that attends his gulling lies solely with the audience. Furthermore, serious questions about sexual mastery and property rights are central to the Harebrain subplot. We are directed beyond Harebrain's vices to the vices of his society and to the audience's stake in them. In *The Dutch Courtesan*, the emphasis throughout the subplot is on the vintner's suffering and his torturer's cleverness. Mulligrub is a tame fool. It is precisely the failure to exaggerate sufficiently his sins, or to connect them with the community, that keeps the audience from questioning his assigned role. The ease with which we identify with Cocledemoy (unlike Penitent Brothel) robs us of the distance that our mature judgment requires. The subplot takes us in and allows us to preserve our certainties. Perhaps the "popularity"[17] of this portion of the play is less encouraging than we might have thought.

If Mulligrub is something of a failure, then his subplot is an exception to the pattern we have been examining. It is more characteristic of city comedy to suggest the inadequacy of contemporary elaborations of social roles by parodying the accepted story. The play arouses the spectator's self-consciousness to the extent that it can be read not only as a conservative reaffirmation of traditional values but also as a progressive challenge to them. City comedy operates as a potential social critique and, inevitably, as a critique of its antecedents (whether they be Roman comedy, Renaissance comedy, morality plays, or verse satire). When Chapman, Jonson, and Marston joined together to write *Eastward Ho*, this self-consciousness seems to have guided their composition of the entire play.[18] Starting with traditional apprentice-makes-good (cf. Heywood) and apprentice-goes-bad (cf. prodigal-son plays) stories, the collaborators wittily upend every assumption behind them at the same time that they carry them out to the letter. Alexander Leggatt has argued that the genial goldsmith Touchstone is a special variety of the merchant-playwright whom we have already encountered. Touchstone "wants life to duplicate the plays he has seen. Just as he wants [the apprentice] Golding to be a theatrical citizen-hero, he wants [the apprentice] Quicksilver to suffer the fate of the fictional prodigal." The result is a "satire on those who see life in terms of theatrical conventions."[19] It is not clear whether Leggatt means to apply this judgment to the audience, but certainly this is what would guarantee the play its unmistakable power.

The playwrights present each character as a bold caricature. Touchstone is a Simon Eyre whom we can laugh at as well as with. He is a pastiche of bourgeois proverbs: "I hired me a little shop, bought low, took small gain, kept no debt book, garnished my shop, for want of plate, with good wholesome thrift sentences—as, Touchstone, 'Keep thy shop, and thy shop will keep thee'; 'Light gains makes heavy purses'; ''Tis good to be merry and wise'" (1.1.54–60). Quicksilver is a roistering, spendthrift apprentice who keeps a whore and connives with the usurer Security and the new-made knight Sir Petronel Flash. He boasts to Touchstone that "I am entertained among gallants, true; they call me cousin Frank, right; I lend them money, good; they spend it, well" (1.1.31–33). Golding, on the other hand, has memorized what he has read:

> Whate'er some vainer youth may term disgrace,
> The gains of honest pains is never base:
> From trades, from arts, from valour honour springs;
> These three are founts of gentry, yea of kings;
>
> (1.1.172–75)

All in good form, the industrious Golding marries Touchstone's obedient daughter and rises at a miraculous pace to the rank of alderman's deputy. Just as surely, Chapman, Jonson, and Marston see to it that we find Golding a precise, unpleasant little conformist. And although they take Quicksilver through his paces as prodigal, prisoner, and penitent, he is always brimming with attractive bravado and exemplary wit. It is in this chiasmus, implicit in most city-comedy caricatures, that *Eastward Ho* catches its audience. By splitting the apprentice/citizen figure into sharply opposed careers, by having good fun with the merchant-master, and by humiliating the usurer, the play shifts all emphasis from character (the given) to characterization (why the given is the given). Advertising its own technique at each step along the way, *Eastward Ho* dutifully meets every requirement of the scholar's definition of city comedy.[20]

Chapman, Jonson, and Marston's play is at once a straightforward city comedy and a sophisticated send-up of the genre's familiar types. Their expectation that the Blackfriars audience would have been alert to the ways a play might parody its own assumptions may have influenced Francis Beaumont when he offered *The Knight of the Burning Pestle* at the same theater, probably in 1607.[21] However, Beaumont's play has an agenda different from *Eastward Ho*'s: in his play, the straightforward city comedy is suppressed. Or, at least, it is severely tested. That Beaumont followed an unsuccessful program is suggested by publisher William Burre, in his epistle printed in the first quarto edition. This "unfortunate child" of a play was "exposed to the wild world, who for want of judgement, or not understanding the privy mark of irony about it . . . utterly rejected it" (ll. 3–6). The whole that emerged from the various parts of *The Knight of the Burning Pestle* was not easily grasped. Satire on citizens and gallants is coupled with satire on city comedy and chivalric romance. The play is, unexpectedly, a celebration of the theater and the imagination, not an attack on mercenary merchants like Venturewell or unsophisticated grocers like George.[22]

The Knight of the Burning Pestle begins with the citizen grocer George demanding that the boys put down their title, *The London Merchant*, that they may "present something notably in honour of the commons of the city" (Induction, 25–26). What George has in mind is something like the Legend of Whittington. What he will not tolerate is another staging of stale, stereotypical roles that he is certain will add up to an attack on the City. Beaumont *is* having fun with George, and with George's lack of sophistication; however, if we are to understand Beaumont's attitude, it is essential to note that he is in at least partial agreement with the grocer. Beaumont, like George, is not interested in a hackneyed ambitious-merchant/cheeky-apprentice/clever-gallant play. Indeed, *The London Merchant,* or that part of it which we do get to see within Beaumont's play, is mitigated by the presence of Humphrey, a ludicrous would-be gallant, not the customary wit of city comedy. A no-holds-barred satire on the City would have called for a clever Humphrey, and it would not have countenanced the success of an unrepentant Jasper. Still, our overriding sense is that *The London Merchant* does not count for very much. Tired, uncritical city comedy with its predictable intrigue and conventional romance is at best a secondary concern for Beaumont. He focuses our attention instead on role creation. In contrast to the trite re-creations of *The London Merchant,* we are offered the unexpected, if equally conventional, roles created by and for Rafe. This knight of the burning pestle is imprisoned in the available roles of chivalric romance just as surely as Jasper and Luce are predetermined by bourgeois romance. But Rafe brings an energy and inventiveness to his performance far exceeding the boundaries that establish a role like Venturewell's or Humphrey's. Repeatedly erupting in the midst of the boys' weary satire, Rafe displays a vitality before which the conventional roles played out in *The London Merchant* pale.

Beaumont has no patience for the tactics employed by a playwright like Middleton to stage and examine conventional urban roles. Where Middleton plays out the roles of stereotypical citizens and gallants and in so doing intimates their origins in status-group conflict, Beaumont asserts directly, in the Induction, that status-group rivalry produces typical city-comedy characters. He then moves on to populate his city with Rafe in his many incarnations. Beaumont relies on George and Nell, who in turn use Rafe, to break free of city comedy's familiar plot. "Plot me no plots," threatens George. With George, Beaumont is willing to "hazard the spoiling" of the play (2.265–66). This risk may have been Beaumont's downfall with the Blackfriars audience; but he cannot be blamed for trying to invigorate city comedy. Nell's prediction that Rafe "will go beyond them all" is delightfully borne out. And Beaumont's play succeeds with us not merely because of what George and Nell thrust forward onto the Blackfriars stage—it succeeds because of the explosion that takes place when bourgeois romance and chivalric romance and city comedy are forcibly brought together.

Generic synergy in *The Knight of the Burning Pestle* produces characters who must give up their expected roles. When Jasper meets Rafe in Act 3, he must improvise. A host, emerging from a place that cannot have been in the plot of *The London Merchant*, presents Rafe with an opportunity for further improvisation. The disruptions occasioned by the *Burning Pestle* plot are mirrored in the anarchic spirit of Old Merrythought. At any one moment, we may be able to assign a particular character a familiar role (May Lord, Lord of Misrule, knight errant, prodigal apprentice, mean-spirited merchant, and so on); however, each and every role is challenged. Even George and Nell, though unable to transcend their middle-class attitudes, are caught up in the imaginative enterprise that is the theater. They stretch their wits even as we recognize the limited scope of their exertions. And the distance they are willing to travel in the realm of the imagination suggests possibilities beyond what a playwright can hope to do with city comedy's standard merchant. For all that Venturewell and George and Nell resemble one another, the grocer and his wife exceed the rich merchant in important ways. They breathe life and excitement into the play that contains Venturewell. And they unleash their man Rafe to travel freely across class and genre boundaries, to create a play that triumphs over the satire on citizenry intended by the boys at Blackfriars.

City comedy was also on the boards in Whitefriars, the private theater housed in a former Carmelite priory. In 1607, the King's Revels produced what may have been a revised version of Middleton's *The Family of Love*.[23] The next year, the same company staged Lording Barry's *Ram Alley*, and when the Queen's Revels moved to the Whitefriars theater in 1609, they offered Jonson's *Epicoene*.[24] The community depicted in *The Family of Love* foreshadows the miniature society of *A Chaste Maid in Cheapside:* in both plays a scheming group of citizens and gallants surrounds a thwarted romantic couple. Furthermore, both plays present gallants and citizens who base their responses to rivals on stereotyped versions of "the citizen" or "the gallant." Bumbling gallants and scheming citizens are sketched in such extreme proportions that they evoke neither our moral approbation nor our disapprobation. They are too ridiculous and so too *unhuman*. We can only ask where such characters come from. And when we are invited to join hands with the Family of Love in the last lines of the play, we are answered: these characters are the nightmares with which the audience populates its own versions of the City.

Both the beginning and the end of this play suggest that Middleton had more in mind than an attack on one of London's more infamous sects. As Margot Heinemann has remarked, "Middleton's sectaries are caricatures," they would seem outrageous even to their own neighbors.[25] But Middleton's evocation of love in *The Family of Love* is meant quite clearly to extend beyond his sectaries. The audience is implicated through its applause at the end, and it is implicated in Middleton's letter "To The Reader" at the outset. We learn that "plays in this city are like wenches new fallen to the trade, only desired of your neatest gallants whiles they're fresh; when they grow stale they must be vented by termers and country chapmen." To attend the theater, or to love, is to look for novelty. In both instances, we can expect to find reflections of ourselves and our prejudices blocking our access to the plays or to our lovers. And this, like the purgations that feature in this play, is an ongoing process.[26] The spectators demand a new play and then another; the characters make it clear that there will be no terminal ministrations. If Mistress Purge's love "must be free still to God's creatures" (5.3.225–26), then we have no reason to imagine that a new, purged, comic society will emerge from the fifth-act trial. Even the romantic lovers of the plot (who have themselves been unromantic enough to allow a premarital pregnancy) are not agents of reform. They too are reconciled to the now expanded, but debased, society they were to have judged. Middleton may have expected something similar from a few in his audience.

The two city comedies that followed *The Family of Love* at Whitefriars do not present merchant-citizen figures. *Epicoene* includes a tippling land and sea captain whose shrewish wife has become a "rich China-woman," but there is almost no concern for this aspect of the City. Lording Barry's *Ram Alley* (1608) substitutes a lawyer-usurer for the merchant-usurers of *A Trick to Catch the Old One* (Barry's play is well in debt to Middleton's). Indeed Barry seems to have been cashing in on the success of city comedy at the rival private theaters. We miss the clear sense of a playwright self-consciously composing types. In *Eastward Ho*, the figures are borrowed and then held up for analysis. In other successful city comedies, characters call our attention to the bases of their characterization. But in *Ram Alley*, we have neither characters with whom we can fully identify nor characters to consider as such. The clichés of the genre (ll. 820 ff., 1207–9, and 1639 ff.),[27] pieced together as they are, fail to suggest their own triteness. They are in the service of the plot and make no gesture toward the audience. Throat, a recognizable lawyer-usurer, is unique in his potential to ask the questions that we have found common to city comedy, but he can do so only by exploiting what in 1608 was already commonplace about the merchant.

The Public Theaters

One of the surprises that follow upon this reading of city comedy is the degree to which the plays staged at the popular theaters match those produced by the boy companies. An examination of dramatic conventions and urban assumptions, and the prevalence of self-conscious characterization (through deliberate exaggeration), continue beyond the private theaters. If merchants seem to receive more favorable treatment, they are no less recognizable as types. We do not need a proper young Golding to prove how easily a type may call into question the very assumptions that generate it. The merchants on the popular stage were also stagings of ideologies that could focus the audience's gaze on social as well as moral suppositions. Alfred Harbage argues that on the private stage, "the cheat and libertine who is a gentleman is treated differently from the cheat and libertine who is a tradesman." We have seen that it was just this perception that city comedies were articulating. The plays underscore this practice and so bring it into question. Thus it is not "fair to say," pace Harbage, "that the difference between the popular and the select drama is the difference between social

consciousness and class animosity."[28] Class animosity finds
its way to the private stage as part of a larger discussion of
social consciousness. And class animosity, within the same
framework, does surface on the popular stage. In either theater, it can be either endorsed or held up for examination. A
patient or genial merchant on the public stage is as much a
product of prejudice (and dramatic convention) as he is just
a good, upstanding member of the urban community. I suspect that we insult the audiences at the open-air theaters
when we limit their reception of these plays to identification with heroes and villains. There was a regular and sophisticated theater audience that was capable of judging enacted versions of its own experience—especially when each
element of city comedy was drawn in such high relief.

We might have found the rich linen draper Candido, in
Dekker and Middleton's *I Honest Whore* (1604), on the private stage or the public stage. It happens that this was a
production of Prince Henry's Men at the Fortune.[29] This
playhouse, erected soon after the completion of the Globe
in 1599 (and constructed by the same builder), represented
a significant part of Henslowe and Alleyn's efforts to keep
in step with their chief rivals. Chambers notes that the theater's northwest London site "would be convenient for the
well-to-do population, which was establishing itself in the
western suburbs."[30] But in the first decade after it had
opened its door, the Fortune began to acquire a reputation
(shared with the Red Bull) for its unruly audiences and its
"vulgar fare."[31] The mixture of humours, romance, and morality plots that we find in *I Honest Whore* is not unchar-
acteristic of the offerings at the Fortune. As the subtitle of
this play makes clear—*The Humours of the Patient Man,
and the Longing Wife*—the merchant-citizen role is played
in a low humours plot. Candido, an unfailingly patient
draper, refuses to snap back at his shrewish wife, Viola, or
at the band of gallants who would try his patience. He is a
"monstrous patient man"; and he "haz no more gall in him
than a Doue, no more sting than an Ant" (1.2.72–73). Yet
for all his patience, we come to see Candido as a successful

shopkeeper. His patience is something of a strategy: we are fond of him for it, and he loses nothing by it.

The patient merchant at the Fortune modifies the poles between which we have seen the private-theater merchant-citizen moving. Justiniano, Quomodo, Lucre, Hoard, and their brethren are alternately (and often at the same moment) childish and menacing. Candido is gentle and politic. He breaks the circle of gulling with his patience as he consistently refuses to be inflamed, but he paradoxically initiates a more subtle form of gulling as he uses his patience for profit. His version of the shopkeeper's creed bears a resemblance to the mottoes Touchstone pronounces (the following year) in *Eastward Ho*. He is even more reminiscent of another successful draper, William Scott, the author of *An Essay of Drapery*. Candido's gentle, or patient, craft is a precursor of Scott's *sancta avaritia* because it combines predatory as well as mild traits into one bourgeois ethic. For Scott, a little flattery and even a little deception is tolerable. The played-upon Candido turns out to be no more innocent than Scott's ideal shopkeeper: "Oh, he that means to thriue, with patient eye / Must please the diuell, if he come to buy" (1.5.127–28). This is not to suggest that Candido is an intriguer comparable to Quomodo. Nevertheless, it is fair to say that Candido's patience represents a defensive strategy deployed in a world that is manifestly antibourgeois. The fact that his journeyman and apprentices, at moments of crisis, stand behind their master, points to the citizen's need for a solid line of defense. The apprentices attempt with cudgels only what Candido more politicly accomplishes with patience.

The Candido subplot parallels the honest-whore main plot. The patient draper ends up in a madhouse with the chaste heroine. But the feminization of the shopkeeper does not stop at his passivity or his wife's claim that "hee haz not all things belonging to a man" (1.2.58–59). Dekker and Middleton make it quite clear that the alternatives offered to women and citizens by the prevailing ethos of the gentry are equally unsatisfactory. It is fitting that the whore Bellafront end up in a madhouse—once she has been rejected as a whore and as a chaste woman, there is little left for her to choose. Similarly, Candido is intolerable as a man of patience, as a gentle husband, and, implicitly, as a successful shopkeeper. In the final scene, even the Duke rejects Candido's patience: "Twere sinne all women should such husbands haue. / For euery man must then be his wiues slaue" (5.2.512–13). That the healthiest members of the society are judged unfit is an obvious, if not especially original, satiric statement about the values of that society. In the case presented by Candido, however, the Fortune audience is asked to applaud his patience at the same time that it is expected to laugh at it. The audience is offered the citizen in caricature, as holy fool and as prosperous "senator." Whatever the poles, the citizen is not available as an unequivocal role model.

In Dekker's sequel to *I Honest Whore*, Candido is a figure of considerably less interest.[32] Or perhaps he is simply more confusing. Candido is still "the Patient Man," but he is no longer passive; he allows the knight Lodovico to goad him into a confrontation with his new wife. In *II Honest Whore*, Candido characterizes his first wife as "curste Cowes milke . . . ranke in taste" (2.2.72–73), and he sets out to tame his new wife because the marital conflict is now "for the breeches." This is a new, *im*patient Candido, a husband with at least something of a will to mastery. But Dekker is not interested in sustaining this side of the draper, and by Act 3, scene 3, Candido is once again the imperturbable shopkeeper of *I Honest Whore*. In the 1604 play, Candido presents one version of the untenable role assigned the Jacobean merchant-citizen; in the sequel, it is Dekker's characterization, not social prejudice, which undercuts the draper. In his first scene (with his wife) he is assertive; in his second scene (in which he is played upon by the gallants), he is knowingly patient; but in the third scene (in which he is caught up in the thievery of the main plot) he is merely a pawn. Like Mulligrub, Candido (in *II Honest Whore*) will not provoke any qualms in the audience about his sufferings. He is peripheral to the play and inconsequential to the polis. At the end of the play, when Bellafront and Candido find themselves (this time) in Bridewell, only the honest whore's presence asks us to evaluate the trajectory of a social career. Candido as a "thief" in no way reflects on his activities as a draper, and the Duke's closing words—commending Candido's patience as a "Patterne for a King"—bear absolutely no relation to the events that brought the draper to prison.

In *I* and *II Honest Whore*, the characterization of the merchant-citizen is related more to humours conventions than to the current debate over the merchant's role; but, as we have seen was the case on the private stage, it was just this humours characterization that could call prevailing assumptions into question. The shopkeepers in the audience at the Fortune were staged as both winning fools and wealthy businessmen. The double bind that distinguished the stage merchant was an accurate articulation of the spectator-merchant's dilemma. And the dynamics of the shopkeeper as lovable fool were rehearsed once again in 1611, in Dekker and Middleton's *The Roaring Girl*.[33] At the center of this play, overwhelming every other character, is the roaring girl Moll Frith (alias Moll Cutpurse). We will return to Moll in a later chapter, when we consider the women in city comedy; but it is appropriate to point out now that the gender reversal figured in her character also characterizes the merchant-citizen couples that appear in the second, third, and fourth acts of the play.

The citizen scenes in *The Roaring Girl*, beginning with Act 2, scene 1, present us with a cityscape unrivaled on the Jacobean stage. The stage directions call for "three shops open in a ranke: the first a Poticaries shop, the next a Fether shop: the third a Sempsters shop . . ." The audience is linked to the actors who shuttle back and forth, from one shop to the next on the open city street. Cheapening, punning, bantering, and trade intersect as the exchange of capital infiltrates customer, marital, extramarital, and master-servant relations. The customary cry of the shopkeeper—"what ist you lacke"—acquires new overtones as the entire economy of the City is sexualized. Mistress Gallipot, the apothecary's wife, dallies with Laxton, who in turn is extorting his keeping from her. The lecherous gallant Jack Dapper seeks vainly the favors of Mistress Tiltyard, the featherer's wife. And Goshawk, still another city fop, provokes Mistress Openwork by telling her that her husband is unfaithful to her. As was the case in *Westward Ho*, the women in Dekker and Middleton's play derive their pleasure from sporting with, but not quite consummating, adultery. The sexual unsettledness of their marriages makes for good dramatic plotting at the same time that it suggests the precariousness of their domestic economies.

In fact, as Peter Laslett has argued, there "was no sharp distinction between [the man at the head of the household's] domestic and economic functions. His wife was both his partner and his subordinate, a partner because she ran the family, . . . a subordinate because she was woman and wife."[34] Thus the domineering citizen-wives that were regulars on the private stage (we see this type most vividly in Mistress Otter in *Epicoene*) catered to obvious, ideologically motivated prejudices concerning citizens. Uxoriousness filtered into middle-class economics and was righted by the self-assured gallant who redressed the balance by using the city wives. On the public stage, in plays like *The Roaring Girl*, this balance remains precarious because neither husband nor gallant is afforded full command of the relation. The three triangles in this play elaborate several permutations of this theme but decide in the end for what cannot be imagined to be anything but comedy's enforced amicable settlement. Laxton and Mistress Gallipot contrive an elaborate story to rob Gallipot of his money, but before long Mistress Gallipot asks her husband's pardon. Laxton calls the whole plot a test of her fidelity to her husband, and they all go off to dine together. Mistress Openwork's initial suspicions of her husband's unfaithfulness give way to a reconciliation and a plot of their own to catch Goshawk for disturbing their marriage. Finally, we are presented with

Mistress Tiltyard, the one wife who never gives her gallant a chance.

The solution to all the citizen plots is citizen solidarity and a generous widening of the community to include the city gallants. However, the play yields center stage to the disarray of the citizen marriages, not to their reestablishment at the offstage feast following Act 4. Here, just as on the private stage, the wives have little patience with their men. Mistress Gallipot tells her husband that his "loue is all words; giue mee deeds, I cannot abide a man thats too fond ouer me, so cookish; thou dost not know how to handle a woman in her kind" (3.2.22–24). He is an "aperne husband" and a "cotqueane" (3.2.29–30). Mistress Openwork complains that her husband's business trips rob her of the pleasures of her vigor: "I send you for hollands, and you're ith low countries with a mischiefe, I'me seru'd with good ware byth shift, that makes it lye dead so long vpon my hands, I were as good shut vp shop, for when I open it I take nothing" (2.1.202–6). Throughout Act 2, Mistress Openwork refers to the sempster's shop as her own, while Openwork speaks timidly of his "mouse" and consistently refrains from crossing her (2.1.137–51). As for Gallipot, his wife is his "mouse" or his "honey Pru." All the wives seem to resent or distrust Moll (2.1.86–87 and 209–11), and yet they fail to see their own urges toward domination as versions of the roaring girl's role. The husbands are discredited for not being like Moll; their wives are discredited when they imitate her, and they forfeit our interest when they reassume their "rightful" roles as obedient wives.

The citizens in *The Roaring Girl* are not so much triumphant over their wives or the gallants as they are, finally, left undamaged by them. They are allowed their profit but must pay for it by being accounted, at least temporarily, fools. But like the audience at the private theaters, those at the Fortune would have been well equipped to see a Gallipot or a Tiltyard as an artificial type. Since an attack on the citizen that confirmed prevailing aristocratic notions would be least expected at a public theater, we may interpret the equivocal and confusing characterizations in *The Roaring Girl* as an exposure of the contradictions inherent in the denigratory citizen type. City comedy at the open-air theaters presented a citizen no more encouragingly than its competition indoors. This suggests that we must examine the degree to which audiences identified with characters. By exaggerating the worst traits of gentry and merchants alike, city comedy distanced its audience, and it enforced the discrepancy between spectators' perceptions of themselves and their socially conditioned perceptions of others.

It is another such extravagant depiction of a society populated by figures who exploit one another on the basis of mutual misperceptions that Middleton presents in his great multiple-plot comedy *A Chaste Maid in Cheapside.*[35] We see a profoundly bankrupt society. Like its abused romantic heroine Moll, we are "led through gutters" (3.3.31) of morality, sexuality, and theology. The story of hope and renewal figured by the Lenten/Easter context is consistently upended or desecrated. Fathers deny their offspring (Whorehound), debase them (Yellowhammer), consider them their ruination (Touchwood senior, Sir Oliver Kix), and even when celebrating them (the christening scene, 3.2), devalue the very rituals that make such celebrations meaningful. Mothers are adulteresses (Lady Kix and Mrs. Allwit), they abuse their children (Maudline Yellowhammer), or they dispose of them (the Country Wench).[36] No one is spared in *A Chaste Maid*, whether merchant, wife, knight, noble, gentry, civil servant, prostitute, mistress, Puritan, or academic. Indeed, Middleton seems self-consciously to have stuffed this city comedy with the *reductio* of every conceivable role in the genre. Because there is no one worth identifying with (the lovers Moll and Touchwood junior have almost no voice and are fairly overwhelmed by everyone else), we are left to witness the at once mechanical and ruthless energy with which the representatives of these roles take advantage of one another. But it is not life that is meaningless, or bankrupt, for Middleton; it is the society that can envision itself only in roles which derive their substance from hatred and self-

interest. This is the most conventional of all city comedies—each type and its role are defined by excess—and it is
the demise of just this conventionality that is staged.

In the following chapters, we will have occasion to return to *A Chaste Maid* and to the roles enacted by the
women and gentry in the play; for the moment we may
confine ourselves to citizens Yellowhammer and Allwit.
They, like the other figures in this play, exemplify the
"comic distortion and violent coloring" that Middleton applies to stock characters.[37] Yellowhammer, a goldsmith, has
a son who is a graduate of Cambridge (the Puritan university) and a daughter whom he would like to see marry Sir
Walter Whorehound (instead of poor Touchwood junior). He
is also busy with preparations for his son's marriage to a
"Welsh Gentlewoman," who is in fact Sir Walter's cast-off
mistress. The prestige that would accompany Yellowhammer's offsprings' marriages to socially respectable wealth
circumscribes the goldsmith's entire play life. Looking after
his son and daughter as he might an investment, he warns
that "We cannot be too wary in our children" (1.1.166). Indeed Yellowhammer suits himself entirely to the role that
Sir Walter has cast him in. Overreaching but easily over-
reached, he embodies the prime contemporary version of a
"citizen's life." In *A Chaste Maid in Cheapside,* Yellowhammer is but one of a cast of players Middleton uses to work
out the consequences for a society populated by conventional types. As each figure fails to have his way, one and
then another inadequate social role is revealed.

The more Yellowhammer answers to his rivals' and the
audience's expectations, so much more does he display the
fabric from which he is fashioned. When Allwit informs
Yellowhammer that his prospective son-in-law is a whoremonger, the goldsmith receives the news calmly: "Well,
grant all this, say now his deeds are black, / Pray, what serves
marriage but to call him back? / I've kept a whore myself
. . ." (4.1.240–42). He is just the hypocrite we expect, and
our laugh is a laugh of recognition. We know this type, and
we know that Middleton knows it too. Whether Yellowham-

mer is reacting to his daughter's assumed death by worrying over what the neighbors will think of him (5.2.92–93), or rejoicing over the economy of letting one feast serve for two marriages (5.4.113–15), he is literally true to form. He plays an entirely conventional part with a prescripted social identity that has replaced any vestige of autonomy.

The excess caricatured in Yellowhammer is his monomania; Allwit's excessiveness may be located in the way he plays out his role as cuckold. He is a wittol, a "complaisant cuckold,"[38] whose role inscribes him in a remarkable matrix of power relations. Allwit is head of a family, but he is not the father of the offspring; he is his wife's husband but not her mate; and although he is a citizen, he has no need to employ himself as such (Sir Walter supports the family). Like Tim Yellowhammer, who would use logic to prove a whore an honest woman, Allwit has set out to prove that the conventional and miserable citizen-cuckold can be an eminently satisfied wittol:

> I am like a man
> Finding a table furnish'd to his hand,
> As mine is still to me, prays for the founder,—
> 'Bless the right worshipful the good founder's life.'
> I thank him, 'has maintain'd my house this ten years,
> Not only keeps my wife, but a keeps me
> And all my family: I am at his table;
> He gets me all my children, and pays the nurse.
> Monthly or weekly; puts me to nothing,
> Rent, nor church-duties, not so much as the scavenger:
> The happiest state that ever man was born to!
> (1.2.11–21)

If anything, Allwit boasts, it is the founder (Sir Walter) who is the jealous one, not the husband (1.2.52–55). Richard Levin concludes that Allwit carries the "commercialization of love to its logical conclusion," or perhaps to its absurd reduction.[39] He is not interested in his wife, his family, or the community. His motivation is exclusively self-interest: "I feed, laugh, or sing" (1.2.55). Irresponsible as long as things are going his way, Allwit turns vicious just as soon as he sees his means of support giving way. But then he is only a shocking personification of the same poles of infantile desire and authentic menace that have delimited the stage merchant-citizen throughout the decade.

Middleton explodes the entire convention of merchant-citizen cleverness with Allwit. Unlike Quomodo, or Hoard, he is not first clever and then shown to be a dupe; rather he is always perceived as a fool (in spite of his cleverness). It makes little sense to argue that Allwit alone escapes punishment—he is always a mark of derision, and he is his own tormentor. As Alexander Leggatt has written, Allwit "is in many respects the most enslaved character in the play."[40] If Allwit is all wit, he is nothing else. Having emptied the citizen role of nearly all value, Middleton stages the results of an anticonduct book. His wittol endures because he does not father children and does not earn a living; beyond his food, his laughter, and his song, he does not do anything. The wittol enacts an antirole. He is an absence in the urban community, a voyeur, and a preposterous staging of the ideologies that generate merchant-citizens. It is fitting that Allwit, recycled into a new social role beyond the boundaries of *A Chaste Maid in Cheapside,* will return in the Strand as a brothel keeper. Once again, others will take "labour all out of [his] hands" (1.2.51).

What we see in city comedy, then, is the enslavement of all merchants in predetermined social roles. They are threats to the community or they are miscalculating fools (often they are both at once), they are sexually inadequate or they covet their wives and relatives, they are clambering out of their status group and aiming for a country estate or they are intolerably proud of their citizenship. City comedy offers a consistent analysis of the social or cultural contradictions that are expressed in these contemporary conventional accounts. To borrow from a statement on the function of art that was developed in a different context, we may say that city comedy employs "popular codes to address itself to social-political contradictions in the actual world."[41] And we must not be fooled by the prevalence of these popular codes: dividing stage and audience, they call attention to themselves, and, potentially, to their shortcomings or contradictoriness. The successful city comedy points to the discrepancy between ideologically motivated accounts of urban social relations and the actual experience of London merchant-citizens. This is not to say that the playwrights, or, for that matter, the pamphleteers and the preachers, would ever have been able actually to mirror this experience. All articulations of social roles are filtered through interests and ideology—but it is precisely this important truth that city comedy could stage. It could show that the calculating merchant answered to the aristocrat's fears, as well as to the requirements of first-class comedy of intrigue. And *we* can best understand the city comedy of this period by reading it in the context of late Tudor and early Stuart London. The uncertain status of the merchant-citizen on the streets bears upon his staged surrogate in ways that any contemporary theatergoer would have been quick to recognize.

4

The Gentleman-Gallant

Historians do not agree on the size of the population of Jacobean London. Depending upon whether or not one includes the liberties, the outparishes, and Westminster, figures have ranged from 160,000 to 250,000.[1] Between ten and fifteen percent of these Londoners were members of an elite minority.[2] They filled the ranks that began with squires and knights and rose to dukes, they were called courtiers and gallants, and they were referred to, generically, as gentlemen. City comedy has little to do with gentleman-courtiers (though very many European and English writers were interested in this group) because citizen drama travels only rarely to Westminster and the royal chambers. Instead, city comedies concern themselves with men whom we may, for convenience, divide into gentlemen and gallants. These are the men whom we found at odds with the merchant-citizens discussed in the preceding chapter. We have seen that in the late Tudor and early Stuart period, commentators were attempting to fashion "the merchant"; we find, as well, that they were attempting to redefine "the gentleman" at a moment when his economic and social stability was being tested.

Lawrence Stone suggests a broad historical perspective within which we may locate the changes that generated new definitions of the gentleman:

In the Middle Ages war was a time-absorbing and honourable occupation; by the late seventeenth century some noblemen had developed a passion for reading, collecting, and antiquarianism, others busied themselves in the hunting-field or on the benches at
Quarter Sessions, while yet others were absorbed in the intrigues
and ceremonies of the Court. At first [under Elizabeth and the early
Stuarts], however, nobles and squires found that the end of military
service left time lying heavily on their hands, for administration of
the estate was no longer a very time-consuming occupation now
that most of the estate was let out on long lease, and little was kept
in hand.[3]

Whereas lineage had once been sufficient to determine gentility, now "virtue, education, and the capacity to serve the
State" were also important factors (p. 27). Or at least this
was what men like James Cleland, Richard Brathwait, and
Henry Peacham were arguing. Ruth Kelso concludes that
"True nobility is almost always defined as that of race and
virtue."[4] The gallant is thus reminded that "it was only the
inclination to virtue, not virtue itself, that was inherited"
(p. 23).
   The distance between gallant and gentleman is either
the implicit or explicit text of much of the commentary
devoted to this status group. In his address "To the Knowing
Reader," Richard Brathwait asks, "For who knowes not, (if
he know any thing) how the *Gentry* of this age, through a
depraved effeminacie, must be in custome with the fashion,
to purchase him the title of Gentleman? Where he is to
enter commerce with Taylor, Haberdasher, Millener, Sempster, and sundry other appertinences of a *Gentleman:* which
intime, worke *Gentility* out of love with *Hospitality*, engag-
ing him so deeply to vanity, as by a strange *Catastrophe*, he
ever ends with misery."[5] In Stuart London, we need not look
far for what Brathwait called "depraved effeminacie." According to Stone, between 1608 and 1613, King James
"bought a new cloak every month, a new waistcoat every
three weeks, a new suit every ten days, a new pair of stock-
ings, boots, and garters every four or five days, and a new
pair of gloves every day. Silks alone were costing the King

and Queen over £10,000 a year, and the wardrobe expense altogether was running at over £25,000 as early as 1610" (p. 563). By 1618, there were 148 foreign tailors in London (pp. 585–86). Even in the 1590s, Roger, earl of Rutland, found a way to spend £1,000 or more a year on his clothes; the earl of Salisbury spent £40,000 on construction at Hatfield between 1608 and 1612; and in 1612, the earl of Cumberland had a painter gild and paint his bakemeats (pp. 565, 554, and 560). It is no wonder that the viscount of Conway boasted that "we eat and drink and rise up to play and this is to live like a gentleman; for what is a gentleman but his pleasure?" (p. 27). We recall citizen Allwit's "I feed, laugh, or sing."

Jacobean London had become what F. J. Fisher has called a "centre of conspicuous consumption."[6] Lawrence Stone explains, "Over-consumption led to sale of land, which generated social mobility and psychological insecurity among the purchasers; in its turn insecurity caused a struggle for status, exacerbated by the inflation of honours, which found expression in competitive consumption" (p. 185). And to consume as well as to be seen consuming, one was best off in London. Sir Anthony Denton wrote (c. 1601–5) to Thomas Isham that "London is the garden of England whear we may all live together" (p. 387). Thomas Wright, with what may be more than a hint of sarcasm, wrote that "our Northern and Welshmen, when they come to London, are very simple, and unwary, but afterward, by conversing a while, and by the experience of other men's behaviours, they become wonderful wise and judicious."[7] All the expenses of housekeeping could be channeled into high living once one had moved to the capital. James, who set new records for profligacy, was not above complaining that "Soon London will be all England."[8] Stone cites his 1616 declaration that "one of the greatest causes of all gentlemen's desire, that have no calling or errand to dwel in London, is apparently the pride of women . . . because the new fashion is to be had no where but in London" (p. 391). Ben Jonson pointed to the same problem: "First, to be an accomplished gentleman— that is, a gentleman of the time—you must give over housekeeping in the country and live together in the city amongst gallants where, at your first appearance, 'twere good you turned four or five acres of your best land into two or three trunks of apparell."[9]

There was, of course, a serious attempt on the part of some men to identify aspects of post-Elizabethan gentility. For example, in 1626, Sir William Vaughan listed the "means to discern a gentleman":

First he must be affable and courteous in speech and behaviour. Secondly, he must have an adventurous heart to fight and that but for very just quarrels. Thirdly, he must be endowed with mercy to forgive the trespasses of his friends and servants. Fourthly, he must stretch his purse to give liberally unto soldiers and unto them that have need; for a niggard is not worthy to be called a gentleman.[10]

Brathwait spoke of mildness, munificence, fortitude and moderation:

A gentleman is a Man of himselfe, without the addition of either the Taylor, Millener, Seamster or Haberdasher. Actions of goodnesse he holds his supreme happinesse. . . . Hee scornes pride, as a derogation to Gentry. . . . He admires nothing more than a constant spirit, derides nothing more than a recreant condition, embraceth nothing with more intimacie, than a prepared resolution. Hee viewes the *City*, with a princely command of his affections. No object can with-draw him from himselfe; or so distract his desires, as to covet ought unworthily; or so intraunce his thoughts, as to admire ought servilely.[11]

Peacham repeats the call for "temperance and . . . moderation of the mind";[12] but he replaces liberality with frugality and adds religiosity and learning. Peacham is careful also to remind his reader that the gentleman must be "beneficial and useful to his country . . . for they hardly are to be admitted for noble who, though of never so excellent parts, consume their light as in a dark lanthorn in contemplation and a Stoical retiredness."[13]

Time and again, it turns out that commentators who

sought to distinguish a gentleman from a gallant, or a man of virtue from a profligate, had to distinguish first between gentlemen and commoners or plebians. James Cleland accounts for the old saw "When Adam delved, and Eve span, / Who was then a Noble man?" by agreeing that "in respect of beginning . . . [and] our ending too, we are all equals . . . but in the middle course, betweene our birth and burial, wee are ouerrunne by our betters, and of necessitie must needes confesse that some excell & are more noble than others."[14] But Cleland goes on to remark that "be a man neuer so wealthie, neuer so highlie preferred, if he lack the character of vertue, he is to be valued but as a stampe of honor set upon base bullion."[15] While men believed that wealth and lineage went a long way toward constituting gentility, they wanted, as well, to make it clear that a true gentleman was more than his name and his estate. The idea that gentility meant gentle birth would never be put by, but many worked hard to add onto this foundation. Kelso cites a tract translated from the French in 1598, which informs us that "The stocke and linage make not a man noble or ignoble, but use, education, instruction, and bringing up maketh him so: for when a man from infancy is instructed in good manners, all the rest of his life he shall be inclined into acts of nobility and vertue" (p. 24). Perhaps one of the most popular (and succinct) definitions of a gentleman is to be found in Sir Thomas Smith's *De Republica Anglorum:* "whosoever studieth the lawes of the realme, who studieth in universities, who professeth liberall sciences, and to be shorte, who can live idly and without manuall labour, and will beare the port, charge and countenance of a gentleman, he shall be called master, for that is that title which men give to esquires and other gentlemen, and shall be taken for a gentleman" (p. 26).

For every serious attempt to delineate "the gentleman," this figure, like "the merchant," had to contend with witty and satirical renderings of his character. Men like Dekker, Nashe, and Greene turned often to the gentleman-gallant as a subject for their satire. Clever character writing on the

"Gentery" comes also from the pen of Thomas Gainsford. In *The Rich Cabinet*, he sums up the gentleman's life in a half a dozen different ways:

A Gentleman wihout meanes, is a painted bardge without oares; faire to looke on, but their is no use of him, neither in calm, nor storme. (sig. 51ᵛ)

. . . if some luckie and vnlookt-for *Neptune* ioyne not with *Venus*, to hale him in, and land him in the lap of some lustie Lady, or rich widow, he is driven into some dusty ditch, where he rots, if not unseene, and unknowne, yet unpittied and unrespected for all his rich painting. (sig. 52)

A Gentleman without meanes, is like faire house without furniture, or any inhabitant, saue onely an idle house-keeper. (sig. 52)

He railes on Usurers, the dearth, bribery and corruption of the times. He abhors Bayliffes, Sergeants and Sheriffs. He hunts on Sundaies, and wrangles for tythes; yet sildome or neuer goeth to law with his neighbours. He is alwaies in pursute of some good widow. . . . The dislike of his owne, inclines him to seeke better fortunes in other countries. . . . He well approues necessarie warres, for those that haue bodies fit for cold and hard beds . . . but onely desperation of meanes driues himselfe to the warres . . . (sigs. 54ᵛ–55)

With a little Labour, he would proue a prettie excheator, a prowling promoter, or a good land-spaniel, or setter for a hungry Courtier, to smell him out a thousand pound sute, for a hundred pound profit. (sig. 55ᵛ)

For conclusion, this beggarly Gentleman, is too good to be a seruingmen, to poore to be a Merchant-man, too weake to be a husband-man, too wastfull to be a tradesman, too lazie to be an artificer, too idle to be a scholer, too tender to be a souldier: and yet hath matter in him, to make him fit for all this, with good moulding in tract of time . . . he is potentially apt for anything, but actually good for nothing. (sig. 56)

The second citation, in which Gainsford writes of the gentleman rotting, "not unseene, and unknowne," points to an aspect that we find especially prominent in writings on gentlemen, that of being on view, of visibility and spectacle. The life of the gentleman is characterized by what one biographer of Sir Walter Ralegh has called a "histrionic sensibility constantly striving for a moving presentation of the self."[16] Though many of the gentlefolk in London were not courtiers, all seem to have felt the influence of Castiglione's and Machiavelli's notions of the self-fashioning, role-playing courtier or prince. The courtier, it has been argued, would have been at fault "*not* to behave theatrically, not to be mindful of beholders, not to afford the finest possible spectacle."[17] The gentleman does not merely act magnanimously or virtuously; he dresses himself in these traits. Brathwait writes that "there is no one virtue which doth better adorne or beautifies man, than Temperance or Moderation."[18] Peacham believes that "There is no one thing that setteth a fairer stamp upon nobility than evenness of carriage and care of our reputation."[19] Once "dressed," the gentleman (or gallant) plays out his role before an admiring, or an amused, public. Thus Brathwait concludes hundreds of pages devoted to the English gentleman by remarking that "Hee hath plaid his part on this Stage of Earth with honour; and now in his *Exit* makes heaven his harbour."[20] Ralegh, in a famous epigram, sees himself "drest for this short Comedy," and his life, "a play of passion."[21] Dekker has copious instructions for the gallant who would act his part on the stage—the "mediterranean isle" of St. Paul's. You must "bend your course directly in the middle line, that the whole body of the church may appear to be yours; where, in view of all, you may publish your suit in what manner you affect most."[22] It would seem that the gentry in city-comedy audiences were well aware that their lives might be thought of as roles for which they themselves were in large part responsible. Gentlemen and gallants were at once playwrights, costumers, stage managers, and actors.

The gentry accounted for less than five percent of the population of England, but after 1550, they owned between forty and fifty percent of the land. It was the income and power derived from this land that set off those men below the peerage and above the yeomanry as a distinct social force.[23] Landed gentry garnered significant new wealth as prices rose precipitously between 1550 and 1640. The "price of wool rose fourfold, timber more than fivefold, agricultural produce in general over sixfold, and some products, cattle, sheep and grain, more than sevenfold." Rents were raised, leases were shortened, enclosures increased, more land was cultivated or drained and then plowed up, and mining and quarrying increased dramatically.[24] Between 1575 and 1625, the gentry oversaw unprecedented country-house building while the dissolution of the monasteries presented landowners with even greater opportunities to extend and consolidate their estates.[25] These changing economic conditions (coupled with the uncertain fate of those allied to various factions in Westminster) resulted in well-publicized rises and falls in personal fortunes. Lesser gentry rose into the ranks of the greater gentry, and not a few of the peerage experienced drastic, if temporary, declines in their holdings. But the net effect during the sixteenth and seventeenth centuries "was that the gentry increased their share of the land: indeed they may have doubled it to something approaching half of the total."[26]

Needless to say, social changes accompanied gains and losses in other arenas. We have seen that social prejudice worked against conferring such dignity as might correspond to the role of the merchant in Jacobean London, and not a few, in the face of a profligate court and the conspicuous consumption that I have merely touched upon, had unflattering things to say about gentlemen. Particularly in London, where men of means were strutting up and down the center aisle at Paul's, where they were supporting the brothels in and about the Inns of Court and showing their latest fashions from the most prominent seats at the theaters—in London, many gentlemen were thought of as gallants. And what a gentleman-gallant was said to represent could be taken advantage of just as the role of the merchant-citizen could be fashioned to suit now one interest group, now another. The men who wrote city comedies wrought from such discourse a figure who was, preeminently, self-confident. The playwright who set gallants in motion alongside self-justifying citizens posited that the gallant's faults as well as his virtues were accompanied by his certainty that he could "beare the . . . countenance of a gentleman." Self-confidence is part of the subtext of the conduct books. In city comedy, it is the essence of the gallant's style, whether he is affable or vain, generous or profligate. Indeed, this confidence was largely a matter of style, not substance, and such style was something few citizens could even hope to master.

Self-confidence is that aspect of the courtier's *sprezzatura* available to the gallant and the gentleman. It means that the gallant, even when he is deplored for his lust or his idleness, is rarely on the defensive. He may assume a base of social legitimacy unavailable to the citizen. Unlike the merchant-citizen, who is either stolid or calculating, and who can have no innocent fun, the gentleman-gallant may engage in frivolity. Conversely, unlike the gentleman-gallant, the merchant fails to compensate for his earnestness with charm; he rarely succeeds in suggesting grace or graciousness. Even at a time of economic uncertainty, a bedrock of social sanctions licenses the gentleman. In Middleton's *No Wit, No Help like a Woman's,* the gallant Savorwit distinguishes the gentleman from the citizen: "Our knavery is for all the world like a shifting bankrupt; it breaks in one place, and sets up in another; he tries all trades, from a goldsmith to a tobacco seller; we try all shifts, from an outlaw to a flatterer; he cozens the husband, and compounds with the widow; we cozen my master, and compound with my mistress; only here I turn o'th' right hand from him; he is known to live like a rascal, when I am thought to live like a gentleman."[27] The gentleman who might doubt his credentials when challenged by rival gentry, and who might tremble as the target for a merchant's attack on his fiscal well-being, nonetheless felt remarkably secure about his social status and its attendant prerogatives when dealing with merchant-citizens. The stage gallant is tolerated, not only because he represents a glamorous version of the social order that the audience aspires to, but because he acts with the same spirit and the same exemplary ingenuity that are expected of the gentleman outside of the theater. When the gentleman is presented as a gallant, and when his trickery is not directed toward the amelioration of social tensions, we must choose whether to admire his clever tricks or to reject him for his narrow social vision. In either case, it is the gentleman-gallant's confidence that he is on the "right" side that offers us the possibility of uncompromised complicity.

City comedies puncture this self-confidence from time to time, but they do not examine all of its ramifications. The plays permit the gallant or gentleman bravely to play out his frequently borrowed version of a role, but these are dramas unwilling to draw the conclusion that the gallant or gentleman is, solely, his role. In fact, we encounter a curious reversal in city comedy: the merchant-citizen, the man associated with Puritan strictures against acting and spectacle, is figured as master pretender, one who eternally adopts roles that will lead to greater prosperity, while the gentleman-gallant, a type which parades its finery and purchases the props indispensable to a public (almost ceremonial) life, is figured as a man with an essential social identity, a core self that underlies a set of theatrical personae. The merchant-citizen is an obsessive actor (or intriguer) whose obsession has gotten the better of him; the gentleman-gallant is a confident actor, a master of his craft who feels sure that he can turn aside from his playacting when it has served its purpose.

City comedy is content with disabusing the gentlefolk of their self-confidence, and it limits itself to the examination of the mere social utility or morality of their roles. This in itself constitutes a valuable critique of urban gentry; but what appears to be the genre's own confidence (or faith) in the bases of the society that it stages is never undermined. (Jonson's plays are an exception.) The merchant-citizen is presented as an untrustworthy Proteus assuming socially harmful roles. Even if this presentation is what the drama means to discredit, to add a gentleman-gallant who is but another agglomeration of roles would be to set in motion a vertiginous whirligig of hollow identities. If the gentleman-gallant turns out to be the hero of city comedy, it is because he is not obsessed with his role playing. A character like Witgood (in *A Trick to Catch the Old One*) is in control of his act, and he has a good time putting it on. He knows that he can return to himself. If the gentleman-gallant turns out to be the butt of city comedy, it is because he is a considerably less accomplished actor than he believes himself to be. He too can return to himself; however, there is a smaller self to fall back on.

If the theater were to rely on the endorsement and patronage of the merchant-citizen, it would have the support of a group that itself lacked a stable social identity. The playwrights may take part in fashioning this identity, but they stand to gain little from figures that the plays themselves demonstrate to have minimal social legitimacy. By contrast, city comedy can disconnect the gentleman-gallant from his role(s). The gentleman is recognized as a solid basis for the dramatist's vision of the City. If a playwright were to question this solidity, he would undermine his relations with the class that supported and protected the theater, and he would deprive himself of a standard of identity. It may be that the availability of this self, beneath its role, is the factor which helps us to distinguish comedy from tragedy. G. B. Jackson argues that the "comic contract between playwright and audience depends heavily on a conviction, established early, of where basic or stable reality lies."[28] The comic spirit informing city comedy does not despair over a world of endlessly shifting roles that are nothing but roles; it locates a secure self in the gentleman, the sponsor of prevailing ideologies, and it suggests (perhaps only tacitly) that equivalent selves must be found for the merchant-citizen and for women. The society that is absent from city comedy is one in which the merchant has the same self-confidence or security as the gentleman. This is not to say that merchants want to be gentlemen; rather it is to argue that merchants desire what the gentry already have: a legitimacy proper to their own group. A perverse understanding of the merchants and gentry like Quomodo's—they take our wives and we take their money—ignores the contemporary commentators who envisioned a society sustained by merchants and governed by gentlemen. Quomodo's (or Allwit's) ontology equates being with role. When city comedy accepts the primacy of the gentleman's self over his roles, it holds out the same possibility to the merchant.

Neither gallant nor merchant could expect to interact in society without adopting the features of one or another role. City comedy does not suggest that the City would be a better place were men to strip themselves of their roles and, somehow, commingle as transparent selves. The genre is not nearly so naive in its social vision. Neither do the playwrights of city comedy pretend that a role is necessarily a disguise and, necessarily, something to beware of. We should expect a playwright, a man who fashions roles, to be sensitive to elements of role playing that suggest more than mere deception. An adopted role might enhance a core self, or display it to better advantage. A public role might be a man's chosen way of publishing his real virtue. Thus a king's careful display of his royal aspect for the good of his realm, and a playwright's elaboration of roles for the profit and entertainment of his audience, are always potentially salutary activities. However, role playing, like wit, may also be an indication of narcissism. When a witty gallant acts parts that he believes are expected of him, parts that he believes will confirm his cleverness for others, he puts aside responsible, or constructive, self-consciousness. City comedies take gallants to task for their preoccupation with the figures they cut, not for their desire (or need) to adopt a role in and of itself. These plays insist that a role which conforms to conventional strictures, whether the precepts are set down by moralists, courtiers, or the writers of courtesy books, must be judged in a social context. The familiar gallant who can exercise his wit only at the expense of a merchant casts doubt on the value of wit. He is not sufficient cause to argue that wit, per se, is useless; however, his example does suggest that gallants were notorious for abusing their wit (and the wealth that afforded them the leisure to exercise their wit). So, too, a critical examination of role playing and wit does not line up necessarily against the theater. Wit on stage can be irresponsible and it can be conscionable. What we discover in city comedy is a blend of the two: at the very moment that the plays seek to disabuse their audience of prejudice, they implicate themselves in these same prejudices by reenacting them. This is a tricky business; but short of inventing an entirely new discourse based on attitudes that were *not* current, this is the path toward entertainment and profit that city comedy is left to follow.

In the decade following the reopening of the theaters in 1603, the stages at the song school, at Blackfriars, and at Whitefriars were crowded with gallants. Dekker and Webster, Middleton, and Chapman, Jonson, and Marston wrote city comedies that portrayed the gallant interacting with his companions, with citizens, and with assorted father figures. When these playwrights developed their versions of the merchant-citizen, they were able to suggest the inadequacy of the denigrating stereotype by exaggerating and parodying it. The citizen was ridiculed, but the gentry might recognize that the citizen whom they saw on the stage embodied their own prejudices. When the playwrights developed their versions of the gentleman-gallant, they again suggested the deficiencies of the popular conception. But the gallant was seen to be self-consciously casting his own parts. To analyze the city gallant was to explore the various postures one might assume in relation to one's roles. A gallant might simply play the prodigal or the lecher for lack of something better to do. He might approach such roles with too much confidence, or he might not even see that he is playing a role. The gallant might play his part cynically, he might let others decide his role for him, or, occasionally, he might retain control over his role playing and put it in the service of his authentic self and the community. Finally, the would-be gallant might prove to us that he is no gallant at all. There is no evidence to suggest that the stage gallant or gentleman became more cynical, more foolish, or more or less anything else between 1603 and 1613. Early and late in this decade, we find callous, naive, and self-assured gentry. The playwrights were exploring different types of gentry whenever they turned to urban drama, and this variety may be seen in individual as well as collaborative efforts, in public- as well as in private-theater productions.

The Private Theaters

Gallant Frank Monopoly, in Dekker and Webster's *Westward Ho*, keeps his distance from the roles he enacts. There is even an element of casualness to Monopoly's performances—he does not appear to put much of himself into his roles. Monopoly is nephew to an earl, and he is identified deferentially by the citizen Tenterhook as "A Courtier, a gentleman" (3.1.16). In debt to Tenterhook and dallying with his wife, Monopoly, one of a group of "gallants" (2.2.236) that includes a knight, a captain, and an alderman's son, crosses back and forth between the gentle and *bürgerlich* worlds. It is his self-consciousness in both of these realms that allows him to maintain a distance from the roles he enacts within them. His power resides in his unwillingness to risk the self that he offhandedly engages in social interactions. This quality of half-hearted involvement is especially obvious in Monopoly's relationship with Mistress Tenterhook. He plays with her desire, keeping her on tenterhooks and flirting with her, though in fact he is not at all interested in the woman herself. When a letter from her is brought to him by the bawd Birdlime, Monopoly asks, "Are there no Pottecaries ith Town to send her Phisick-bils to, but me" (2.2.210–11). He knows that he has excited the city wife, but he wants the relationship on his terms. When the bawd reminds him of his "wanton," he argues that *he* is the victim, that his mistress is abusing him: "pray thee stretch

me no more vpon your *Tenterhook:* pox on her" (2.2.209–
10). Monopoly wants to play out his fantasy of the marriage-
spoiling gallant, but Mistress Tenterhook's forwardness impinges on this fantasy with a little too much erotic energy.
It is not that Monopoly has no sexual designs; rather he
wants to "have" her according to his precise design. This
turns out to be a version of the conventional rendezvous
between gallant and citizen's wife beyond the city walls.
The drama latent in a clandestine meeting at a "Brainford"
inn whets Monopoly's appetite more than the woman he
plans to sleep with.

Were there enough of Monopoly to be truly concerned
about, we might locate real pathos in his inability fully to
engage himself (his self) with an other. But this is not the
business of *Westward Ho;* Dekker and Webster are more
interested in setting up (for a fall) Monopoly's wit and off-
handedness than in exploring his psychic immaturity. The
gallant's first comeuppance takes place just outside the
Lion, in Shoreditch (3.2). Master Tenterhook, Sergeant Am-
bush, and yeoman Clutch have come to arrest the drunk and
"unbrast" Monopoly for his failure to pay his debts. In the
encounter that follows, the tipsy gallant maneuvers his way
in and out of a series of roles, trying to avoid arrest. First he
acts as a haughty gentleman-courtier, calling the sergeant
and yeoman "varlet" and daring them to arrest "one of the
Court" (3.2.41–43). Next he tries to bluff his way free. When
this fails, he plays the threatening gallant; then, in a last
effort, Monopoly appeals to the arresting trio as "Christians" and asks for mercy. Monopoly loses the argument
because he expects others to be as ready to adopt fantasy
roles as he is. But the sergeant and yeoman are unrespon-
sive; they miss their cues and refuse to be varlets, good
pitiful rascals, Christians, or honest faithful drunkards.
They know only their assigned roles and prove incapable of
improvisation.

The paradigmatic city-comedy gallant enacts his role,
or roles, because he has an important goal in mind—a mistress, wealth, or both. In *Westward Ho,* the most prominent

gallant has no overriding interests. He plays his parts (Mistress Tenterhook speaks of "my young gallant who . . . has plaid his part"—3.1.4) because he has nothing better to do. If he is a threat to the City, it is as much because he fails to take his role seriously as because he is "an arrant knaue, a cogging knaue, who if . . . suffered to ride vp and downe with other mens wiues, hee'le vn-do Citty and Country" (5.4.174–76). If Monopoly cannot take an interest in the appointed roles of a gallant, it may be because these roles are so thoroughly exhausted and banal. Dekker and Webster stage and restage the fatuous roles that actual men of property saw fit to cast themselves in. By taking these roles to their comic conclusions, the playwrights show that whether or not the gallant takes his part seriously, his actions have implications for everyone else in the City. And if, as was noted in the preceding chapter, the gallants turn out to be among the gulls in *Westward Ho*, it is because they never bother to consider what the roles or fantasies they casually accept are setting them up for. The gallants' final comeuppance, at the hands of the citizen wives and the playwrights, is a result of the former's down-to-earth propriety and the latter's conventionally plotted play of urban relations.

The example of *Westward Ho* makes it clear that though the "coterie" playwrights acknowledged the availability of the gentry's "absolute self," they were prepared to criticize the ways that self-confident city gentry conducted themselves. When Dekker and Webster cried "Northward ho!" they presented the song-school audience with another example of what we may call the disengaged gallant. The plot is set in motion by the gallant Luke Greenshield, who, having failed to secure the attention of Mistress Mayberry, plans to assuage his ego (but not his libido) by convincing citizen Mayberry that he has actually seduced his wife. As was the case with Frank Monopoly, the gallant is motivated by his conception of conventional city roles: Greenshield's "main motive is not love for a woman but a desire to translate into action his cynical belief that all city wives are lecherous."[29] Greenshield depends on the way others perceive him. He is secure in his role only when he can convince others he is acting like a gallant. When his companion Featherstone suggests that perhaps Mabel Mayberry is indeed chaste (and not merely exhibiting a "puritanical coynesse"), Greenshield replies that "this art of seeming honest makes many of our young sonnes and heires [i.e., gentry] in the Citty, looke so like our prentises" (1.1.11–12). Greenshield, like Monopoly, believes that "seeming" is a universal mode of living. He adopts a plot that preserves conventional city roles—roles as they were recognized by the gentry alone. And it is this narrow vision that makes Greenshield's cuckolding by a member of his class—his friend Featherstone—so wonderfully appropriate.

Like the pamphlets and treatises in which the gentleman was defined and the gallant, explicitly or implicitly, satirized, *Northward Ho* draws a few conclusions about gentility. The distinction that we have made between role and self corresponds to the equally traditional distinction between appearance and reality. It had become one of the standard arguments among those who were refashioning the gentleman that gentility was not simply an external quality. But such thinking was far from congruent with contemporary social customs, and it comes as no surprise that Greenshield is not the only one who has faith in his outward appearance. Citizen Mayberry is well aware of the fact that "lyes that come from sterne lookes, and Sattins out-side, and guilt Rapiers also, will be put vp and goe for currant" (2.2.24–26). Still, it is Greenshield who provides us with the most clear picture of a man who thinks that gentility can, quite literally, be put on. Late in the play, Greenshield offers to doff his gentle exterior and put on the borrowed clothes of a country player in order to play the part of a pander: "But how? be a Pander as I am, a gentleman? that were horrible, Ile thrust my self into the out-side of a Fawlconer in towne here" (5.1.80–82). It is tolerable for a gentleman to play parts—even the part of a falconer/pander—so long as his assumed identity does not impinge on his real self. But when Greenshield realizes that his friend has been dallying with his wife, Kate, he is less eager to accept the new role: "Ile go instantly take a purse, be apprehended and hang'd for't, better than be a Cuckold" (5.1.173–74). The threat to Greenshield's confidence arises when he learns that he is, not that he must play, the cuckold.

Dekker and Webster catch Greenshield in a fundamental contradiction: he wants to live like a gallant and yet be a gentleman. Indeed, it is part of his fantasy that he may behave like a gallant because he has the authority of a gentleman. Yet for a while, and despite the control that he believes he exercises, Greenshield's part (his self as gallant) takes over. This is not the case of an actor who suddenly begins to believe himself to be the character he is playing; rather the logic of the role entraps the actor whether he likes it or not. Greenshield's ability to play a part is proven beyond a doubt. Those around him not only take him to be a gallant but treat him as one too. We see how inappropriate (and unfair) it is of Greenshield to turn to Featherstone and cry, "thou hast not vsed me like a Gentleman" (5.1.176). It is a considerably ironic temperament that any gallant must bring to his roles, but the irony in Greenshield's exclamation belongs to the playwrights and the audience. And perhaps to Featherstone, who answers, "thou a gentleman: thou art a Taylor" (5.1.177; "tailor" being not merely a term of ridicule and a punning name for a lecher or pander—see 2.1—but another role or part as well).

The two *Ho* plays at the song school remind us that the conventional role of the gentleman-gallant as it was elaborated in Jacobean London might be seen, once it was staged, to be both as foolish and as dangerous as that of the citizen. When Greenshield's wife "sleepwalks" out of his bed and into Featherstone's, the stage gallant is mocked in exactly the same way that we have seen the citizen mocked. So, too, the merchant-citizen and the gallant are equally embarrassed at the end of *Westward Ho*. That the gentry (despite their assumed legitimacy) and the citizenry are open to identical attacks should suggest a basis for their mutual solidarity. Together they might defend themselves against the narrow roles that were used to define them and that they were thought to embrace. Social conventions might fall into line with an economic reality that included gentleman-apprentices and merchant-landowners. But in exacting his revenge, Mayberry perpetuates the struggle that sets gentry against citizens, then citizens against gentry. And Dekker and Webster have a stake in the conflict too. Their comedies and their theater profit from this struggle even as their drama exposes the roles we have identified. The play ends when the citizens have played *their* last trick. But Dekker and Webster might have ended it when (just one trick earlier) Mayberry tells Featherstone that "what parts so euer you haue plaid with mee, I see good parts in you" (5.1.436–37).

The *Ho* plays present us with cool, disengaged gallants who know their way around the City. If they are put down, it is because their confidence in themselves runs a little too high. In *Michaelmas Term*, Middleton comes at the gallant's self-confidence in a different way. Here, the playwright turns his attention to the different levels of self-consciousness, as they are related to roles, that three distinct types of gentry manifest. The most extreme example is presented by Andrew Lethe (né Gruel). A bogus parvenu who sees himself as a courtier and a city gallant, Lethe conveniently forgets his origins (his father was a Scottish toothdrawer—1.2.251), abuses his mother, corrupts his mistress, and proposes simultaneously to the draper Quomodo's daughter and wife. What makes Lethe's actions particularly disturbing is the realization that he not only forgets who he is (his real self) but has no self-consciousness about the things that he does. There is simply no distance between the self and its roles. Lethe is categorically not a gentleman or a gallant because of this lack of self-consciousness; he is morally not a gentleman because of his perverse activities. He is so engaged in the part he plays that he forgets—and this is the most telling aspect of his forgetfulness—that he is playing a part. Indeed, for all his egotism and vanity, Lethe has forgotten himself:

he passes for Lethe "'Mongst strange eyes / That no more know him than he knows himself" (1.1.149).

Andrew Lethe is only one of several characters in *Michaelmas Term* who come up to the City and are tested by it. He succeeds in London to the extent that he dissolves his old self into a new one that is appropriate to the exaggerated sordidness of Middleton's London. He fails because he has no idea that others see through his mask (or learn to see through it) to the toothdrawer's son whom he thinks he has left behind. To Rearage, Lethe is "One that ne'er wore apparel but, like ditches, / 'Twas cast before he had it" (1.1.63–64). Thomasine Quomodo tells Lethe's mother that he "has forgot how he came up . . . those parts that are covered of him looks indifferent well, because we cannot see 'em; else, all his cleansing, pruning, and paring, he's not worthy a broker's daughter" (2.3.9–17). Thomasine sees him playing the parts that he no longer realizes he is playing.

If we turn to the play's other would-be gallant, Richard Easy, we find the opposite extreme: Easy plays no roles at all. Easy, a landowner from Essex, is a "pure, fresh gull" (2.1.172). He is "yet fresh, / And wants the city powd'ring" (1.1.55–56), and he is a "fair, free-breasted gentleman, somewhat too open" (1.1.53). To be "open" is to be frank, transparent, and honest. Easy is simply himself, he plays no part. He is as unselfconscious as Andrew Lethe. However the problem with such openness is that others will take the initiative to cast parts for the man who scripts none for himself. Lethe guarantees that he is not a true gallant when he dresses himself in "cast" apparel; Easy fails as a gallant because he never thinks to dress himself at all. And this, as the gallant Cockstone notes, is the "gentry-fault at first" (1.1.55).

There is probably no one who has written about *Michaelmas Term* who has not addressed this question of apparel. The play returns again and again to the effects of costume, disguise, adopted roles, and so to the question of appearance versus reality (or surface versus substance). We begin with an "Induction" in which the personified Michaelmas Term exchanges his white, country cloak for "civil black" (Ind., 4) and we conclude with a series of typically comic discoveries. The City demands that its inhabitants distinguish themselves in habits and roles, but it is suggested that real success in the City requires substantial control over one's costume and actions. Those who forget that they are playing a part inevitably fall victim to their illusions. Those who fail to play a part in the first place run the risk of losing sight of themselves. Thus Quomodo, through his "spirit" Shortyard, works with Easy, fashioning him into the gull he needs to satisfy his own part (that of the greedy merchant). Shortyard teaches Easy (though with little success) how to give himself out (2.1.31). He tells him that "there's a kind of bold grace expected throughout all the parts of a gentleman" (2.1.92). A gentleman-gallant must hide his self—he must learn to "smile upon . . . ill luck" (2.1.103). But Easy never learns to create a part for himself. When he is left on his own and must find a way to meet his debts, he is reduced to a rather pathetic lament: "Methinks I have no being without his [Shortyard's] company" (3.2.6). Even as the play moves through its final turns and restorations, Easy is more a beneficiary of circumstances than an active director of his fate. It is Thomasine who goes after Easy, and then it is Thomasine who watches Quomodo sign the quit-bill that releases Easy from his obligations to the draper. Similarly, it is Shortyard, not Easy, who tricks Sim Quomodo and so recovers the deed to Easy's land. Comic reversals and the wit of all those around Easy triumph over Lethe and Quomodo. Easy himself never makes anything of himself. Perhaps this is why, unlike the conventional marriage-seeking prodigal gallant, he fails to find a wife.

The gallant who does get the girl (Susan Quomodo) is Rearage—another prodigal and the third variety of gentleman-gallant in the play.[30] Rearage, and his friend Salewood, come from the same stock as Frank Monopoly. They play the gallant and they know perfectly well what they are doing. Both characters have the gallant's requisite cynicism and his passing interest in whores and wives. They see Lethe for the "coxcomb" that he is, and Rearage, Lethe's rival in pursuit of Susan Quomodo, organizes a little comedy of his own in order to catch out the upstart with his whore. But neither Rearage nor Salewood plays an entirely pleasant part. Their names imply their prodigality, and they appear to support themselves in London on the rent that they extract from their tenants (2.1.165–67). Moreover, Rearage is not ignorant of the fact that Susan Quomodo comes with a sizable dowry (1.1.58). He and Salewood balance the extremes represented by Lethe and Easy, just as Rearage's marriage to Susan balances Lethe's marriage to his whore and what turns out to be Easy's continued bachelorhood. As Cockstone explained to Easy at the beginning of the play, "Here's [in London] gallants of all sizes, of all lasts" (1.1.44). Middleton offers his spectators no authentic gallant-hero. He permits them to maintain their own gallant-like distance from the stage gallants. From a distance, they may perceive the foolishness of Lethe and Easy, as well as the thin veneer of sophistication applied to Salewood, Rearage, and Cockstone. But these gallants' versions of the gentry are no more adequate than Quomodo's version of the merchant-citizen.

The gallants, grotesque, naive, or cynical, play parts which ensure continued deceit and class divisions in the City. It is ironic that the only ones banished from the City at the end of the play are the citizens (perhaps merely city residents) Shortyard and Falselight. It is not they who come up to London to dally with merchant wives and heiresses, to gamble and whore, or to disturb the economy of the City. These two "spirits" are undoubtedly duplicitous, but after all Easy *offers* himself as a target. While the gallants may seem "inherently more congenial,"[31] their forgetfulness and their prodigality represent threats to social order equal to Quomodo's rapaciousness. Lethe spurns his mother, corrupts a "country wench," and ends up married to a whore. Easy squanders his patrimony and can hope to reestablish himself only by marrying a city widow. Rearage self-consciously repeats what simply happens to Easy. No one is willing to respect his class or status origins because no one can imagine a role model which would allow him to do so. This dilemma lies at the center of Middleton's dramatization of the unprecedented social mobility during the Jacobean period. One's discontent with his social status does not only correspond to a desire for financial gain; it also reflects a failure of imagination. Certainly this is a large part of Easy's problem; it may well be Middleton's problem too. For if we discount the future implied by Lethe's marriage to his wench and Easy's continued bachelorhood, we are left with the progeny of Rearage and Susan. But Susan's few lines in the play suggest her vapidity, and Rearage's last words (save three inconsequential lines in the final scene) only reinforce our impression that he is a cynical opportunist (5.2.12).

Michaelmas Term was followed quickly by the song-school productions of *A Mad World, My Masters* and *A Trick to Catch the Old One* (also produced at Blackfriars). Though set in London, *A Mad World, My Masters* eschews for the most part city comedy's typical conflict between citizens and gentry. In its main plot, Middleton stages what was to become standard fare after the Restoration: gentlemen calling attention to their own pretensions. Sir Bounteous Plenty pretends to hospitality, and his grandson, Follywit, pretends to wit. And while the confrontation between them is going on, in his second plot Middleton presents us with Penitent Brothel, who lacks the one quality of a gentleman that Follywit possesses.

Certainly Penitent Brothel has very little of the typical self-confidence of the gentry. He meditates on adultery and concludes that he is a "wretched unthrift, that hast play'd away / [His] eternal portion" (4.1.4–5). For the first three acts of *A Mad World*, Penitent Brothel is a slave of passion; in the last two acts, he is overwhelmed with penitence. As his name suggests, the same reactive personality is at the mercy of opposed emotions. Whereas most of the major characters in the play are both master and mastered in their mad world, Penitent is exclusively one of the mastered. He cautions Mistress Harebrain to be honest, "then the devil will ne'er *assume* thee" (4.4.44; my emphasis), because he conceives of the self as a form or vessel which others (or other forces) may fill. The unconscious desires that drive him to commit adultery are as much beyond his control as the unconscious self that confronts him with a succubus at the beginning of Act 4. While Follywit is busy planning the play that will allow him to trick his grandfather one last time, Penitent's tortured conscience produces a play of its own, confirming our belief that he is his own passive spectator. Indeed he is suitable as Harebrain's rival, for neither is master of his fears or desires.

Sir Bounteous Progress and his grandson Follywit compensate for all the self-confidence that Penitent lacks. They both pursue fantasies of unlimited power, and each in his way is mildly checked. Neither their faults nor their plots impinge directly on those around them (Frank Gullman may be an exception to this), and our knowledge that they are fond of one another (Follywit speaks of his "frolic grand-sire"—1.1.40; Sir Bounteous has every intention of bequeathing his money to his grandson) relieves us—and Middleton—of the need seriously to censure them. We are left, then, with a foolish old man and an overconfident gallant who have their laughs and take their lumps. Although both are taught that the world is not entirely as their fantasies suggest it is, neither shows any sign that he has learned the lesson.

As an urban good housekeeper without rival, Sir Bounteous opens up a space in which Follywit may play out his repertory of tricks. The knight is not unaware that his graciousness is "above ordinary" (2.1.52), but he must admit also that it is "a kind of art which naturally slips from me, I know not on't, I promise you, 'tis gone before I'm aware on't. Cuds me, I forget myself" (2.1.56–58). Sir Bounteous is the festive spirit that prepares the way for comedy. His temporary refusal to bankroll his grandson is less a contradiction of his openness than a necessary adjunct to it. This well-meaning tightfistedness is precisely what enlarges the comic world—it brings Follywit home and forces him to enter his grandfather's festive world. The young man must operate within Sir Bounteous's magical, comic space, and it makes little difference what tricks he plays there. No matter what setbacks the knight experiences, he is flexible enough to bounce back and resume his madcap ways. Indeed it cannot be otherwise; Sir Bounteous can forget himself because his spirit will always emerge on its own: "Is not my name Sir Bounteous? Am I not express'd there?" (4.3.91). Even Follywit recognizes that his grandfather is the preeminent figure of bounty in London (1.1.58–66). He is mistaken merely in his belief that he can take advantage of the older man by robbing him. Sir Bounteous is concerned about his hospitality, not his riches, and he is upset when he thinks that his guests have been threatened, not when he himself is abused (2.4.34–37). Thus when Follywit, already playing the part of a lord visiting with Sir Bounteous, disguises himself as a thief, binds the knight, and pretends that he has done the same thing to the visiting lord, he comes closest to undermining his grandfather's fantasy of an open-house world. There are some uneasy moments when the played-upon host commiserates with the "lord" (Follywit in disguise) over the insult he is supposed to have suffered at the hands of the thieves, but even here the comic spirit reasserts itself in preparations for a feast. Sir Bounteous concedes that the attack on his guest was "the commodity of keeping open house" (2.6.51), but he starts right up again by inviting everyone from the Harebrains to the thieves themselves to his next supper.

Middleton is interested in Sir Bounteous as a staging ground. The knight's perpetually open doors lead to a theater space, complete with banquet hall and pipe organs. In every disguise that Follywit adopts for this space, whether he is a lord, a thief, a courtesan, or a player, he appears as an actor. Even his desire to rob his grandfather succumbs to his need to upstage the old man. As Penitent Brothel remarks, Follywit is "a fellow whose only glory is to be prime of the company" (1.1.87). But there is a good deal of the grandfather in the grandson. The former would live out an ideal of absolute hospitality ill suited to the City; the latter believes that he can do himself good in the world (1.1.55) by playing parts among men and women who either are what they seem to be or who are not what Follywit thinks they are. In fact, Follywit is twice deluded: he thinks not only that he is the best actor, but that he is the only one who can act. And this applies to his companions as well as to his gulls: "Call me your forecast . . . 'tis *I* must cast your plots into form still; 'tis *I* must manage the prank" (1.1.4–6; my emphasis). Follywit's illusions (or his self-confidence) break down when he runs into Sir Bounteous, who plays no roles (as he says, he is himself and his name expresses that self), and then into Frank Gullman, who is playing a role that Follywit fails to distinguish as such. He treats the world as his stage but forgets fully to account for the other actors. As a result, he believes that Frank Gullman is "a woman as she was made at first, simple of herself, without sophistication" (4.5.55–57). It never occurs to him that this is merely the part that she and her mother have cast her in.

Middleton does not reject role playing. He prefers that the playing self be responsible and that it have a social consciousness, a mature awareness of others. Fantasies that do not, at some point, account for the real world—or, minimally, for the fantasy world of others—are bound to fail in Middleton's City. But Middleton's interest in the actor-gallant has still another, and more poignant, side. When Follywit decides to marry, he looks for a woman who plays no roles, one who is herself, not "impudently aspected" (4.5.59). For all his commitment to acting, Follywit betrays a profound desire for stability, identity, and an end to the strain of fashioning roles. If he is not permitted to settle down in peace, if he goes on with his acting after his betrothal, and if he discovers that others play parts too, it is because for Middleton the absolute self has no choice but to enter into social roles. Middleton cannot relieve his audience of this fundamental alienation; he can only stage the consequences when men and women deal with this dilemma with too much self-confidence and too little maturity. Follywit's comeuppance is a signal to look back at his activities and to judge his version of the gallant dispassionately. The members of the song-school audience are cautioned that they must find better ways to play their parts. If they really do want the stability that comes with mature role playing, they must forgo some of the pleasures of shape changing and assume some of the risks of self-exposure.

In *A Trick to Catch the Old One*, Theodorus Witgood finds something of the requisite balance between the self-concealment of the guller and the vulnerability of the plain dealer. Witgood is a clever gallant, but he has in mind more than self-interest and dissembling for its own sake. *A Trick to Catch the Old One*, like *A Mad World, My Masters*, begins with the young gallant casting parts that will further his intended deception. But unlike Follywit, who sets himself up as a rich lord, Witgood casts himself in a role identical with what he claims he actually is—a reformed prodigal. Witgood realizes that with a little help from his friends, he can "be himself" and still count on others to mistake him. Thus he persuades his "honest drab" to test the "power of [her] performance" (1.1.53 and 51) by turning herself into "a rich country widdow foure hundred a yeare valiant" (1.1.61–62). By pretending that he plans to marry the courtesan, he can trick his mean-spirited uncle (Lucre) into returning his estates. Witgood plays the part of a fiancé because it is the only way he can regain his inheritance (and so marry his true beloved). Beyond this simple part and the one elaborate ruse it permits, he is a man who is what he seems to be. Before the play opens, he not only played the spendthrift and the rakehell, but actually saw himself as an indebted lecher; once we meet him, he is the reformed prodigal that he gives himself out to be. Although he tells others, "You will not see me now" (1.1.105), he keeps sight of himself and those around him. For Witgood, the return to selfhood after a successful exercise in stagecraft is but a short step.

Middleton offers his audience cues that allow it to distinguish the hero of *A Trick* from his other heroes. Whereas Richard Easy and Richard Follywit bear names that mitigate whatever virtue we might find in them, "Theodorus Witgood" signifies unironically a salutory cleverness with a touch of divine approval. Moreover, Middleton introduces Witgood as a conventional gallant only to reverse our expectations immediately after by showing us an unanticipated side of the hero. The courtesan greets Witgood as "My love" and he responds by calling her his "lothing." For a moment we are sure of where we stand in relation to this typically cavalier gallant. But in a matter of lines, Witgood has apologized to his mistress: "Forgive—I do thee wrong, / To make thee sinne, and then to chid thee fort" (1.1.39–40). We may still doubt Witgood's sincerity and suspect that he makes up to the courtesan merely to take advantage of her; in fact, he does use her, but to their mutual advantage. As one editor has noted, in Act 3 "Witgood voluntarily shelves his project of tricking Lucre into returning the mortgage, in fact, dangerously imperils the plan, in order that the Curtizan may be assured of wealth and respectability."[32] Witgood's precise words are "Wench, make up thy owne fortunes now, do thy selfe a good turne once in thy Dayes . . . twould ease my conscienee well to see thee well bestowed, Ia have a care of thee ifaith" (3.1.95–101). Witgood puts role playing in the service of the comic community. He casts himself and the courtesan in parts that will allow the two of them eventually to validate their true selves. They are not naive, and there is never any doubt that financial matters are of real importance to them (Witgood looks forward to Joyce Hoard's portion, and the courtesan has everything to gain by marrying the wealthy usurer Hoard); but their special understanding of human nature, as shown in their speeches of repentance at the conclusion of the play, set them apart. At the end of *A Trick*, Witgood and the courtesan offer their version of conformity shaped by sophistication. Their repentance is neither entirely formulaic nor entirely sincere; they have simply found an acceptable way to balance the claims made by an authentic self and a society that can encounter that self only in one of its various roles.

Your Five Gallants, Middleton's last city comedy to be performed by the boys at the song school (and at Blackfriars),[33] again substitutes conflict among the gentry for the genre's expected confrontation between merchant-citizens and the gentle class. There is nothing subtle about this play, nor is it especially original. It consists of a frame story that encloses a string of dupings and cony catchings drawn from the popular pamphlet literature. Fitsgrave, an authentic if rather wooden gentleman, disguises himself as a "credulous scholar" so that he may keep an eye on the five unscrupulous gallants who are competing with him for the hand of Katherine, the orphaned daughter of a wealthy knight. Katherine appears only at the beginning and the conclusion of the play; for the most part, she disappears from even the thoughts of the five gallants. It is left to Fitsgrave to discover the gallants' true colors and to expose them before Katherine in a masque of his own devising.

The five gallants are as monochromatic as the hero. One is a pawnbroker, another is a pimp, the third a whoremonger, the fourth a pickpocket, and the fifth a cheat. They are entirely interchangeable, and indeed this would appear to be Middleton's point. Much of the action of the play concerns the slippery passage of a "chain of pearl" as it is stolen first by one gallant, then by another, and then by still another. What links these figures together as gallants is merely the persistence with which they call each other gallants. Middleton's "five gallants" are in fact neither gentlemen nor gallants; they are simply rogues who imagine that their impudence makes them gallants.[34] Goldstone, the cheat, asks, "What cannot wit, so it be impudent, / Devise and compass?" (4.8.55–56). Pursenet, the pickpocket, goes after his mark with an impudent salute (4.6.15). Primero, the pimp, declares that "Nothing in women's hearts sooner win[s] place /Than a grave outside and an impudent face" (1.1.279–80), and Frippery sums this up from the gallant-rogue's point of view when he argues that "Since impudence gains more respect than virtue / And coin than blood, which few can now deny, / Who's your chief gallants then but such as I?" (1.1.334–36).

Impudence is a graceless variety of the overconfidence that we have already noted. It is exactly contrary to the spirit of *sprezzatura*, and it is just the characteristic we would expect the least genteel would-be gallant to seize upon. However, the brazenness and the magnified ego that are peculiar to the impudent have a special significance in city comedy. Where people live close together and when social classes are continually running one against the other, the premium on tact must be high. The impudent, like Dampit in *A Trick*, are "trampler[s] of time" who abuse our goodwill. Fitsgrave, as Presenter and as Middleton's surrogate, joins the gallants in calling our attention to their impudence; but as we would expect, he is not of their opinion: "The devil scarce knew what a portion he gave his children when he allowed 'em large impudence to live upon . . . surely he gave away the third part of the riches of his kingdom; revenues are but fools to't" (4.5.69–73). In the ironically entitled *Your Five Gallants*, Middleton significantly qualifies the genre's definition of the gallant. There are certain traits which make for unattractive gallants and others which allow us to identify clever or knowing or charming gallants. There are also taxonomic features, such as impudence, which allow us to determine that a figure is not a gallant at all. Like Andrew Lethe in *Michaelmas Term*, the five "gallants" have no justifiable claim to their title. They do not even know how to play the part.

Marston's *The Dutch Courtesan* and Chapman, Jonson, and Marston's *Eastward Ho* present considerably more sophisticated treatments of the gentleman-gallant figure than we have encountered thus far in the plays of Thomas Middleton. Malheureux and Freevill, in *The Dutch Courtesan*, are not merely wits engaged in casual gulling. Each represents serious opinion on the conduct proper to a gentleman. Os-

tensibly, the severe, moralistic attitudes figured in Malheureux are tempered by the reasonable, Montaignian outlook
of Freevill. Freevill is something of a Witgood invested with
the kind of obvious philosophical pretensions that Middleton would not permit one of his comic characters. Marston's
gentlemen allow us to measure some of the thinking that
went into the production of gentleman-gallants. His characters play parts because they have something more than a
notion of what it means to be worldly-wise. By testing carefully articulated beliefs, they ask us to question appealing
motivations for acting the part of a gentleman-gallant.

Marston's "man of snow" participates in a psychological study of the discovery of passion. The aptly named Malheureux, a figure for whom Marston may owe some debt to
Shakespeare's Angelo, comes on decrying his friend Freevill's easy attitude toward his whores. Before long, this "man
of sense" has fallen for Freevill's cast-off punk and finds
himself admitting that he is passion's slave (2.2.111). Malheureux moves from a secure, if false, sense of self to a loss
of self ("I am no whit myself"—2.2.97), and finally to the
recovery of a perhaps wiser self ("I am myself"—5.3.61). His
career is not that of a conventional city-comedy gentleman-
gallant: Malheureux does not engineer a series of changing
roles; rather we witness alterations that reach right to his
central self. We encounter Malheureux as an initiate, not as
a gallant or a gentleman.[35] He is defined psychologically
before he is given a social identity.

The more easily recognizable gentleman-gallants in
The Dutch Courtesan are Freevill and Tysefew. In the next
chapter, these figures will be considered in relation to the
women they consort with; however, we may note at present
a few of the ways Freevill works to present himself as a city
gallant. Marston borrows heavily from Montaigne in his depiction of Freevill. He is a man who adapts himself to a
fallen world while at the same time he believes that he can
carve out an inviolate space for his true, untainted love.
Freevill would teach Malheureux to "Let wise men alone"
(2.1.95), to accommodate himself as a "reasonable man"

(1.1.144) to the fact that "Nothing extremely best with us endures" (4.2.40). But Freevill, for all his ability to articulate his philosophy, lacks the sophistication of a Witgood, who can intermingle freely his concern for a whore and his love for a virgin by tempering both. Although Freevill argues against Malheureux's extreme formulation of virtue and vice, he fails to see that his own compartmentalization of his desires is equally extreme. Freevill is never able to draw the conclusion that, "if nothing extremely best with us endures," then his pure, devoted, romantic attachment to Beatrice will eventually fail too.

Freevill acts the part of a disengaged gallant to his whore, an engaged gentleman to his beloved, and a cool, worldly gentleman-gallant to his friend Malheureux. In each instance, he is careful not to risk himself. He justifies whores and whoring ("do not better persons sell their souls? Nay, since all things have been sold—honor, justice, faith, nay, even God Himself—Ay me, what base ignobleness is it / To sell the pleasure of a wanton bed?"—1.1.119–22) and we believe that he means what he says, but his wit continually undermines the seriousness of his argument. Is he in earnest, is he playing the part of a city gallant, or is he trying to avoid revealing himself? It is the same fear of vulnerability which governs the way Freevill tests his beloved Beatrice till she nearly breaks. Freevill must allow it to be said that Malheureux has killed him in order that his friend may enjoy the whore, but this plot entails deceiving Beatrice as well. Under the protection of his disguise, Freevill (like Quomodo) can observe the "suff'ring sweetness, quiet modesty, / Yet deep affection" (4.4.86–87) with which Beatrice receives his death. He thinks to reveal himself, but then checks this impulse, arguing that "Grief endears love" (4.4.79). Safe at this distance, Freevill assuages the guilt engendered by previous libertinage while stalling a frank commitment to Beatrice. Freevill declares that his soul has shown him the imperfection of his body (1.2.90–91), but he has admitted that "better persons" have sold their souls

(1.1.119). He says that his love has never been false to Beatrice (5.2.55), but he has already argued that it is "not in fashion to call things [like love?] by their right names" (1.2.99–100). While Marston centers his interest in character psychology in Malheureux, he can offer Freevill up to his plot and to Inns of Court men in the audience. As a dramatic figure, the gallant augments the suspense by keeping himself hidden till the last moment. As a role model, he seems to have found a way to manage whoring as well as proper love. But Freevill's cynicism undercuts his stature as Marston's hero. His (read Freevill's and Marston's) solution to the problem of lovemaking and friendship may be appealing, but it is not conclusive.

When Marston collaborated with Chapman and Jonson on *Eastward Ho*, he joined them in pursuing a social, not a psychological, analysis of London's types.[36] The gentry figures are developed in terms of their relationships to members of classes other than their own. Quicksilver, the goldsmith Touchstone's high-living apprentice, chafes in his city dress and attempts to assert his gentle origins by playing the gallant. Sir Petronel Flash, one of the day's new-made knights, sees himself as a Virginia adventurer and as a courtier; he encounters the merchant's world when he marries the goldsmith's pretentious daughter and makes off with her inheritance on his ill-fated journey eastward. Chapman, Jonson, and Marston employ city comedy formulae only, and they allow none of their formulae to escape their parodic judgment. Quicksilver and Sir Petronel fashion typical get-rich-quick plots, have some measure of success, and end in prison. For the playwrights, however, it is the conventionality of the apprentice-gallant's and the knight's careers, not their deeds in and of themselves, which lands them in prison. Quicksilver's and Sir Petronel's very notions of what it means to be a gallant constitute their prisons. So too, Touchstone's idea of how a repentant prodigal should act conditions his response to his imprisoned apprentice and son-in-law. In *Eastward Ho*, there is no passage from role to self—the characters are, wholly, their roles. And their roles refract the at-once comic and self-defeating social economy of the City.

To argue that Quicksilver and the knight are accounted for entirely by their roles is not to neglect the parts that these characters are seen to fashion for themselves. Quicksilver, like many city-comedy gallants, changes into the clothes of a gallant (2.2) and leaves his master in order to play the part. Sir Petronel finds himself a city heiress and cuckolds a city usurer. But there is no self behind these schemes, no core to which the traits of a city gallant are appended. Rather, all of Quicksilver's machinations and all of Sir Petronel's aspirations, when joined together, become the stuff of a cheeky gallant or a £4 knight. The plot, as well as the morality, of *Eastward Ho* depends upon the character types who set it in motion. The play is not unlike a deftly drawn cartoon: we see the nuances of types, not of individuals. Characters do not stand out, as do Quomodo or Witgood, breaking free of their conventional role designations; they appear as personified social integers—first as knight, then as Sir Petronel, first as gallant, then as a youth with a name (and in both cases, with names that refer first to types, then to individual men). Their desires are less their own than those of their types, and once again we may say that it is these "species-specific" desires which constitute the men. Neither knight nor gallant (nor, for that matter, any of the characters in *Eastward Ho*) is felt to generate needs peculiar to himself. Without selves, their needs can correspond only to their roles.[37]

At the beginning of this chapter, it was argued that city comedy refrained from drawing the conclusion that a gentleman or gallant might be his role, and nothing more. In the Blackfriars and song-school productions that we have considered, there has been a common, if in many ways variable, relation between an enacted role and a central self. If *Eastward Ho* seems to approach the position which it has been argued city comedy avoids, it must also be seen that this play skirts the issue by never raising it. The play is not troubled over its self-less protagonists because it never suggests that they should have selves (or uniqueness) in the first place. The play is made up exclusively of types. It is wittier than the other *Ho* plays, but it is also cold and bloodless. Like Sir Petronel, for the moment we must believe that "A man in the course of this world . . . [must] like a surgeon's instrument, work in the wounds of others, and feel nothing himself. The sharper and subtler, the better" (3.2.216–19). *Eastward Ho* is a playwright's play: it displays the criteria of its own composition and makes of these criteria one of the subjects for a drama. This suggests, as well, an explanation for the (heretofore unsatisfactorily explained) successful collaboration of three playwrights on one wonderfully homogeneous play. They would have agreed upon a style or an approach and they would have known that the formulae with which they had agreed to work could lead in only one direction. *Eastward Ho* has been seen as a parody of city comedies; but we may just as easily think of it as a source book.

If for a moment we step out of the rough chronology being followed here, and turn to a play written by Ben Jonson for performance in 1598 by the Lord Chamberlain's Men, we may examine a city comedy that *is* concerned with the availability of a central self. *Every Man in His Humor* in its quarto version is set in Florence. But the play was reworked by Jonson, sometime between 1604 and 1614, performed at court in February 1605, and in its folio incarnation is set in London. Indeed it is possible, though not probable, that Jonson moved his gulls from Florence to London at about the same time he was working with Chapman and Marston on *Eastward Ho*.[38] On the periphery of *Every Man in His Humor* is a city-comedy plot: gentleman-gallant Edward Knowell meets and marries Mrs. Bridget, the sister of merchant Kitely. There are, of course, obstacles; but Knowell's father's man, Brainworm, effectively overcomes them. This plot is brought some distance from the periphery to the play's center because of the attention Jonson pays to Kitely. The merchant both is and is not typical of the genre. His humor consists of his uncontrollable fear of being cuckolded and his consequent obsessive suspicion of city gallants. However, he is a humours character who recognizes and is even pained by his humor. Jonson dignifies Kitely by allowing him to grapple, comically and at times pathetically, with his pathology. Kitely also recognizes the economic and social configuration that threatens his mental health. He is busy with business throughout the play, but must simultaneously find a way to manage the extraordinarily idle gallants who frequent his house. If Kitely's plight never quite comes together in his own mind as a social pathology, it appears as just this sort of city disease to us.

Kitely's partial self-consciousness allows us to place him along a scale that runs from pure type (that is, no central self) to available self (set off by roles). Kitely is close to the middle. Near Kitely on this scale we find Knowell, Sr., a man who speaks sanely but acts foolishly, who is comic to the extent that he is a complete failure as a *Menschenkenner*. Also near the center of the scale, though closer than either Kitely or Knowell, Sr., to the available-self end, is Justice Clement. He is Jonson's deus ex machina. He resolves the intrigues and metes out fit rewards and punishments, though it is hard to imagine that he can do much to improve the next day's goings-on in London. "Mad, merry" Clement is filled with good sense, but he is not sufficiently sensitive to appreciate just how little he can do to alter men and their humors.

If we look for more extreme registrations on the scale, we find at one end Wellbred and Edward, and at the other end, Captain Bobadill, Mr. Stephen, and Mr. Matthew. Jonson puts his art primarily in the service of the interactions among these characters. The town and country gulls are prototypes for Sir Politic Would-be. They are inept pretenders who ape any style or fashion that hints at gentility. They offer conclusive proof that Knowell knows at least whereof he speaks when he says that gentility "is an airy and mere borrowed thing" (1.1.84). Each gull is "a gentleman-like monster, bred, in the special gallantry of our time, by affectation; and fed by folly" (3.4.20–22). Stephen and Matthew expose "the emptiness over which the social self endlessly constructs itself."[39] They seek to construct selves out of what they can borrow or steal from others: Marlowe's verse, Bobadill's oaths, and Downright's cloak are all fair game. Imitating Bobadill, they take up scraps of a language that is itself the articulation of a type. The Captain is all bluster and fustian, but the gulls are impressed. That he can cut a figure, whatever it might be, is sufficient reason for them to hang onto his every word or pose. Stephen and Matthew exceed Jonson's fear, expressed in *Discoveries*, that in our insistence on imitating others, we cannot return to our selves. They have no selves to which they may return.

Wellbred and Edward Knowell represent clear alternatives to the hollow shells that describe Bobadill and the two gulls; however, two other, opposing characters are less easily found on the scale. Downright and Brainworm represent the totally inflexible and the uncannily flexible self, respectively. The former is ill equipped to cope with life in London because he lacks even a drop of the tolerance that social commerce in a busy community demands. His decorum and probity are a straitjacket. Unbending, wooden, finally tiresome, Downright can play his role, but not roles. His finger is ever on the trigger, and he resorts to violence without hesitation because he has none of the urban *sprezzatura* that makes force unnecessary. Brainworm, on the other hand, is a constant shape shifter. Unable to stand still, he intimates Jonson himself, as creative and witty artist. But his deceptions are amoral, and his playing, though a sign of flexibility, is (unlike Jonson's) an end in itself. Each new day will find Brainworm in motion again, not so much without a self to return to as without the will or good sense to try. His career foreshadows Volpone's: he must keep recreating himself through new and more clever deceptions; when he ceases, he ceases to be.

Stephen and Matthew look forward, for us, to the likes of Sir Politic, and Brainworm hints at both Mosca and Volpone. Wellbred and Edward may be said to intimate the clever gallants of *Epicoene*. *Every Man in His Humor*'s two *self*-confident gallants, like Truewit and his companions, look to the City for their entertainment. Wellbred's letter draws Edward to town with the promise of a "present" for him greater than that given by the Turkey Company to the Grand Signior. He has in store for Edward a "rhymer . . . worthy to be seen" and an "other" too wonderful to describe (1.2.75–83). Edward takes great pleasure in his knowledge that he can "furnish our feast with one gull more toward the mess" (1.3.60–61). The gallants' typical day in London is thus not taken up with getting Edward a wife—this turns out to be merely incidental—but with amusing themselves at their gulls' expense. They are idle, witty young men looking, in Volpone's words, "to make the wretched time more sweet." Neither malign nor cynical, they nonetheless are best able to confirm their own integrity by exposing the superficiality of Bobadill or Stephen or Matthew. When Jonson created Truewit, he was ready to fashion a city wit whose entire role is to expose gulls. In *Every Man in His Humor*, he does not yet go this far. For one thing, Edward is himself tricked by Brainworm. And unlike Truewit, both Edward and Wellbred are members of (what constitute finally the same) extended families. Incidental though it may be to Jonson's play, Edward's idling leads to marriage. Wellbred is already kin to Kitely, and by the play's end he is, through Kitely, kin to Edward. For all that they are preoccupied with themselves, everyone from Stephen to Kitely to Knowell, Sr., to Wellbred is bound together by family. This family, ratified by Justice Clement and supplied by Cob, is a city in miniature. Its bonds are at once indisputable and fragile. Its various members are to one degree or another cousins' and neighbors' constructions. Brainworm is brought into relation as Clement's "mistress" (5.5.82) just as Wellbred explains that Edward now "belongs" to his sister Bridget (5.5.4). Only those entirely without selves of their own, Bobadill and Matthew, must wait to be forgiven or forgotten, finally brought into the family or let go forever.

But neither of these gulls is the gentleman-gallant, sure of his self, upon whom city comedy depends.

The sophisticated comment on city types found in *Every Man in His Humor* and *Eastward Ho* is generally missing in *The Puritan* (1606).[40] There is a "Lady-Widdow," "a gray Gull to her Brother, a foole to her onely sonne, and an Ape to her yongest Daughter" (1.2.133–35). There is also an oath-swearing corporal, an old soldier, and three very undistinguished gentlemen who hope to marry the rich widow and her two daughters. If this is Marston's work, then he borrowed from his earlier, collaborative effort versions of Touchstone, Sir Petronel, and Gertrude.[41] However, George Pye-boord, the figure who initiates the play's intrigue and holds our interest when lesser characters grow tedious, deserves some attention. Pye-boord is introduced in stage directions as "a scholler and a Cittizen." When he speaks for himself, he describes himself as a "poore Gentleman, & a Scholler." His rivals are clearly gentlemen, "men of estimation both in Court an Citty" (5.4.101–2), and Pye-boord is just as clearly a wit, well aware that "the condition of the age affoords creatures enow for cunning to worke upon" (1.2.118–19). Pye-boord goes to extraordinary lengths, setting up gullings within gullings to get what he has taken aim at—the widow, Lady Plus, and her daughter Frances. But then, all of a sudden and at the very last moment, all that Pye-boord has just begun to grasp is snatched away from him. Although he has won our sympathy and sustained the intrigue when not one other character reveals even a jot of imagination, he is exposed and bested.

Unlike *Eastward Ho*, *The Puritan* lacks mature city comedy's awareness that neither citizens nor gentry are admirable when they merely play to type. The play gets carried away with its elaborate intrigue only to pull up short, to dispose of its protagonist, and to champion unthinkingly the faceless, if respectable, gentlemen endorsed by the play's nameless "Noble man." Pye-boord is working toward comedy's fifth-act marriages, but his credentials do not seem to be in order. His cleverness is unexpectedly renamed "knavery" and he is deemed unworthy of the marriage prize. Yet his "coozenage" never strikes us as villainy, and his defeat seems a rebuke to his energy as well as to his imagination. The expansion of possible roles that might have followed upon the success of a scholar-gentleman-citizen is forfeited by a playwright who is also content to end his play lecturing Lady Plus with tired clichés about widows. She, not the playwright, has made the "mistake" of falling for Pyeboord's (and his henchman, the Captain's) wit and inventiveness. For this she is reminded that "such is the blind besotting in the state of an unheaded woman thats a widdow" (5.4.7–9). But we too, though never deceived by Pyeboord, have been "besotted." We have been teased with the possibility that Pye-boord is a scholarly Witgood (a contemporary on Paul's boys' stage) and then asked to accept Frances' marriage to inconsequential Sir Andrew Tipstaffe.

The real victimization of the widow and her daughter Frances is not at the hands of Pye-boord, though he certainly looks forward to their money. Lady Plus is victimized by a condescending and paternal noble, and by a playwright who cannot see beyond the stereotypical widow's role. She is aware of her husband's duplicity but pretends otherwise; she will remarry shortly but laments that she has survived her husband; and she is duped by fortune hunters. Men can manipulate her, and men must save her from disgrace. It is never hinted that she, like so many of city comedy's women, has little to gain from marriage. Nor is it this playwright's intention to examine the roles of widows or "respectable" gentry. The only deviation from conventional casting in *The Puritan* is to be found in the treatment of Pye-boord, the clever-gallant figure who, in this rare instance, is foiled completely. As a result of this turn of events, the most conventional of urban economic and marriage relations are endorsed, and the admittedly gentle probing that these relations have undergone is quickly halted. This is city comedy fully complicitous with conservative and unimaginative ideology. The widow, the Puritans, the scholar, the citizens—

all are exposed, admonished, and accommodated by members of the gentry and nobility who thrive on stereotypes of the city that plays like *Eastward Ho* deem ludicrous.

Whitefriars city comedy followed close on the heels of the city comedies at the song school and at Blackfriars. In *The Family of Love,* in *Ram Alley,* and in *Epicoene,* we recognize the gentry of the earlier plays while at the same time we find new strategies for the presentation of the equivocal relationship between self and roles. In *The Family of Love,* none of the gentry has an adequate way of expressing his love.[42] For Lipsalve and Gudgeon (who aim at Glister's niece, at Mistress Purge, and at Mistress Glister—at times pursuing two at once), the problem is not merely their farcical attempts at seduction; it is as well their conception of love and the language they use to prove that they are true gallants. At least as much as Glister, who divides his time between making a cuckold of his neighbor and administering clysters, the two gallants represent the inseparability of sexuality and anality that pervades the play.[43] They are gallants because they know how to talk about love: Lipsalve has memorized the right sayings ("a wife brings but two good days, that is her wedding-day, and death-day"—1.2.7–8); he knows the right emblem for the lover (a naked man, with a "wench" tickling him on one side with a feather and pricking him on the other with a needle—1.2.18–30); and he can sing the gallant's love songs ("Since every place now yields a wench; / If one will not, another will"—1.2.48–49). Gudgeon, referring to Mistress Purge, tells Lipsalve that "I had thought to have bound myself from love, but her purging comfits makes me loose-bodied still" (2.3.59–60). Just as the title of the play undermines whatever certainties we may have had concerning faith, family, and love, the recurrence of the word "love" throughout the play makes clear that its abuse is as common as its use. When Gudgeon tells Glister that "I love mistress Purge," we think of words already spoken by the very lady: "Of all men I love not these gallants; they'll prate much, but do little: . . . they use great words, but little sense" (1.3.21–24). Or, as Glister puts it, "these great-breeched gallants; they love for profit, not for affection" (1.1.7–8). In the "close-stool of [Gudgeon's] mind," a gallant is his talk, his witty, dirty, passionless way of expressing his love. A gallant clothes himself, and so identifies himself, with a way of speaking. *The Family of Love* stages types which animate all the city jokes about sex, city wives, and cuckoldry. Its language is scatological not because the City was in fact a sewer, but because this is the variety of self-expression that follows upon a conception of the City wherein wives and privies have equal value.

The gentleman-gallant Gerardine's love for Maria is another, if less obvious, version of the gallant's love in *The Family of Love*. Before turning to his high-flown, rather vapid rhetoric of love (what, when referring to Gudgeon and Lipsalve, the page Shrimp calls "their mouldy, fly-blown compliments"—2.3.9), it is worth noting that even Gerardine is tied to the more coarse lovers in this play. He first appears on stage as a friendly companion to Lipsalve and Gudgeon, and we learn as well that Gerardine is a cousin of Mistress Purge's (1.2.165): he too is related to the disreputable Family of Love. But where the libertines show themselves gallants by their cheap talk, Gerardine thinks to prove his gentle status with what has been called "pious, frigid verse" in a static, "romantic story."[44] Gerardine, like Freevill in *The Dutch Courtesan*, can take love seriously only when it is pure, almost unearthly. He cannot find an everyday language for his love that would allow him to speak of it to Lipsalve or Gudgeon. Instead, Gerardine fails to communicate with them, responding to their low humor with such oracular lines as "Profane not . . . the sacred name of love" (1.2.15) and with self-conscious conceits out of the sugared sonnet tradition:

> This is the chamber which confines my love,
> This is the abstract of the spacious world:
> Within it holds a gem so rich, so rare,

That art or nature never yet could set
A valued price to her unvalued worth.

(1.2.54–58)

Like the gallants, Gerardine imagines that he can assume a
rhetorical style and thus confirm his status as a gentleman.
But his ornate, literary language is nothing more than another of the play's instances of "fustian above . . . understanding," serving only to "make asses' ears attentive"
(5.3.47–48). Once again, it is Doctor Glister who unwittingly diagnoses the chief malady in this play: "truth needs
not the foil of rhetoric" (5.3.340–41).

Although Middleton relates Gerardine to the debased
Family by blood (Mistress Purge), by deed (the seduction),
and by his unreliable rhetoric of love, it remains for Gerardine to give the appearance, at least, of a salvaged society at
the play's end. However, even here we note that his superiority to those around him serves the plot—it is not meant
to hold up under close scrutiny of his character. And we
need to take only one more step, with Lording Barry (*Ram
Alley*, 1608), to see what happens when even the appearance
of the gentleman's superiority and the merest hope for a
rejuvenated community are dispensed with altogether. The
alley was a stone's throw away from the Middle and Inner
Temples, and Barry fills the stage with precisely the Whitefriars types (a whore, a widow, a blustering captain, a counterfeit lawyer, a foolish justice, and a brace of gallants) that
satirical verse and rogue pamphlets tell us lived there. We
have seen that in skillful hands, the dramatization of such
types as the merchant-usurer or the city gallant challenges
the audience to reexamine the prejudices that such figures
embody. The merchant is revealed as the personification of
the gentry's fears, and the clever gallant represents the gentry's will to sexual mastery at a time when its social and
financial potency was uncertain. Whether citizens like Mayberry triumph over gallants like Greenshield (*Northward
Ho*), or whether the gentry humiliate Quomodos (*Michael-*

mas Term), the full range of city comedy suggests the inadequacy of the ways men figured the contemporary social economy. Each play rests upon an assumed hierarchy—here the merchants are superior to the gentry, there the citizens best the gallants—which is undermined or finally jettisoned. However, in Barry's play, it is not easy to establish this initial hierarchy. Borrowing heavily from Middleton's *A Trick to Catch the Old One*, Barry would have us sympathize with the gallant William Smallshanks and applaud his gullings. Yet the gallant is at all times a thorough knave. Instead of starting with seemingly admirable figures who turn out to be less than they pretend, Barry introduces us to a cast of discredited types and, whatever his intention, never permits us to see them as anything else. When every male character is an Andrew Lethe or a Dampit, the audience cannot be expected to acknowledge versions of itself on the stage. Where Middleton can subvert current ideologies, Barry leaves them in force.

As we might expect, Ben Jonson's examination of the gentleman-gallant is considerably more discriminating than that of a theatrical dabbler like Lording Barry. Whereas city comedy's paradigmatic plot entails conflict between classes, comedy of the City simply presents us with a plot suited to the City. In the case of *Epicoene*, Jonson turned to London for its noise and for its young men about town—knights, gentlemen, or gallants who keep an eye on the court, live in the metropolis, but do not think of themselves as city men. These are the men who "come abroad where the matter is frequent, to court, to tiltings, public shows and feasts, to plays, and church sometimes; thither they come, to show their new tires too, to see and be seen. . . . The variety arrests [their] judgment" (4.1.52–57).[45] Jonson's urban gentry range from the outrageously antisocial Morose to frivolous social butterflies like Daw and La Foole. Somewhere in between, on what has been called the "*via media* between the polarities of courtly folly and alienated virtue," we find Clerimont, Dauphine Eugenie, and Truewit.[46] As most critics have recognized, it is with these figures that we must come to terms. In this discussion, I shall concentrate on Truewit, the most outspoken member of the trio.

While most readers find Truewit a particularly delightful character, Jonas Barish's writings on *Epicoene* have forced them to sharpen their appraisals.[47] Barish argues that Jonson, perhaps in spite of himself, was caught in a "stalemate" between a temperament at once Ovidian and Juvenalian. The self that would accept life seems to win out over the self that satirizes life, but the victory is "highly equivocal," and it demands a mighty distortion of the satiric spirit. At the center of this equivocal victory is Truewit, "tentative," and "one who is still experimenting with a variety of attitudes and has not yet allowed any to take full possession of him." He is "an ideal of equivocal detachment, equally unable to commit himself wholeheartedly to the world and to let it alone." Neither cynic nor sensualist, Truewit's indifference "reflects the carelessness of the young gallant about town." In recent years, critics have responded to Barish's reading by suggesting that Truewit (along with Clerimont and Eugenie) is considerably less equivocal than Barish makes him out to be. W. David Kay, for example, locates Truewit in a tradition of "urbane wit, of the critical yet detached attitude toward experience which permits good-humored dissent from the world."[48] Kay, like Michael Shapiro (to whom Kay refers), writes of Truewit in terms of serious play, being in the world but not of it, "urbane criticism," and "judicious aloofness." (Shapiro's terms are similar: "deliberate aloofness," "truly detached," "cool observer," "amused rather than outraged," "urbane insouciance," "virile audacity.")[49] Truewit fits within "humanistic contexts" consonant with Erasmus' formulation (in the *Enchiridion*): "Though I want you to differ stoutly from the world, I do not want you to take up a kind of churlish cynicism. . . . Adapt yourself to all men outwardly, so long as your resolution remains firm inwardly."[50]

Does Truewit possess "inward resolution"? He is a figure just elusive enough to bring some of his admirers near to the point of contradiction. Barish argues that Truewit "never ceases to keep one foot planted solidly in the real world," but that the self that owns this foot is less solid: "Truewit speaks through so many masks that one is not sure when, if ever, he is speaking *in propria persona.*"[51] Shapiro argues that Clerimont, Eugenie, and Truewit are "a model for the audience's behavior in ethics as well as in fashions, in life as in theater," but asserts later that they are independent "of all positions, values, and convictions, even—or especially—their own."[52] Truewit has "a *certain sprezzatura,*" a "nonchalance" that is "*close*" to sprezzatura, and he is idle, but with a "*sophisticated* idleness."[53] Indeed, Jonson has Truewit playing the gallant so well, and with such self-confidence, that we believe Truewit can locate his central self even if we cannot. He is, as Salingar has written, a "farceur," and to a large degree we are as played upon as are his stage victims. We want to have faith in Truewit's taste and judgment because he, with Clerimont and Eugenie, is alone in his ability to see through folly and pretension. If Truewit lets us down, proving frivolous when put to the test, then we are in just that precarious position that city comedy most often avoids—within a society with no solid ground and no absolute selves.

Jonson's art lies in his unwillingness (not, pace Barish, his inability) to make a final judgment concerning Truewit. He gives his Whitefriars audience enough material to make their own judgments and so to reveal their own prejudices, tolerances, and desires. He gives them the perfect gallant playing his part to perfection and then asks them what they make of this figure. Truewit is a touchstone: we speak ourselves when we emphasize his wit over his aggression, his carelessness over his frivolity, or his detachment over his engagement. Each discrimination that we make associates us with Truewit's own sharp-eyed way of seeing and further commits us to a way of seeing Truewit. In the end, it is we who must admit our Ovidian or Juvenalian biases. Jonson offers us a figure that allows us to judge ourselves better than we can judge the character we contemplate. Truewit's advice to Clerimont as to how he ought to appear to women describes Truewit's own "approach" to the audience: "You must approach them i' their own height, their own line" (4.1.84–85). He is one of those Shakespearian characters who are as we like them or what we will. His "variety arrests [our] judgment." Professing total indifference ("I have learned to lose as little of my kindness as I can. I'll do good to no man against his will"—1.1.61–62), Truewit slips out of our categories, now an ironist, a satirist, a farceur, or a trickster. He joins "fashionable men" in their exercises, but only "for company" (1.1.37–38). He outdoes all the gallants that city comedy had been offering for six or seven years, playing his part with faultless detachment, with self-confidence and amusement, but hardly a touch of cynicism.

If we are to discover evaluative terms for Truewit, we must look beyond his easy, pliant gallantry, to both his social context and his daily activities. He is, after all, the "young man about town" that Barish takes him to be. His business is nothing more serious than to exercise his wit. And he can be witty and aloof because he is at his leisure, because he knows the courtier's and the gallant's styles, and because he has neither family nor finances to tie him down. When he does get down to business, we find him tormenting Morose, amusing himself with the Otters and the city wives, and making fools of Sir John and Sir Amorous. Except for what he does to Morose, there is (for Truewit) hardly anything of weight in these activities. Even in the case of Morose, Truewit sees his work more as jest than as torture (note his line about another trick of his: "How! Maim a man forever for a jest?"—4.5.119). For all his coolness, we perceive the smallness and, occasionally, the harshness of Truewit's preoccupations. He is a perfect city gallant, but that role does not, after all, add up to a great deal for Ben Jonson. While waiting to fill a position of responsibility in the commonwealth (or while preparing to sidestep the responsibilities of wealth altogether), Truewit passes his time by amusing himself. It is not that he fails to strip the ragged follies of the time; rather we begin to realize that Jonson sees Truewit's youth and confidence as merely youthful confidence. As with his play, Jonson would have us enjoy True-wit's wit, perhaps even applaud it, but not "apply" it (as we are warned in the second prologue) to ourselves. Truewit is a model for the stage gallant that would entertain the White-friars audience; there is no need to praise him as a model for the audience itself.

Jonson's qualified approval of Truewit springs from his mature perspective, not from his ambivalence. He is tolerant of the young wit even if he would prefer to see London's Truewits engaged in more serious affairs. What has been seen (and praised) as Truewit's "detached attitude toward experience" may have been, for Jonson, a sign of *im*maturity, of an unwillingness to engage experience head on and at one's risk. Truewit stages little dramas but keeps his safe distance; for Jonson, the "true Artificer will not run away from Nature, as hee were afraid of her."[54] The gallant's self-confidence elicits our approbation, but we must remember how easily Truewit comes by his confidence. It is doubtful that Jonson, who tells us that "Who casts to write a living line, must sweat," was as taken in by Truewit's charm as were the Whitefriars gentry.[55] Surely Jonson was as "detached" from Truewit as Truewit is from experience. And it is this same detachment (bordering on cynicism) that the playwright feels toward his next-year's wit—*The Alche-mist*'s Lovewit. In a play filled with the greed and wild am-bition of Sir Epicure, a London knight, and Kastril, a would-be gallant, it is something of a relief to encounter the cool, relaxed "master of the house." Like Truewit, Lovewit is above (literally, beyond) the follies of the City. He too is not going to risk himself: the plague sends him running to the country. And though Lovewit turns out to be less an exposer than a conniver, he, like Truewit, has for the audience a wink denoting self-knowledge. Jonson is not carried away by these wits, but he seems willing to settle for Truewit and Lovewit as the best the city gentry can offer. As these char-acters stand above the follies that encompass them, so, Jon-son would say, must we—perhaps a little less confident of ourselves and a little more seriously engaged in improving the City.

Lovewit is less attractive than Truewit because he is an "old man" and because, by collaborating with Jeremy, he allows us to associate him with the rogues of the play. But Lovewit is no dupe; he is "A little indulgent to that servant's wit" (5.5.150) because it serves his turn.[56] Lovewit gives nothing away to his confused Blackfriars neighbors. He admits to his ignorance with great care, usually turning onlookers' comments into jests: "He [Jeremy] hung out no banners / Of a strange calf with five legs to be seen? / Or a huge lobster with six claws?" (5.1.7–9). And Lovewit prepares both his neighbors and himself for his servant's latest "device" by making it clear to all that he loves "a teeming wit" as well as he loves "his nourishment" (5.1.16). He is a true gentleman-gallant: confident but careful. He knows the city game and he knows to play coolly. More intrigued than anxious because of his neighbors' stories, Lovewit responds to the smith as "the alchemists" answer their gulls: Yes, smith, "Thou art a wise fellow"; now "lend me thy help to get this door open" (5.1.42 and 44). Once the door has been opened and Jeremy has begun his account, Lovewit can dismiss his neighbors as "rogues" and "changelings." Before long, Lovewit realizes that Jeremy is telling less than the truth, but he remains the "indulgent master," asking, "What's your mid'cine, / To draw so many several sorts of wild fowl?" (5.3.78–79). From the last line of Act 5, scene 3 ("Well, let's see your widow") to the end of the play, Lovewit takes over as the final sanction for all that has preceded his appearance and for what follows too. He obtains for himself a wife and some added riches, and he has the pleasure of outfacing all the gulls and perhaps Jeremy/Face too.

Jonson could fashion foolish or downright unpleasant gentlemen-gallants like Daw, La Foole, Mammon, and Morose as well as Middleton could. He invests more art in their language than a Middleton or Dekker could hope to do, but his efforts serve purposes identical to theirs—he would point to the discrepancy between the pretenders' self-conceptions and their actual, woefully small substance. These figures are parodies of city gallants. Figures like Truewit, Clerimont, Dauphine Eugenie, and Lovewit are considerably more complicated. City comedy rests the ethics and the cohesiveness of the City on their shoulders. They must remain clearly their own men, grounded in their secure selves and thus apart from the changelings. However, while *nosce teipsum* should be their motto, Jonson suggests that these wits are unreliable heroes. They are either a shade too engaged in (or aggressive about) their trickery, or they are just a little too disengaged and so frivolous. Jonson implies that urbanity, the city gallant's *sprezzatura*, is not the sole mark of a gentleman in the City. There are more serious concerns for a man of wealth and family. When Jonson writes that "Our scene is London, 'cause we would make known, / No country's mirth is better than our own" (Prologue, 4–5), or that he means to show us "natural follies" (l. 23), he implies that there are more weighty activities than those of clever wits exposing greed and pretension, or, for that matter, than playwriting. The conventional depiction of the foolish gallant indicates the obvious social inadequacy of one role model; but the equally traditional figure of the cool and witty stage gallant is, for Jonson, as flawed as the typical stage merchant is for men like Middleton and Dekker.

The Public Theaters

Were we to accept Harbage's rigorous separation of the public and coterie theaters, and his belief that whereas the former theater was affirmative and communitarian, the latter was satirical and elitist, we would expect to find public-theater gallants who were more warm and generous than their private-theater counterparts. Or we might expect that the wit of the gallant would be directed toward improvements in the community. However, we find that public-theater gallants are very much like their cool, offhanded private-theater brethren. To explain this likeness, we must reject the sort of moralism that ascribes beneficent or nasty intentions to the plays and playwrights of the two theaters. On both stages, gallants and merchant-citizens were unmistakably conventionalized figures. Public-theater audiences did not identify with exaggerated citizen heroes any more than they reveled in the shortcomings of clever gallants. In both public and private theaters, the gallant was recognizable as a type, and as the embodiment of traditions. A Walter Whorehound's entire existence is bound up with his exploitation of merchants. Quomodo's life centers on gulling gentry. Such figures do not "represent" pride or greed or wit; rather they are elements in city comedy's staging of relations in the City. Their activities spring from the ways men thought of one another in the City, and they point to the fears and aspirations of the contemporary theater audience. I turn to two rather dissimilar plays—Dekker's *II Honest Whore* and Middleton's *A Chaste Maid in Cheapside*—and their representative gentry, in order to explore this argument.

Dekker's sequel to his collaborative work with Middleton presents the courtier-gallant as good fairy (or "happy man"—1.2.49), and as knave. Matheo, the knave, busies himself with two related activities: he torments his wife, the honest whore Bellafront, and he plays the gallant. At the beginning of the play, we learn that Matheo stands accused of killing a man (1.1.124 ff.). Dekker allows us a moment during which we may want to give Matheo the benefit of the doubt ("'twas a faire fight, yes, / If rumors tongue goe true"—1.1.129–30), but it is not long before we are convinced that Bellafront is yoked to one of the preeminent scoundrels in Jacobean comedy. Freed from prison, Matheo has only one thing on his mind—he would prove himself a gallant, or, as he cries repeatedly, he would "flye hye." But the high life costs money, and Matheo's limited imagination leads him to robbery, planned robbery, and debt. Along with these nasty practices, Matheo is continually suggesting that Bellafront return to her former profession to bring in addi-

tional money. In a scene that passes quickly from melodrama to sordidness, Matheo, foaming like a madman
("Must haue money, must haue money, must haue a Cloake
and Rapier, and things"—3.2.27–28), begins to tear at Bellafront's clothes. He tells his man that he is "fleaing" her,
that he will pawn her to her "very eye-browes," and that it
is really no matter because "it's Summer: your onely fashion
for a woman now, is to be light, to be light" (ll. 45–56). Two
scenes later, Matheo's compulsive stutterings start up again,
but this time he takes up a stool, ready to "beat out the
braines" of Bellafront. Matheo's humor becomes his "humour": coolness and self-confidence give way to an all-
consuming mania. Sick and raving, Matheo is in no shape
to play the part of a gallant.

To check Matheo's violence, Dekker introduces his
chief addition to the dramatis personae carried over from *I
Honest Whore*, Bellafront's father, Orlando Friscobaldo.
Hazlitt found Friscobaldo "unforgettable," while other readers couple him with Dekker's memorable Simon Eyre.[57]
With the help of the Duke, Friscobaldo manipulates the action, testing the former whore, the prodigal son-in-law, and
his whoremongering friend. However, *our* interest in Friscobaldo lies less in his plotting than in his character. He is,
like Sir Bounteous Progress in *A Mad World*, more a comic
spirit than a courtier or a gentleman. When he gives up his
"Lodging at Court" and disguises himself as the servant Pa-
checo, he metamorphoses into the agent of comic reconciliation. However clever or testy we find Friscobaldo, we remain certain that he alone will be the engineer of the
expected happy ending. It cannot be otherwise because Friscobaldo comes right out of the book containing an "Italian
Painter's" picture of the "happy man":

After the picture . . . doe I Striue to haue my face drawne: For I am
not couetous, am not in debt, sit neither at the Dukes side, nor lie
at his feete. Wenching and I haue done, no man I wrong, no man I
feare, no man I fee; I take heed how farre I walke, because I know
yonders my home. I would not die like a rich man, to carry nothing

away saue a winding sheete: but like a good man, to leave *Orlando* behind me. I sowed leaues in my Youth, and I reape now Bookes in my Age. I fill this hand, and empty this, and when the bell shall toll for me, if I proue a Swan, and go singing to my nest, why so? If a Crow! throw me out for carrion, and pick out mine eyes. May not old *Friscobaldo* . . . be merry now ! ha? (1.2.67–78)

Like a Zen master, Friscobaldo boasts, "I haue a little, haue all things; I haue nothing" (1.2.80). It is the mature Friscobaldo, not Truewit, who is in the world but not of it. And his worldly dealings are of unquestionable import: Friscobaldo sets out to reclaim his daughter, to chastise Hippolito, and to reform his son-in-law.

In *II Honest Whore,* the obstreperous father has become a good angel. Dekker's romantic, or melodramatic, inclination leads him to extreme varieties of conventional figures. We may find here that all old men in city comedy are not Lucres and Hoards, but we are still left with types unsuited to the extratheatrical world. Typecasting which borrows from popular versions of whores and citizens and jolly old gentlemen makes for successful city comedy, not viable urban relations. City comedy succeeds as more than entertainment (the "profit") when it stages its spectators' sense of the City and lets them know that it is doing so. Theatergoers see that their own prejudices are embodied in the types that populate the stage. When they refuse to dream of Friscobaldos and men like Sir Bounteous, and when they no longer pin their dislikes on Moroses and Matheos, spectators begin to refashion the gentleman-gallant for themselves and for London.

And such refashioning is called for in *A Chaste Maid in Cheapside.* In this, the finest of Middleton's city comedies, none of the gentry are allowed successfully to enact the role of the self-confident gallant. Touchwood senior's sexual prowess threatens his own health (2.1.17) and that of the commonwealth (2.1.61–62).[58] Touchwood's opposite, Sir Oliver Kix, is impotent. He represents the total dissolution of the gentry (no progeny) as he sheepishly offers to "make good deeds my children" (2.1.145). Sir Walter Whorehound appears to be a successful gallant, arranging his marriage to a wealthy city heiress while cuckolding Allwit. However, we know from the start that Sir Walter is bound to lose Moll Yellowhammer to Touchwood junior; we learn, later, that Walter is dependent on the Kixes and that he is in fact exploited by, not exploiting, Jack Allwit. Finally there is Touchwood junior, Moll's chosen but thwarted lover. In Act 1, he is every bit the gallant: he sports with Yellowhammer and speaks of Moll as "that choice spoil" which "whets / My stomach" (1.1.138 and 140–41). But unlike Witgood in *A Trick to Catch the Old One*, young Touchwood fails miserably with his stratagems to secure his bride and must rely finally on his brother and the Yellowhammer maid to bring about his marriage. Moreover Touchwood junior, the ostensible source of regeneration in the play, is all but lost amid the unpleasant stirrings of the Allwits, the Yellowhammers, and the Kixes. He is anything but the self-sufficient, controlling gallant of city comedy.

By qualifying his approval of every figure in the play, Middleton is able to suggest the uniform inadequacy of the roles assumed by his gentry and citizens alike. Because there are no heroes in *A Chaste Maid*, the spectators at the Swan could depart either in disgust, or prepared to find more tolerable versions of the citizen and the gentleman. If Middleton is any help in the latter course, it is because he has fashioned antitypes. By fixing the limits of negative characterization, Middleton asks us to start over again, with a new cast of characters that will be better suited to living together in the City. By depriving both the gentry and the citizens of champions, he disallows all self-righteous class superiority in his audience. His awareness extends beyond the immorality of his gentry and citizens to the need for a general rejuvenation of the urban community. In the typical city comedy, these groups are set apart. In the series of perverse subplots in *A Chaste Maid*, however, Middleton insists on the mutual dependence and interrelatedness of gentry and citizenry. As in Jacobean London during the decade of city comedy we are examining, the two social classes in the play are bound to each other. The Touchwoods determine the fate of the Kixes, the Yellowhammers' daughter, and the Allwits. Whorehound depends on the Kixes, maintains the Allwits, and would join the Yellowhammer family. And the Allwits' fate depends on the Yellowhammers, Whorehound, and the Touchwoods. The logic of the plot demands that the solutions that are found—Touchwood senior as Lady Kix's stud, Touchwood junior's "stomach" appeased, and Tim Yellowhammer married to a whore—be unsavory, but Middleton implies that solutions, and more constructive solutions, must be found for the problems created by contemporary class antagonisms. In *A Chaste Maid*, these antagonisms produce humiliation, not victory and defeat. Yellowhammer would have his son Tim called "Sir" but must suffer Tim's marriage to a whore. Contradictorily, he insists that, as the daughter of a goldsmith, Moll is no gentlewoman (1.1.181), yet he tries to marry her to Sir Walter and agrees finally to her marriage with Touchwood junior. Allwit's "exploitation" of Whorehound is the obvious source of the wittol's own humiliation. By settling for "the erecting of bridewells and spittlehouses" (2.1.143), Sir Oliver admits his failure. Touchwood senior has the gallant's potency but cannot support his family. And Sir Walter's cavalier arrangement with the Allwits, along with his attempt to secure Moll's two-thousand-pound dowry, ends in one of London's "counters."

At stake for the citizenry, and even more for the gentry, is wit.[59] Sir Walter, Touchwood senior (vis-à-vis the Kixes), and Touchwood junior all think of themselves as clever schemers. The last is rather naive, and his brother is cynical (2.1.100), but Sir Walter is totally confident. If the knight, the most self-assured wit, ends in prison, it is because there is no other place in the City for the gallant's destructive wit. Sir Walter's fate is a consequence of the disruptiveness of all the antisocial tricks played by all of the comedy's gallants. His personal comeuppance comes when this once-brash knight must repent in the midst of the callous Allwit "family." Whether or not his repentance is sincere (or motivated merely by the fear of death), it represents a complete reversal of his self-confidence. For Walter, "The game begins already" in the first act, but by the fifth act, he is crying "Gamesters, farewell, I have nothing left to play" (5.1.149). The city role that is filled by the cool gamester, and the genre whose plots are motivated by witty gallants, are judged along with Sir Walter. Wit, "the disease, that fit employment wants," in the form of Allwit and Whorehound, is sentenced to its appropriate prisons.[60] Where cleverness ends, social responsibility must begin. If, however, there seems little hope for such responsibility in the world that survives Yellowhammer's words at the close of the play, it is because Middleton's characters are still caught in their unsatisfactory roles. That Middleton wrote city comedy at all may testify to his belief that actual citizens and gentry could find new and happier roles for themselves.

5

Wives, Whores, Widows, and Maids

There was a wide divergence of opinion on the status of women in late-sixteenth- and early-seventeenth-century London. Women were alternately praised and damned. They were either virgins or they were whores. The praise might be sincere: women "performe and publish the most happy and joyfull benefits which euer came to man-kinde"; or, to borrow Hermione's words, if not her intention, it might be hollow: "cram's with praise, and make's / As fat as tame things."[1] The invective might be choleric, as in Swetnam's "Bear-bayting of women"; it might be traditional, as in Overbury's or Breton's character sketches of common or "wanton" women; or it might be equivocal: "A woman is a stinking rose . . . a flattering wound."[2] Women were discussed as daughters, wives, widows, or whores. They were portrayed as children and as temptresses, as treasures or commodities, and as the usurpers of conventional masculine roles. And London was as much "a paradise for women" where "females have great liberty and are almost like masters" as it was the home of theaters, where "Every fastasticke Poetaster . . . will striue to represent vnseemely figments imputed to our sex."[3]

Given this range of opinion, it is not surprising that modern historians arrive at dissimilar conclusions when they make generalizations. Roger Thompson argues that

"Although women had their defenders in Stuart England, the great weight of public opinion deemed them mentally, morally, psychologically and physically inferior to men."[4] Ruth Kelso suggests that a woman was "formed to play her part, as man his, to yield obedience as an inescapable condition for the performance of her duty and the realization of her perfection. This was the prevailing belief, which of course fitted existing conditions."[5] Louis B. Wright concludes that "During the late sixteenth and early seventeenth centuries, middle-class writers ... prevailingly defended her."[6] Religious historians point to the influence of Puritanism, but they disagree on the extent to which women were seen as men's companions, not their servants.[7] And economic historians tell us that as household industry gave way to larger manufacture and out-of-home business, women were relegated to housekeeping and child rearing.[8] More recently, Linda Woodbridge, a scholar whose primary interest is Renaissance literature, has suggested that the constant stream of advice directed through marriage pamphlets at women of this period reflects men's discomfort with the women of independent spirit in their midst. Woodbridge concludes that "Middle-class marriage [which "arose as much in reaction against women's intractable pursuit of independence as it did in reaction against Catholic ascetic philosophy"], as institutionalized by the rising mercantile classes and rationalized by lay moralists and Puritan divines, was not by any stretch of the imagination a feminist institution." Woodbridge argues that although women might be portrayed as equal and even superior to men, the English "Renaissance did not generate a workable body of feminist theory, especially theory that could cope with changing economic conditions."[9]

Hence it should come as no surprise that the women in Jacobean city comedy were not all of one sort. In the plays, as in the pamphlets and sermons, there were pure, innocent virgins and shrill, threatening whores (the presence of one always figures the possibility of the other). And there were

clever, wise, or self-sufficient women at or near the center
of many of these plays. Such women have "the last word,"
and they allow us to perceive the follies common to both
the gentry and the merchant-citizens. In many plays they
are the structural hinge, the covert instigators of much of
the action or the prize men would secure. A woman may
don the breeches (but only temporarily) to gain recognition
for herself, to remind her spouse or lover of her valid claim
on his affections, and to make it clear that she is not blind
to male shortcomings.

Thus Doll Common must manage Subtle and Face;
Moll Firth (in *The Roaring Girl*) trips up the gallant and
protects the gentleman; Maria (in *The Woman's Prize; or,
The Tamer Tamed*) demands the respect of Petruchio; Mistress Allwit (in *A Chaste Maid in Cheapside*) tacitly (though
not with our approval) signals the depravity of Sir Walter
and Master Allwit; Sindefy (in *Eastward Ho*) reminds
Quicksilver of his precarious position; Thomasine (in *Michaelmas Term*) chastens Quomodo and aids Easy; the wives
in *Westward Ho* trick their husbands and their gallants; the
silent "woman" turns the tables on Morose; the whore
Frank Gullman (though she too is deceived) tricks Follywit
and disparages Sir Bounteous (in *A Mad World*); the Courtesan (in *A Trick*) finds a husband as she hoodwinks Hoard;
and Field's ladies receive their amends. Few of these feminine victories are unequivocal. Yet throughout the decade
of city comedy we are examining, playwrights were presenting independent, capable stage women.

Unlike the merchant who seeks dignity, or the gallant
who burdens himself with the need to prove his wit, women
are presented as requiring something more fundamental of
themselves. They must be certain that before they are
"wives, daughters or lovers," they are integral, independent
people.[10] When the stage woman confirms her power and
her own needs, she simultaneously breaks free of conventional whore/virgin typecasting and acquires enough security to *play* the same roles that were formerly imposed on

her. Middleton's or Jonson's women are not Shakespearian heroines; but they do dramatize the constrained roles made available to them by male typecasters.

Ruth Kelso has made several important observations regarding the protocols that governed discussion of the "second sex." While the thinking that informs the ideal for a gentleman appears to be pagan, the ideal woman is described in unmistakably Christian terms. Masculine virtues take shape in the public realm, whereas feminine virtues are private. Conduct books for men foster "self-expression and realization," but writings on women call for "suppression and negation of the self." Finally, men are considered, among other ways, according to their rank (for example, gentlemen and commoners); women, however, are treated without attention to rank—the theory of the lady is nearly identical to the theory of women (pp. 25, 28, and 36). Although rank may not have been a significant factor in the debate over women, "role" was available as an alternative structuring principle. Women were anatomized as virgins, wives, widows, and whores. And each role had economic, moral, and social implications. Thus the morality of prostitution might focus on promiscuity, the economics of prostitution engenders a discussion of profit, and the social dimension might allow men to point to the removal of sexuality from the private to the public sector.[11] Such an analysis has all the delights of orderliness, and it is precisely order that is at stake. Even a whore is tolerable if she can be classified. But if women are merely actresses, filling roles without commitment, or if they blur distinctions between roles (like the adultress, who is both wife and whore), then orderliness, and the control that it allows, is threatened. Before returning to the city comedies, I shall examine briefly some of the features of the virgin's, the whore's, the wife's, and the widow's roles in an orderly society.

The chaste maid was of particular interest to all men. In a society where the transmission of property was contingent upon the legitimacy of heirs, it was essential that a man could be certain of his wife's chastity before, and her fidelity during, marriage. Indeed, next to her dowry (over which she had no control), a woman's chastity was her sole resource.[12] As Kelso points out, chastity was a bargaining chip: "Let a woman have chastity she has all. Let her lack chastity and she has nothing" (p. 24). The proximity of this situation to the feminist argument, that marriage is a version of prostitution (trading sexual availability for financial security), may well have been obvious to seventeenth-century commentators.

Of course, chastity was not merely an economic issue. A sexually pure woman was thought to have a pure soul. In Greene's *The Royal Exchange*, physical beauty, honest habits, and chastity of mind are among the supreme feminine attributes.[13] A chaste woman led a chaste life: her diet and clothing were simple, her house was clean, and she was free of wanton fancies. Chastity implied modesty; a woman who failed to blush was a whore at heart. But she had to follow a tricky path: the unchaste woman was wanton, but the chaste might be called proud. Or, as Joseph Swetnam cleverly arranges matters in a pamphlet concerning "lewde, idle, froward and unconstant women," if you object to his reasoning you are one of the women he is writing about ("for this booke toucheth no sort of women; but such as when they heare it, will goe about to reproue it").[14] Chastity entailed also a refusal to befriend women of uncertain virtue, and, unexpectedly, an unwillingness to be "too easily suspicious of her husband: . . . 'it is better for her to couer his faults then to disclose them.'"[15] Perhaps this double standard may be explained by yet another double standard. A man's honor depended on his word, but a woman's honor was her chastity.

In a society in which the plague killed at least two men for every woman (or, to put it another way, where there was a shortage of marriageable men and an abundance of women) it was easy to undervalue women.[16] A woman might be forced to marry a man below her station, and this in itself was sufficient reason to call into question her chastity. Furthermore, women were usually assumed guilty; theirs was a heritage of lasciviousness, of temptation ("Then who can but say that women sprung from the Deuil, whose heads, hands & hearts, minds & soules are euill. . . . For women haue a thousand wayes to intise thee, and ten thousand waies to deceiue thee"),[17] and of madness (hysteria, "the mother," had its etymological, and supposedly physical, source in the womb). It was unusual for a man to argue that women were no more wanton than men, that "he desires, as much as she delights."[18] And, beyond modesty, a woman's only defense was to reverse all commonly held assumptions. But there were few Moll Friths, and few "Ester Sowernams" who would commit to print the belief that "no woman is bad except shee be abused" by a man.[19]

The antitype to the virgin is the whore; however, "The difference betwixt the love of a courtesan and a wife"[20] (or a chaste maid) is not a simple matter. If the chaste maid is prized for her sex, the prostitute is a figure who impinges on the maid's power. By making sex available, the prostitute both robs the virgin of some of her value and increases the scarcity of virgins. And the prostitute *dis*orders sanctioned attitudes toward sex. Whereas a wife trades her sex for security, family, and social status, a prostitute must be paid for her services because of her (loss of) status in the society. And whereas a wife is her husband's property and is assumed to delight in his company, a prostitute is independent of her client. She can humiliate a man: the very thing he craves, she denigrates ("a whore is railed and reuiled of euery body for her filthy condition, and yet courted and embraced for wanton allurements").[21] Chastity bespeaks order in the family, and by example, order in the state. A prostitute, treated by the law like a madman or a monster, is an emblem for anarchy. Richard Brathwait writes of the whore "haling downe the hand / Of vengeance and subversion on the state."[22] The prostitute deceives men by playing a role but not actually filling it. She is an actress who plays the part of the chaste maid. She sets an example for wives who are unhappy in marriage, teaching them to pretend affection where there is none to be found.

However, the prostitute was not simply a *threat* to the family and state. Augustine was cited frequently: "Remove prostitutes from human affairs and you would pollute the world with lust" (*De Ordine*, ii, 4). Others argued that the prostitute was not entirely responsible for her actions: she was simply "acting in accord with her sexual character."[23] She might be tolerated as long as her property rights were curtailed and her inferior social status was acknowledged. Because handsome profits could be made from prostitution, numerous brothels—some two dozen, at least, by the mid-1590s—opened for business in Southwark. The law went after procurers, then clients, and then, finally, the prostitute. The owners of brothels (men like Edward Alleyn and Philip Henslowe) were held responsible for the spread of prostitution and venereal disease. Indeed, some representatives of the state, like Duke Vincentio in *Measure for Measure*, could make the prostitute disappear altogether: "Why, you are nothing then, neither maid, widow, nor wife?" The prostitute rematerialized as a person when, against all odds, she converted. She might enter a Magdalene order, or she might (with the proper dispensation) marry.[24]

That a structure was available for turning a prostitute into a nun or wife reflects the tremendous desire for orderliness that I have already noted. Since women were deemed unreliable on their own and incapable of self-government, they were best dealt with as wives, daughters, nuns, or wards. A sometimes strategic "infantilization" of women was common.[25] When a woman was denied an education and had no part in running a family business, it was easy to dismiss her as trivial and self-indulgent. What made the prostitute a threat was her unwillingness to conform to contemporary measures of social and feminine order. "Her eyes are like Free-booters" and "Her modestie is curiositie."[26] "The sinnes of other women shew in landscip, far off and full of shadow; hers in State, neere hand, and bigger in the life."[27] By emphasizing the fact that "a whore is a hie way to the Divell," men could compartmentalize their love: all that was corrupt and lustful was saved for a prostitute; all that was pure and morally unobjectionable was directed toward a chaste wife. A prostitute was expected and allowed to be willful and clever while a wife was expected to be obedient and simple. When a woman combined any of these traits, she was no longer identifiable by role. She was then either a monster, or a human being to be reckoned with.

As a wife, a woman was subjected to an inordinate amount of counsel. Numerous Puritan conduct books directed at the London bourgeoisie—in particular, at middle-class wives—outlined the purposes of marriage and proper domestic relations. Precisely how innovative were the views of men like Robert Cleaver, William Whately, and William Gouge is the subject of some debate.[28] It has been argued that beginning in the late sixteenth century, conduct books articulated a broadening consensus that companionship, not procreation, was the basis for marriage. Puritan divines are said to have retreated from the Thomist conception of marriage as a discipline so that they might increasingly stress love and the relief of man's essential loneliness. A marriage based on companionship was understood to entail a combination of duties and love. Wives continued to be expected to obey their husbands; but the latter were expected to love their wives. When marriage was envisioned as a society for procreation, God's will and the needs of a growing commonwealth provided the necessary theological and political authorities. When marriage was seen as a society for mutual solace, another political model was invoked: the family, "society's microcosm," was set above the state.[29]

Such attitudes gave rise to new tolerances. For the most part, forced subjection of a wife was considered irresponsible. Men and women were counseled to choose apt or fit mates. William Heale wrote that "it is the greatest folly of all follies, for a man to aggrandize his owne misfortunes by quarreling with his owne choice."[30] William Whately preached that "Most men enter this estate [marriage], and being entred complaine thereof. They should rather complaine of themselves."[31] But as much as enlightened attitudes may have altered a man's idea of marriage, they did not alter certain basic facts. To survive, a woman had to marry, and once married, she owed her husband obedience.[32] "Puritan writers were at one with their predecessors in believing strongly in male dominance."[33] The Hallers have written that in matters of conscience, a wife was fully equal to her husband: they are "equal in sin and alike in their appointed inheritance of death, therefore they are the heirs together of the grace of life."[34] But Kathleen M. Davies argues convincingly that practical behavior advocated by men like Whately and Gouge "seems to have left little room for a tender conscience. . . . And even if we accept that these [the Puritans'] statements allowed some liberty of conscience to wives, it seems to be no greater a liberty than that described by pre-Reformation writers who discussed the same problems."[35] Throughout our period, marriage remained an institution designed to keep the male line intact, and to secure monetary or political advantage. Men continued to think of love as a duty of the already married, not as a prerequisite of marriage. "First he must choose his love, and then he must love his choice."[36] Marriage was always a serious *business*, and Elizabethan and Jacobean drama that made much of the sex-money equation was only exaggerating the assumptions that underpinned marriage in every social class.

Few moralists failed to enumerate the responsibilities of a good wife. For Whately, her "main duties" were chastity, benevolence, cheerfulness, and willingness. "Euery good woman must suffer her self to be conuinced in iudgement, that she is not her husbands equall; . . . out of place, out of peace," etc.[37] And these are the words of a man who believed that marriage "ingageth them to each other, in a reciprocal debt."[38] Whatever love a husband was expected to show his wife, the same list of wifely virtues appears whenever the subject of women or marriage is broached. According to Kelso, her virtues were "humility, sweetness, simplicity, peaceableness, kindness, piety, temperance, obedience, patience, charitableness," and chastity. Her faults were "licentiousness, instability, disloyalty, intractability . . . gluttony, pride, vanity, avarice, greed, seditiousness, quarrelsomeness, vindictiveness, and . . . talkativeness" (pp. 24 and 12). The wife marries for shelter and nourishment, but the husband, according to Robert Burton (following Jacobus de Voragine) has a dozen advantages ranging from financial gain to comfort and increased kin.[39] A husband could expect his wife to avoid contention. Where he failed to have his way, we recognize the source of many city comedies and satirical pamphlets.[40]

We may end this summary examination of women's roles by turning to the widow. There is a good deal to be learned from the very first line of the Overburian character of "A Vertuous Widdow": she "Is the Palme-tree, that thrives not after the supplanting of her husband."[41] The sketch goes on to explain that a woman marries for her "Childrens sake . . . and for their sakes she marries no more." In other words, a woman is canceled out entirely in favor of her departed husband and her offspring. The widow is compared to gold (again, woman as treasure) that "never receives but one mans impression." She is to occupy herself with works of charity and with setting an example "for our youngest Dames." In contrast to the virtuous widow, "an ordinarie widdow is like the Heralds Hearse-cloath; shee serves to many funerals, with a very little altering of colour."[42] She is proud, she is cunning, she is a cozener, and her chief interest is in her jointure. It was asserted that a widow was "habituated to the sex act," and it was common to ridicule her if she remarried.[43] Men were advised to marry a young girl because, as Swetnam wrote, "thou must vnlearne a widdow."

From the standpoint of the widow, however, hers was a unique position of independence. For the first time she was guaranteed an important role in choosing a husband. If her first husband left her financially solvent, she was in a position to control her own destiny. Many women might look forward to widowhood as the only period in their lives when they were not directly controlled by men. For some, this freedom meant the opportunity to direct a business enterprise; for others it meant a chance to assume complete responsibility for a household. But for the moralist, as Kelso writes, widowhood entailed nothing less than the "intensification" of the demands made upon a wife (p. 127). Unprotected and ungoverned, a widow was expected to be even more modest than a wife. "One feels considerable anxiety in the minds of writers as to what use widows will make of their freedom from the rule of husbands. That concern seems at odds with the general advice not to remarry, but it is obvious that all the rules on behavior, interests, virtues, and aims in life are carefully framed to curb as much as possible their independence and freedom" (pp. 131–32).[44] Freedom from caring for a husband, from cares of the flesh, from care of children, from the need for colorful garments, and from the need to associate with men, meant nothing more nor less than a new freedom to devote oneself entirely to God.

I began this chapter by citing a contemporary opinion that London was a paradise for women. This was the opinion of men who feared and disapproved of self-assertion on the part of women. It was both a man's authority and his sense of cosmic and social order that were threatened when "*Megge* lets her Husband boast of Rule and Riches, / But she rules all the Roast, and weares the Breeches."[45] Sir John Wynn of Gwydir wrote to his eldest son that "sootherne weomen, and those that bee bredd aboute London . . . are able to overthrowe anie man's estate what soe he bee, both in minde (which is most) and in his fortune. Therefore I resolved with my-selfe you shoulde marrie a country gentlewoman . . ."[46] The playwrights of city comedy took up the women's issue, staged much of the conventional wisdom, and lampooned those women who were either proud or ignorant of their own follies. But the playwrights went still further when they parodied the too-chaste maid or the too-obedient wife. And they introduced a more significant figure into the discussion when they created able, witty and self-sufficient women. The conventional stage woman was most often the brainchild of the stage gallant or stage merchant; the independent woman suggested a role model that was not utterly contingent upon men.

It is not clear why this "new woman" should have appeared in *the theater*. Her appearance on stage predates, by more than a decade, the outbreak of the *hic mulier* controversy of the 1620s. The "female transvestite movement" dated back to the 1570s; however, during the 1590s and early 1600s, little attention was paid to women in male attire.[47] Nor does the fact that contemporary women usurped male fashions in itself explain the stage's independent women. Perhaps she exists because, as Linda Woodbridge suggests, a theater populated by Patient Griseldas would be unbearably tedious.[48] Perhaps only the theater, predicated as it is on the elaboration of created roles, could "see" that women were docile or talkative or shrewish merely by convention. The power and subversive potential of Shakespeare's heroines would have been familiar to playwrights of city comedy. Or perhaps independent women in city comedy owe their presence to the considerable number of (often unchaperoned) women in the audience. Like contemporary apprentices, women seem to have found a limited area of freedom within the confines of the theater. A Moll Cutpurse might dramatize the fantasies of Jacobean women, just as a Witgood or a Truewit embodies fantasies common to city gallants. Whereas Queen Elizabeth held a place in the realm beyond even the wildest fantasies of common women, the clever wives of city comedy might suggest more available role models. Nonetheless, city comedy was not feminist theater. The women on stage were the creations of male playwrights only, and they were played by boys and young men. No doubt the women in the audience, like Cleopatra, were not always pleased with the "quick comedians," the "squeaking" actors who "boy[ed their] greatness / I' th' posture of a whore." Even within the freedom of the theater, women were liable to discover that their fantasies were, if not fully censored, then mediated by the competing fantasies of men. The play-wrights of city comedy represented women in their best aspect when they staged *men's* follies. It proved impossible to fashion an independent woman without first making room for her amidst the strictures, the fears, and the desires of men.

City Wives

In *Westward Ho*, Dekker and Webster present their song-school audience with city comedy's obligatory whore (Luce), and with an unusually large dose of the genre's familiar bawd (Birdlime). But the action of the play centers on its city wives—Mistresses Justiniano, Honeysuckle, Tenterhook, and Wafer—who are the victims of jealous, inept, and un-faithful husbands, and/or cavalier and foolish gallants. The women respond to their men by taking matters into their own hands; they exercise their native wit in attempts to free themselves from the "intricate laborinth of a hus-band"(3.1.35). As much as Justiniano (see Chapter 3), they work to shape their own drama and thus to gain some mea-sure of independence. Their wit, unlike the gallant's, is a means to self-assertion, or it is a device that will permit them to act with self-respect. When they proclaim that the gallants (with them in "Brainford" and in the song-school audience) "shall know that Cittizens wiues haue wit enough to out strip twenty such guls," they make it clear that, in a city filled with vain gallants and hypocritical hus-bands, they must look out for themselves. Whereas the gal-lant uses his wit to humiliate his rival, the city wife needs all her wit to guarantee *her own* integrity.

The Justiniano–Earl–Mistress Justiniano plot stages a classic woman's dilemma: Mistress Justiniano is caught be-tween a jealous and apparently insolvent husband, and a lecherous, old, would-be lover. Act 1 opens with Birdlime, in the Earl's employ, making a visit to Mistress Justiniano. As the Earl's surrogate, it is not surprising that the bawd should echo the standard complaints that pamphleteers directed toward women. We have already noted Ruth Kelso's argument that the theory of the lady is nearly identical to the theory of women; Birdlime merrily rehearses this line when she explains that "ther is equality inough betweene a Lady and a Citty dame":

They [city wives] haue as pure Linen, as choyce painting, loue greene Geese in spring. . . . Your Cittizens wife learns nothing but fopperies of your Ladie, but your Lady or Iustice-a-peace Madam, carried high wit from the Citty, namely to receiue all and pay all: to awe their Husbands, to check their Husbands, to controule thier husbands; nay they haue a tricke ont to be sick for a new goune, or a Carcanet, or a Diamond, or so . . . (1.1.27–34)

Birdlime's account repeats the contradictions inherent in popular versions of women. She describes a woman who is simultaneously frivolous (interested in "fopperies," in dainty foods and jewelry) and overly assertive or mannish (out to control her husband). A wife loses whether she is retiring or self-confident. In Mistress Justiniano's case, the no-win situation is even more frustrating. When she admits to her husband that the Earl has solicited her love, and that she has returned him "most chaste denials," Justiniano accuses her of a "prouoking resistance" (1.1.168). When she is most a wife, Mistress Justiniano is still a whore.

Ironically, it is Justiniano himself who, by disguising himself and seeming to be bankrupt, assumes a conventionally feminine role (deceitful and dependent). And if there is some sad truth to his comparison of his wife with a tradesman, a traditionally masculine role, it is only because he himself has left her without means of support. She *must* consider turning tradesman (her ware is of course her person). Hence she quite rightfully reminds him, "let not the world condemne me, if I seeke for mine owne maintenance" (1.1.204–5).

Westward Ho is not a feminist tract. Nor is Mistress Justiniano the first woman on stage to be unjustly accused by her husband and compromised by a wealthy old man.

However, it is unreasonable not to consider Mistress Justiniano's dilemma in the context of contemporary women's
issues. The old earl covets her even as he admits that if she
returns his love she will be damned: "if [I] possesse, I vndo
her; / Turne her into a diuel, whom I adore" (4.2.43–44). As
Thomas Gainsford wrote, men curse the whore before
whom they abase themselves (in *Westward Ho*, cf. 2.2.70
ff.). The more fundamental women's issue, the question of
survival without a husband, is also raised in this play—in
no uncertain terms:

> Poverty, thou bane of Chastity,
> Poison of beauty, Broker of Mayden-heades,
> I see when Force, nor Wit can scale the hold,
> Wealth must. Sheele nere be won, that defies golde.
> But liues there such a creature: Oh tis rare,
> To finde a woman chast, thats poore and faire.
> (2.2.142–47)

It is not too much to say that Mistress Justiniano has discovered the economic basis of women's dependence and social inferiority. She has also come to recognize the role alternatives available to her: "tho my husbands poore, / Ile
rather beg for him, then be your Whore" (2.2.119–20).

Where survival is at stake, wit is little help. Mistress
Justiniano spurns the Earl and, we learn later, decides to
take her life. She is saved because her husband comes to his
senses, puts away his jealousy, and acknowledges his wife's
integrity. Only then is the cynical edge taken off Justiniano's
earlier address to the audience ("Haue among you Citty
dames? You that are indeed the fittest, and most proper persons for a Comedy"—1.1.225–26). His words take on new
meanings, as women *are* found to be fit and proper, and
comedy—the process of defining a healthy society—becomes their mode. So too, new meanings for Justiniano's
words are suggested by the comedy enacted by the remaining city wives in *Westward Ho*. Mistresses Honeysuckle,
Tenterhook, and Wafer are, like Mistress Justiniano, sus-

pected by their husbands; however, they are not nearly as badly off as the Italian merchant's wife. In their less melodramatic plot, they are free to stage "the wit of a woman when she is put to the pinch" (3.1.44–45).

Dekker and Webster's conception of the three city wives is not entirely consistent. The women are clever and resourceful, but they are also vulnerable and open to their own share of ridicule. In either case, assertive or dependent, these women may serve to validate men. Monopoly takes advantage of Mistress Tenterhook by dallying with her emotions. Justiniano deceives the wives for his own purposes; and Dekker and Webster are not above poking fun at the wives' malapropisms (5.1.94–100). More seriously, the playwrights have Mistress Wafer imitating men's nasty appraisals of women when she compares "widdows" with "theeues" (1.2.134). Nevertheless, there is an overriding sense of sport and mutual solidarity that pervades the women's actions. In Act 2, Mistress Honeysuckle advises Mistress Tenterhook to spurn Monopoly ("vse him as thou dost thy pantable, scorne to let him kisse thy heele"—2.3.19–20). Later, Mistress Honeysuckle speaks as one woman to another when she exhorts her friend, calling her "wench" (the word "sister" is used in a similar context in *The Woman's Prize*). In the next scene (3.1), Mistress Tenterhook makes her move, convincing her husband to arrest Monopoly for failure to discharge his bond.

When the action finally does move westward, to "Brainford," the three city wives join together for their chief comedy. It had been their intention to enjoy themselves beyond the "laborinth of a husband" (a fine epithet for the City), and they mean to continue their sport with their gallants. An admirable sanity underlies the women's action. Their wisdom—"tho we are merry, lets not be mad" (5.1.159–60)—prevents them from cuckolding their husbands and provides a fitting motto for the most appealing figures in the play. They pretend illness, lock themselves in their chamber, and refuse to admit the confused gallants. At this point, the latter manifest a standard feminine trait—

envy—as each makes sure that no one of them gets at the women. The wives' clever plot makes for a good city comedy at the same time that it furnishes the women with a good story: "tho we lye all night out of the Citty, they shall not find country wenches of vs: . . . the Iest shal be a stock to maintain vs and our pewfellowes in laughing . . . this twelue month" (5.1.169–73). In a society where women are naturally on the defensive, the wives in the play and in its audience will be able to tell one more merry tale of women's resourcefulness. But like Thomasine Quomodo, these women must return to their lawful husbands and the labyrinths that they represent. The space of the play, and the space of the theater, allow them some relief. In the end, the women must "Away then to *London*" after a few "howres laid out in harmelesse meryment" (5.4.305 and 308).

From my account of the women in *Westward Ho*, it should be clear that it will not do to describe the offerings at the private theater as a "drama preoccupied with . . . the exhibition of the foolish and the foul." Neither does it make sense to say that "The public plays emphasize actions, the private ones attitudes; the public plays valiant or villainous deeds, the private ones clever and stupid schemes."[49] Actions cannot be separated from the attitudes that motivate them. And foolishness (or a clever scheme) arises out of precisely the community interests that Harbage argues are not the preoccupation of the private theaters. The plots (Justiniano's as well as the wives' in *Westward Ho*) are a response to palpable social conflicts. Furthermore, the "satirists" do not simply "speak against rather than for the middle class."[50] The women in *Westward Ho* are solidly middle class, and they do not lose our affection because of this. They are also evidence of political thinking on the part of Dekker and Webster; but we may argue this only when we enlarge the dominion of politics in an urban setting.[51] Witty women, like greedy merchants, do not arrive on the stage merely because such figures have a theatrical history. They had meanings for contemporary audiences because they were a response to contemporary fears, ambitions, prejudices, and debates. The successfully drawn "resourceful woman" on the stage is both a response to the often re-marked upon assertiveness of women in London and a pos-sibility held out to the audience. Her eventual containment is a measure of the power of the prevailing masculine ide-ology. She represents an attempt to resolve contradictions (the modest vs. the forthright, the chaste vs. the alluring woman), in the imaginary present of the theater, that take centuries to settle beyond its walls.

The companion piece to *Westward Ho*, Dekker and Webster's *Northward Ho*, presents the marital careers of two women. The citizen wife in *Northward Ho* dramatizes the utter dependence of women on their reputation (for chas-tity); the gallant's wife offers us a glimpse of a woman who, when caught in the same predicament as Mistress Justini-ano, decides to commit adultery. In the citizen plot, the merchant Mayberry is persuaded (not unlike Posthumus in *Cymbeline*) that the gallants Greenshield and Featherstone have enjoyed his wife's favors. By the end of the first act, the merchant has confronted his wife, listened to and credited her denial, and he has begun to plot his revenge. Signifi-cantly, it is the merchant, not the wife, who works out (and insists that his wife join him in) an elaborate revenge plot. Neither the false accuser—Greenshield—nor the enraged husband is concerned primarily with the truly aggrieved party, Mabel Mayberry. Greenshield resents her aloofness, what he calls her "puritanical coynesse" (1.1.9). And his friend Featherstone tells us everything else that we need to know:

tell . . . how thou [Greenshield] laiest at her two yeare together to make her dishonest: how duely thou wouldst watch the cittizens wiues vacation, which is twice a day; . . . and where she refused thy importunity, and vowed to tell her husband: thou wouldest fall downe vpon thy knees, and intreat her for the loue of Heauen, if not to ease thy violent affections, at least to conceale it, to which her pitty and simple virtue consented, how thou tookest her wed-ding ring from her, met these two Gentlemen at *Ware:* fained a quarrell, and the rest is apparant. (5.1.279–90)

It is apparent that Greenshield assuages his hurt ego by attempting to humiliate the merchant. Mayberry exacts his revenge because his property (his wife) has been attacked, and because it has been by a gentleman. Male sexual prowess overwhelms the issue of Mistress Mayberry's integrity. The gallant has failed to seduce her, and her husband cannot bear the thought of being a cuckold (or the implication that he is unable to satisfy his wife).

It is the intensity of Mistress Mayberry's denial that convinces the merchant of his wife's innocence. However, there is no apology for his demand that she play the part of a whore for the next four acts. Mistress Mayberry would have done with the whole affair: "O God that I might haue my wil of him and it were not for my husband ide scratch out his eyes presently" (2.2.119–20). But she does not have her will, and her husband needs time to exact revenge *for himself*. Kate Greenshield, on the other hand, has a will of her own, and she is not afraid to express it. Her husband, Luke, "ran away from [her] like a base slaue as he was, out of *Yorke-shire*, and pretended he would goe the Iland voiage" (2.2.123–25). In response, Kate becomes intimate (l. 122) with Luke's friend Featherstone. Faced with a dilemma identical to Mistress Justiniano's, Kate decides to forget her husband. Indeed, her instincts appear to be sound: unlike the Italian wife, who is tempted by a white-haired old moneybags, Kate finds a man who responds to her and who, at a moment of crisis (5.1.335 ff.), offers to salvage her reputation and to maintain her through hard times ahead.

Dekker and Webster sympathize with Kate's plight, but they are uneasy about bestowing her on Featherstone. Like other contemporary moralists, they were not prepared to condone divorce because of marital contention. Nor were they quite ready to deal with what they had created—a married woman determining her own future. Their solution is twofold. They prolong the plotting and trickery in the fifth act until Featherstone is married to the whore Doll. Once Featherstone is spoken for, Kate has no choice but to return to her husband (although she implies that she asks Luke's forgiveness only because she could never love a man who was tricked into marrying a whore—5.1.499–500). Dekker and Webster have yet another way of dealing with Kate, and it is the second aspect of their treatment of the gallant's wife that is most significant. As if to thwart our sympathy for an abused wife who places her own interests before her husband's, the playwrights denigrate her motivations. Kate tells us that Luke has deserted her, but she attributes her affair with Featherstone to the "cracks and flaues" that women are "borne to" (2.2.139–40). In other words, Dekker and Webster will not present an unequivocal portrait of a self-assured woman. Kate "held out foure yeare" with a swaggerer, yet she is still "false" (and so, a "woman") when she leaves him. The independent woman of the comedy must be returned to her husband; but we must judge for ourselves whether it is her understandable sense of being abandoned by a thorough knave, or her woman's "cracks," which explain her self-assertion.

The women's issues in the *Ho* plays at the song school are also explored in *The Roaring Girl*, at the Fortune. Once again, we have to do with a trio of citizen wives and a woman who is able to look out for herself. Mistresses Openwork, Gallipot, and Tiltyard are less resourceful than the wives in *Westward Ho*, and there is less mutual support among Middleton and Dekker's women. Self-assertiveness is intermixed with lechery as once again the women, understandably dissatisfied with their husbands, are deemed incontinent when they act on their dissatisfaction. Thus the sexual economy of the City is not especially happy: because citizen husbands are "cotqueans," citizen wives turn to "whisking gallants" who are but "lame gelding[s]" or "mere shallow things." The wives admit that it is best to return to their citizens (4.2); but their final rejection of the gallants is motivated by bourgeois solidarity, not the hope of contented sexual relations with their husbands.[52] It is significant that despite the conventional, unflattering portraits of citizen husbands and idle gallants, the women still seem forward and independent. They speak in a language of double en-

tendres that rivals the bawdy of the gallants. Mistress Gallipot, who has the least appealing husband, comes off the
worst in her dealing with (the least appealing) gallant Laxton. And if the gallants are finally tricked, it is because
Masters Gallipot and Openwork are enlisted into the fray.
Middleton and Dekker protect us from the effects of fully
independent, sympathetic city wives by giving us as much
of them to laugh at as to laugh with.

The citizen wives in *The Roaring Girl* offer us a convenient yardstick to measure the presentation of such women
in the public theater against those in the private theaters.
However, it is obvious that the consequential woman in the
play is Moll, the roaring girl.[53] Middleton and Dekker create
a "considerably romanticized version" of the woman who
dressed as a man, fought, smoked, and generally scandalized
her contemporaries by refusing marriage, motherhood, and
conventional femininity.[54] Moll in *The Roaring Girl* is a
defender of virtue and a debunker of prejudice against
women. She is perfectly confident in herself ("I please my
selfe, and care not else who loue mee"—5.1.319), and she is
uncompromisingly independent ("I scorne to prostitute my
selfe to a man, / I that can prostitute a man to me"—
3.1.107–8). When she reproaches the lecherous gallant Laxton, she strikes out for all contemporary women at all
such men:

> In thee I defye all men, their worst hates,
> And their best flatteries, all their golden witchcrafts,
> With which they intangle the poore spirits of fooles,
> Distressed needlewomen and trade-fallne wiues.
>
> (3.1.88–91)

When Moll converts old Alexander Wengrave to her side,
she proves that "common voice," or the very prejudices the
city playwrights were staging, is "the whore / That deceiues
mans opinion; mockes his trust, / Cozens his loue, and
makes his heart vniust" (5.2.248–50). She is tough, spirited,
good-humored, and morally upright. She champions the

weak (Mary Fitz-allard), and she defeats evil (Laxton, Trap-door).

All this makes Moll sound like Superwoman, and not a portrayal of a flesh-and-blood woman; and this impression must not be passed over lightly. There is another Moll in *The Roaring Girl*—Moll (or Mary) Fitz-allard is the victim-ized romantic heroine—and as the editor of the Mermaid edition of the play points out, this "doubling is a deliberate, if elementary, device to establish the identity of purpose in the two."[55] Mary would like to be free of male domination (in the form of Sir Alexander's refusal to permit his son to marry her), and while she is off stage through most of the play, her namesake acts as her surrogate. But Moll is more than just a stand-in. She is a fantasy, an embodiment of what an oppressed woman would imagine herself to be in a time or land in which she has real power. As in the fantasies of actual oppressed peoples, the champion takes on the traits of the oppressor. Moll wears breeches and can handle a cud-gel. She smokes and consorts with (and in the language of) shady underworld types. Moll is even that ultimate and per-verse fantasy of the avenging woman, a castrator (3.1.65–66).

When we finally come upon a "forceful embodiment of female virtue," we find that she must act like a man.[56] Real women are like Mary Fitz-allard; independent women are freaks, or outcasts, or monsters (1.2.138; "Some will not sticke to say shees a man and some both man and woman"—2.1.186–87). Moll knows that she cannot marry because no man would tolerate her independence: "I haue the head now of my selfe, and am man enough for a woman, marriage is but a chopping and changing, where a maiden looses one head, and has a worse ith place" (2.2.40–43). But she is wrong when she asserts that a woman "that has wit, and spirit, / May scorne to liue beholding to her body for meate" (3.3.133–34). Wit and spirit are not enough, since even in the best of situations, the witty wife must return obediently to her husband (and his whims). Total indepen-dence comes, as Moll illustrates, at the expense of a real self. The poles are Mary and Moll, recognizable, dependent woman and fantastic superwoman, victim and monster. A woman may call attention to herself only in the extreme: as infinitely patient, as sexually incontinent, or as Amazonian.[57] If she is outrageous, she can help herself; if she is mindful of her place, she must wait for her lover (Sebastian Wengrave) or her fantasy surrogate to protect her. This is the no-win dilemma staged at the Fortune. It is at once an elaboration of Swetnam's attack on women and the unspoken implication of Sowernam's defense. Middleton and Dekker can speak out (in the person of Moll) against the injustices done to women, and their attitude seems to be, as Caroline Cherry has written, "basically affirmative and liberal."[58] However, they have solved very little for contemporary women, and what looks liberal is in fact rather conservative. A clear affirmation of the rights and dignity of women would have meant an unequivocal portrayal of the citizen wives. As it stands, the audience may remain something of a Caesar to Middleton and Dekker's Cleopatra/Moll. The truly spirited woman was best encountered as a male actor, playing a roaring girl in male attire, safely set off within the imaginary space of the theater.

Moll Cutpurse is an extravagant representation of an independent woman: her example is of value only to the extent that women can bring Moll's energy and self-confidence back into the mainstream of society. If Moll remains a freak, then she is good only for entertainment. The balance between entertainment and a serious consideration of a woman's role in marriage *is* maintained in one of two city comedies in our period that focuses on an enterprising married woman. In *The Woman's Prize; or, The Tamer Tamed*, John Fletcher composed a sequel to *The Taming of the Shrew* in which Maria, Petruchio's new wife, successfully chastens her husband.[59] Fletcher gives substance to a humorous, mock-heroic play by reminding his audience of the legitimacy of Maria's claims. No longer content with being called a "beast," or with the metonymous equation of women with "tongue" (1.3.54; 5.2.35 ff.), Maria fights to make it clear that only a "childish woman" allows herself to be used by her man (1.2.136–40). She sets out to demonstrate the equality between husband and wife ("Are we not one peece with you, and as worthy / Our own intentions, as you yours"—3.3.99–100); but she knows that her worth will be recognized only when she has, for at least a moment, established her superiority.

In *The Roaring Girl*, it was Moll whom men referred to as a "monster"; in *The Woman's Prize*, Maria tells her sister that Petruchio must "Be made a man, for yet he is a monster" (1.2.104). From a woman's point of view, a monster is not some fabulous creature that lives on the fringes of society. The real monster is a typical husband, a man who takes for granted his wife's obedience and whose primary interest in her consists in the relief of his loins. Maria would have Petruchio "know, and fear a wife," because, as "a brave wifebreaker," he represents what all men take to be their calling. She acknowledges that her battle with her husband is a public, and political, act that "[will] be chronicl'd" (1.2.176). Maria tells her sister to

> Thinke what women shall
> An hundred yeare hence speak thee, when examples
> Are look'd for, and so great ones, whose relations
> Spoke as we do 'em wench, shall make new customs.
> (2.2.83–86)

Petruchio, on the other hand, sees their battle in more personal terms; he is worried about the "safety of [his] honour" (2.6.10). Of course, in one sense, Maria's concern for the chronicle that will memorialize her deeds is nothing more than bluster and Fletcher's "comic inflation."[60] However, the play itself does in fact constitute such a "chronicle." An army of city wives succors Maria and her confederates at the bedroom ramparts, just as word of the story enacted in Fletcher's play may have brought a few extra citizen wives ("the serious women of the City"—2.2.85) to the theater.

What is perhaps most important is that these women would have witnessed what is at heart a healthy, loving marriage. A comic plot thrives on the conquest of ill will or the righting of unequal relations, and in this respect *The Woman's Prize* is no exception. Petruchio is rough and surly; Maria responds by exceeding all decorum; and in the fifth act the two are happily reconciled. However, at regular intervals, Fletcher lets us know that Petruchio and Maria do in fact love and respect one another. Maria has a point that she must make, but she knows when to stop. Petruchio grumbles and plays the wounded "puppy," but he loves Maria for her energy and ingenuity. Thus Maria, as early as Act 1, scene 3, tells Petruchio that

> were I yet unmarried, free to choose
> Through all the Tribes of man, i'ld take *Petruchio*
> In's shirt, with one ten Groats to pay the Priest,
> Before the best man living, or the ablest
> That ev'r leaped out of Lancashire, and they are
> right ones.
>
> (1.3.152–56)

When Petruchio yields to her terms, Maria does not stand by while his honor is impeached. She breaks off the first round of the battle quickly and generously (2.6.160–61). And even though Petruchio has begun to suspect that she is playing "the devill" with him, he confesses: "I cannot choose but love it" (4.2.45). Confused and beaten down by Maria's stratagems, he tells her, "I love thee / Above thy vanity, thou faithlesse creature" (3.3.128–29). Still later, Petruchio admits, "I married her for: her wit" (4.2.26).

There is a current of love and good humor that flows beneath the surface squalls of this marriage. Petruchio admires Maria's wit but forgets that "dull obedience" and wit cannot coexist in the same woman. For her part, Maria wants and must go to great lengths to gain her husband's respect. Moreover, she recognizes the social implications of a public avowal of esteem from Petruchio, "the woman tamer." "Judge me as I am," she demands, "not as you covet" (5.4.12). This might be the injunction issued by all women who have "leap'd into this gulph of marriage" (1.2.68). It reflects not so much a desire to be free of all roles as a profound longing to be free to shape one's own roles. Maria speaks this line out in the open, and it is directed at the three conventional male figures in the play—her husband, her crabbed father, and the still more decrepit Moroso. She means to throw off the tyranny of men (this has been her project throughout the play), to gain respect for herself, and only then to make a life for herself as a wife now happy to please her husband (5.4.57). To this end, she leads an army of "sister[s]," and she awakens her own sister, Livia, to the woman's cause. There is no reason to believe that the significance of her comic battle escaped its Jacobean audience, at least not any more than it escaped Petruchio. Fletcher does not retreat to comedy or bawdy in order to undermine his heroine. Even as she is humorous, Maria delivers a necessary and poignant message.

City comedy's other enterprising married woman appears in Middleton's *No Wit, No Help like a Woman's,* a play that was probably first performed in the same year as *The Woman's Prize.*[61] Middleton's intrigue depends on three women to resolve its seemingly endless complications. Lady Twilight, though a necessary part of the story, does not take up much of the audience's attention. However, the play's consequential wife, Kate Low-water, and its widow, Lady Goldenfleece (discussed below), reveal Middleton working out unexpected problems and possibilities for women. This is a play that is extremely frank about the exchange value of women. Masters Weatherwise, Pepperton, and Overdon want the Widow Goldenfleece for her money. Sir Oliver Twilight wants to marry off his daughter as cheaply as possible. It turns out that the play's two sought-after maids were exchanged in their cradles. And throughout the play, the gallant Savorwit keeps up a nasty patter about women as salable or lascivious creatures: "Virginity / Is no such cheap ware as you make account on" (1.1.207–8); "a chopping girl with a plump buttock, / Will hoist a farthingale at five years' old, / And call a man between eleven and twelve / To take

part of a piece of mutton with her" (1.1.244–47); "She'll lie
down shortly, and call somebody up" (4.1.71); "The mother
of her was a good twigger [prolific ewe] the whilst" (4.1.179).
Gallants in *No Wit, No Help like a Woman's* desire a woman
only when she is "made as a man would wish to have her"
(2.2.168).

In the face of considerable hostility, Mistress Low-water
foils Sir Gilbert Lambstone's plans, tricks Lady Goldenfleece, recovers her family's wealth, and arranges for her
brother's marriage. She is not able to accomplish all of this
and also play out her role as a wife, however. Indeed, Middleton tacitly acknowledges the powerlessness of women
when he not only disguises Kate Low-water as a man
throughout most of the play, but gives to her the gallant's
foremost attribute: his wit. The wit of this play's title, the
wit that Savorwit lays claim to, turns out to be in Mistress
Low-water's sole possession ("Since wit has pleasur'd me,
I'll pleasure wit"—2.3.245). Middleton here has recourse to
the same solution to the problem of powerless women as
did he and Dekker in *The Roaring Girl*. A woman in London
is empowered when she dresses like, and acts like, a man.
But she does not succeed by acting like just any man. Mistress Low-water's husband is woefully passive and ends up
playing his wife's serving man. Mistress Low-water's
brother, Beveril, is an easily duped scholar. And Philip, the
play's wealthy heir, is so beaten down by his troubles that
he approaches suicide no less than three times. The sort of
man who provides Mistress Low-water with a viable role
model, and so the ability to have her way in the City, is the
clever, witty town gallant. There is even an implicit parallel
between the thoroughly self-centered and degenerate Sir
Gilbert, and Kate. Both plan to "marry" Lady Goldenfleece
that they may put her money to use: Sir Gilbert would purchase a mistress, and Kate would set up her brother (as well
as recover the money Sir Avarice Goldenfleece extorted from
Master Low-water).

At the end of *No Wit, No Help like a Woman's*, Kate
Low-water must return to her ineffectual husband. Had she

been content with her role as his wife, she would have had to accommodate herself to penury, and she would have been forced to suppress her native wit. But the protest against gender-determined roles is limited. Freedom to maneuver means freedom only to swagger like a gallant. Other wives in city comedy have similar lessons to learn once their protests have run their course, and we may consider the story of Thomasine Quomodo, in *Michaelmas Term*, as a representative case. Her scheming husband, Ephestian Quomodo, the foolish and profligate Easy, and the thoroughly disreputable upstart Andrew Lethe are exaggerated types rather than men. Ultimately, Thomasine decides for youth and potency (Easy) against age and wealth (Quomodo); but having observed the chief action of the play—the repeated gulling of Easy—from a distance, Thomasine must know that her new lover is short on good sense. Consequently, her second marriage is important to her not as a chance to marry the man she loves, but simply as a chance to choose for herself. Only when Thomasine believes that she is a widow does she feel free: "I do account myself the happiest widow . . . in that I have the leisure now both to do that gentleman [Easy] good and do myself a pleasure" (4.3.39–41). She marries the man whom she has "pitied," and she marries him for relief. Quomodo "ne'er us'd [her] so well as a woman might have been us'd (4.3.54–55), and Easy is a nice, "proper springall and a sweet gentleman" (3.4.244).

Readers have questioned the speed with which Easy metamorphoses from a dupe into a shrewd young man.[62] A close reading will demonstrate that it is Thomasine, not Easy, who takes advantage of the rapidly changing circumstances. As early as the second act, Thomasine has begun to show a willingness to act contrary to her husband and in support of Easy. She asks:

> Why stand I here (as late our graceless dames
> That found no eyes) to see that gentleman [Easy]
> Alive, in state and credit, executed,
> Help to rip up himself, does all he can?

Wives, Whores, Widows, and Maids

Why am I wife to him [Quomodo] that is no man?
I suffer in that gentleman's confusion.

(2.3.202–7)

The last line of this speech suggests that, as Quomodo's
wife, Thomasine suffers in her own self-respect when the
draper gulls the gallant. It also expresses her pity for Easy.
Once she believes herself to be rid of Quomodo, Thomasine
takes Easy by the hand and helps him find his way toward
their marriage. She had already sent Easy £100 to make up
for some of the losses he has foolishly incurred; now she
reveals that she has carried the plot one step further: Thomasine has found a priest to marry them (4.4.75). Only Thomasine's ingenuity suffices to "Restore [Easy] to more wealth,
[herself] to more bliss" (4.4.78).

I do not mean to suggest that Easy is as bad as Quomodo. Only a ninny would cling to the citizen when the
gentleman is available. I want to argue, instead, that Thomasine experiences a measure of happiness only because she
takes matters into her own hands. Her husband admits that
his jealousy over Thomasine is as great as his envy of Easy's
estate (4.1.110–11). Her daughter seems content to marry a
man (Lethe) who is arrogant (better still, asinine) enough to
believe that Thomasine objects to the marriage because she
would keep him "as a private friend to her own pleasures"
(1.1.210–11). And Easy has gotten in so far over his head
that he must have another's help to bail him out. Thomasine's reward for acting in her own best interest, for suffering
Quomodo, and for succoring Easy turns out to be but a moment of happiness. No sooner is she enjoying life with her
new husband ("What difference there is in husbands"—
5.1.50) than that game is up and Quomodo is demanding the
return of his wife. The judge has no choice but to return
Thomasine to the draper. When she realizes what is going
on, she speaks, perhaps moans, her penultimate line in the
play: "Oh, heaven!" (5.3.56). The play concludes with little
for anyone to rejoice about. Another apparent profligate—
Rearage—gets Susan Quomodo, Easy is back where he

165

started, and so is Thomasine. And we are left to wonder whether Middleton's account of a wife who acts on her own behalf better answers to extratheatrical reality than does Fletcher's.

Of course, some of city comedy's wives are but parodies of independent women, and others are simply crude or vicious. The carefully maintained irony of Chapman, Jonson, and Marston in *Eastward Ho* allows them to depict Mistress Touchstone as a sometimes sensible, but more often than not gullible and downright foolish, city wife. While Touchstone champions the marriage of his daughter Mildred to proper Golding, Mistress Touchstone is swept up in her desire to see one of her daughters (Gertrude) married to a knight. The playwrights locate Mistress Touchstone's intelligence somewhere between that of her proverb-wielding, hyperbourgeois husband and that of her haughty, witless daughter. Touchstone sits back and enjoys the fact that he has chosen to back the right marriage: "My wife has her humour, and I will ha' mine" (1.2.170–71). Gertrude is simply his "wife's dilling, whom she longs to call madam" (1.1.91–92). Mistress Touchstone, however, is not quite as naive as her daughter. She has an idea of what kind of knight Sir Petronel is ("I know where he had money to pay the gentlemen and heralds their fees"—1.2.111–13), and she is not incapable of a little bawdy when Gertrude asks about the possibility of a premarital pregnancy (3.2.37–40). It is just that the city wife cannot give up the hope that her girl will be a lady.

Mistress Touchstone is shown to be something of a booby in comparison with her husband. However, Touchstone is himself the subject of some of the rich parody that distinguishes this play. And his wife, it turns out, is intelligent enough to learn a lesson. When her hopes, along with Gertrude's, are dashed, Mistress Touchstone advises her still-headstrong daughter to "kneel down" and ask her father's forgiveness. When Gertrude, now in the fifth act, continues to act the part of a fool, her mother loses patience and rattles off a string of maxims that rival those of Touchstone. She tells Gertrude that "'Thou shouldst have looked before thou hadst leapd.' Thou wert afire to be a lady, and now your ladyship and you may both 'blow at the coal,' for aught I know. 'Self do, self have.' 'The hasty person never wants woe,' they say" (5.1.131–36). Her newly acquired sententiousness is better than her earlier delusions—but only somewhat better. Mistress Touchstone is indulged by her husband and condescended to by her creators. Chapman, Jonson, and Marston are unfair to London's women, but they make it difficult to object to their methods. Behavior on the part of their characters that a woman would consider exasperating, the playwrights expect men to find tolerant, even generous. Witness Touchstone's refusal to reject his wife outright, as he does his daughter: "she [his wife] has been my cross these thirty years, and now I 'll keep her to fright away sprites, i'faith" (4.2.32–34).

Chapman, Jonson, and Marston, as well as Dekker and Webster, offer a rather benign staging of city wives: self-assertion is admissible, and it is the source of comic plotting; but it is either contained or undermined at strategic moments, and always at play's end. Middleton, on the other hand, creates the genre's crude, stupid, even vicious wives. Like his contemporaries, Middleton stages contemporary prejudice; yet, while they tentatively subvert prejudice with women too sensible to be equated with contemporary stereotypes, Middleton tests prejudice with women who, in their extreme ugliness, gather into themselves all of the worst of traditional, antifeminist diatribes. They are exaggerated stagings of the women figured by prejudice and, as such, they reveal the chaos and harm that would ensue were men's biases accurate reflections of women's ways. Less pleasant than Mistress Touchstone, Mistresses Allwit, Yellowhammer, and Purge are parodies of familiar types and embodiments of contemporary social attitudes. In a morality play, Mistress Purge might have been said to figure lasciviousness (or false zeal or even stupidity); but in a city comedy, her vice is rooted in an obviously social context. She is saddled with a wittol for a husband, and a couple of gallants are stumbling over themselves to seduce her. What, we need to ask, does lasciviousness mean in this context? Does Middleton himself appreciate the degree to which Mistress Purge is a pastiche of male fantasies and complaints? And should we not bear in mind that these women (Allwit, etc.) magnify what were held, by men, to be women's faults? The unattractive city wives stage men's attitudes, and they spell out the unattractive consequences of these attitudes.

Mistress Allwit speaks only a handful of lines in *A Chaste Maid in Cheapside.* Until the fifth act, she is spoken for by the situation we know her to be in. While Allwit sings, laughs, and plays, Mistress Allwit satisfies her "longings" with (1.2.118), and bears the children of, Sir Walter Whorehound. But Mistress Allwit's striking situation keeps her ever on the edge of our consciousness: we want to know what kind of woman would live this way. She cannot be much more than a sexual object, or proof of potency, for the knight; and she is but a social cover for her husband (the neighbors believe that Allwit is the father of his wife's children). If she is anything like the "gossips" who gather for the christening of her daughter (3.2), then we may account her an alcoholic, a hypocrite, and a lecher. Middleton waits for the final act to reveal the Mistress Allwit he has been imagining. Once it is clear that Sir Walter is a liability, Mistress Allwit may pass in one breath from loving him to defying him (5.1.146–47). With audacity equal to her husband's she boasts that "[She] knew he [Sir Walter] was past the best when [she] gave him over" (5.4.66). And she suggests to her husband that they ought now to set up "shop" in the Strand. In a few deft strokes, Middleton alters our sense of Mistress Allwit: instead of mere moral bankruptcy, we discover in her a cold ruthlessness that is usually reserved for obvious villains.

Despite her unpleasantness, we laugh at Mistress Allwit for her sheer audacity. Like the merchant-citizen, she is both foolish and cunning. As such, and as a sexual play-thing, she draws to herself all of the contradictory accusations directed at the city wife. Middleton's portrait of the other city wife in *A Chaste Maid* adds one trait that he was unable to find a way to award Mistress Allwit. Maudline Yellowhammer is vicious and humorous, and she is bawdy. She figures the salty, lowbrow city wife. The play opens with Maudline berating her daughter Moll for showing no signs of sexual desire. Maudline tells her, "When I was a young, I was lightsome / And quick two years before I was married" (1.1.10–11). When she was Moll's age, Maudline boasts, her "dancer . . . miss'd [her] not a night; / I was kept at it" (ll. 16–17). She then encourages her daughter to be happy with the prospect of marrying Sir Walter. At least Maudline is consistent in her interest in her children's sexual development. At the christening, she picks up with son Tim where she left off with Moll: "call him [Tim] up / Among the women, 'twill embolden him well, / For he wants nothing but audacity" (3.2.101–3).

Like Mrs. Allwit, Maudline Yellowhammer becomes progressively more unattractive. In the fourth act we watch Maudline dragging Moll away from the Thames (and away from an attempted elopement) "by the hair." One of the watermen describes her as a "cruel mother!" Maudline plays out the role of the sexually aggressive city wife. She is mercenary, she is coarse, and she is brutal. It remains to single out a Middletonian city wife who is an idiot; and for this we turn to Mistress Purge, in *The Family of Love*. Perhaps it is inaccurate to call Rebecca Purge simply an idiot: she too represents the contradictory nature of the charges made against women. At the same time that she shows herself a fool, she stands accused of being a hypocrite. In other words, she is witless even though she has the wit to speak right-eously while acting lasciviously. The confusion resides in Mistress Purge's language. Almost everything that she has to say about the Family and its nocturnal gatherings is

couched in double entendres. She claims that in their meet-
ings, they "make singular use of feeling" (3.3.47); but we
cannot determine whether Rebecca knows (as Middleton
surely knows) that "feeling" is not "singular," that it can be
both religious and carnal. If it is the former, her language
proves her a fool; if the latter, she is a hypocrite. Middleton,
it seems, wants her to be both.[63]

It is important to recognize that what, in the character
of Rebecca Purge, is meant to be a portrait of Puritan "preciseness" becomes an overdetermined representation of a
city wife. She tolerates her marriage to a wittol; she encourages Doctor Glister's advances; and she accepts the affection
of the play's two lecherous gallants. Mistress Purge is
against the theater (1.3.110 ff.); she is worried about what
she looks like (3.3.1 ff.); and she will lie if she thinks she
can get away with it (5.3.288 ff.). This overdetermination
extends, as I have noted, to her language. When she informs
her husband that her "love must be free still to God's creatures" (5.3.425–26), she presages social as well as linguistic
chaos. Is she a hypocrite, foreshadowing a sectarian's dream
of free love; or is she a fool, foreshadowing the same thing?
And why is Middleton so set on laying bare the sexuality,
the deviant sexuality, of Mistress Purge? Like his character,
Middleton provokes doubts. Are his contradictory images of
women his own (and intentional), or are they just one more
instance of what men were writing in countless pamphlets?
Is Middleton as aware of the discrepancy between the stereotypical and the actual when he fashions the city wife as
when he fashions merchants and gentry? Has the theater
become a forum for titillation, or is it being used to stage,
and so to dispel, ridiculous notions about women? There are
no simple answers to these questions, and they do not even
turn up as questions if we fail to situate city comedy in a
social, or extratheatrical, context. Rebecca Purge stands for
the easy target that the spectator-gallant believed he would
find in the City. But what are we to make of the gallant who
would want her, who enjoys taking advantage of city wives,
if this is what they are like?

Plain Punks

Competing with the city wife, we find the city whore, or prostitute, or mistress. Andrew Lethe says, "I may grace her with the name of a courtesan, a backslider, a prostitution, or such a toy; but when all comes to all, 'tis but a plain pung" (*Michaelmas Term*, 3.1.74–77). Of course, in city comedy, we discover that "all" does not come easily "to all." The stage prostitute has often an integrity all her own, peculiar to those who live beyond the pale. Her loyalty to her client (perhaps, if she is a mistress, to her lover) may rival a city wife's fidelity. Her ingenuity and self-sufficiency are also to be reckoned with. Like city comedy's greedy merchants and witty gallants, the city-comedy prostitute exceeds her theatrical history. She is more than a *meretrix;* she is an index to the covert vices of the City. When an Andrew Lethe abuses a "country wench," he measures his own, more than the wench's, depravity. We have already seen that Witgood's concern for his mistress reflects on his gentility. The prostitute may also be a comment on, or a parody of, her conventional type. Her longing for stability and order belies her assumed independence, and it allows us a new fix on the citizen's idea of order. The city whore, an emblem for the lust in city wives, husbands, and gallants, is (as is generally true of prostitutes) often devoid of lust. She is working to survive, not to feed her pleasure. If she is something of an actress—now feigning desire, now feigning gentility—she is rarely deluded by her role playing. Like the contemporary actor, she has only a marginal place in her society; when she manipulates appearances she exercises the unique power available to her. And once again, her acting makes of her a touchstone: she measures the deludedness (and the delusions) of those before whom she plays. The actor on the stage and the whore in the comedy gauge the follies, the fears, and the desires of their respective audiences. The gallant who jeers at a boy actor playing a whore toys with "her" in a way that cannot help but remind us of Andrew Lethe.

The reversal of expectations that may be figured in the
city whore (the honest whore, the chaste whore, the loyal
whore, the reasonable whore) is observable in Sindefy,
Quicksilver's punk in *Eastward Ho*. The whore (here, the
mistress) is wise beyond her years. Indeed she may be the
norm that critics have been looking for in this play. While
one reader advances the Touchstones, and another suggests
Winifred and Security as a "fixed point of reference," I would
argue that the uninflected voice of reason in the play is
Sindefy.[64] Amidst usurer, merchant, knight, wife, and
daughters, perhaps it was Chapman, Jonson, and Marston's
private joke to champion the whore. Sindefy serves as inter-
locutor to two of the more obvious overreachers in *Eastward
Ho*, and in both instances her determined realism is con-
trasted with their foolish vanities. She alone is given a
chance to speak her mind without becoming herself the
object of the playwrights' humor.

In Sindefy's first scene (2.2), she establishes the fact that
she is not Quicksilver's "lovely Dalida [*sic*]"; rather she is
something of a wise-father figure. Quicksilver fantasizes
about a life at court (he has given up on the "silly city"); but
Sindefy is not particularly impressed:

> *Sin:* Well, Frank, well: the seas you say are uncertain; but
> he that sails in your court seas shall find 'em ten
> times fuller of hazard, wherein to see what is to be
> seen is torment more than a free spirit can endure. But
> when you come to suffer, how many injuries swallow
> you? What care and devotion must you use to humour
> an imperious lord, proportion your looks to his looks,
> smiles to his smiles, fit your sails to the wind of his
> breath?
>
> *Quick:* Tush, he's no journeyman in his craft that cannot do
> that.
>
> *Sin:* But he's worse than a prentice that does it, not only
> humouring the lord, but every trencher-bearer, every
> groom that by indulgence and intelligence crept into
> his favour, and by panderism into his chamber. He
> rules the roast; and when my honourable lord says it

shall be thus, my worshipful rascal, the groom of his
close stool, says it shall not be thus. . . . He that rises
hardly, stands firmly; but he that rises with ease, alas,
falls as easily.

(2.2.76–98)

Sindefy, a punk, is concerned about Quicksilver's integrity.
More important still, she appreciates his energy and worries
about the torments such a "free spirit" is setting himself up
for. The locution "how many injuries swallow you?" suggests not only that the court will take advantage of Quicksilver; Sindefy is thinking of Quicksilver's readiness to debase himself.

In a play that is a pastiche of other plays and of familiar
conventions, Sindefy is uniquely alert to quotations. In her
second scene, she puts up patiently with Gertrude's unre-
mitting foolishness. When the abandoned "lady" appeals to
"chronicle" and romance for solace, Sindefy replies that "it
were but cold comfort should come out of books now"
(5.1.4–5). When Gertrude asks for a "lamentable story,"
Sindefy offers her own biography: "first to be stol'n from my
friends, which were worshipful and of good accompt, by a
prentice in the habit and disguise of a gentleman, and here
brought up to London, and promised marriage, and now
likely to be forsaken, for he is in possibility to be hanged"
(ll. 10–15). It might again be objected that Sindefy's account
is just one more quotation; however, in this instance, the
punk is aware of the conventionality of her own story. Unlike Gertrude, Sindefy has no trouble distinguishing reality
from story, or the Knights of the Round Table from the
knights "of the Square Table at ordinaries, that sit at hazard"
(ll. 48–51). She knows "pretty waking dreams" when she
hears them. It is the reversal of roles, the wise whore serving
the inane citizen's daughter, that comes through when Gertrude describes *herself* as Sir Petronel's "punk" (l. 31).
Sindefy is without doubt a punk, and she does play a part to
deceive Gertrude and Mrs. Touchstone. Nevertheless, it is
Sindefy who joins the playwrights in assessing the follies of

the City, and who might more properly be the play's "Touch-stone."

City comedy's whores are not always as appealing as Sindefy, but they do usually join her in calling our attention to the vices of socially acceptable members of the community. The farcical encounter between Luce and the citizens in *Westward Ho* is wholly at the expense of the latter. Each citizen flatters himself in the belief that he alone enjoys the whore's favors when of course she has little interest in any of them. The whores in *A Trick to Catch the Old One* and *Ram Alley* are instrumental in exposing the lechery of greedy old men. City whores, by fitting themselves to men's desires, play upon men's inability to see through false outsides. The bawd (and mother!) of Frank Gullman, the "courtesan" in *A Mad World, My Masters,* reminds her daughter that "'Tis nothing but a politic conveyance, / A sincere carriage, a religious eyebrow / That throws their charms over the worldlings' senses" (1.1.160–62). With this in mind, Frank is able to practice upon each of the principal male characters in the play. Harebrain greets her as "Lady Gullman, my wife's only company" (1.2.28). Sir Bounteous allows himself to believe that he could get her pregnant: "How soon he took occasion to slip into his own flattery, soothing his own defects [i.e., his impotence]" (3.2.85–86). And Dick Follywit, having just met Frank, declares that he cannot "abide . . . artful entertainments." He prefers "a woman's simple modesty" (4.5.58 and 64).

In fact, we have reason to think that Middleton himself sees similarities in the careers of Follywit and the courtesan. Frank's mother's words about deception (quoted above) are suspiciously applicable to Follywit, as is the conclusion to her speech, when she argues that "Who gets th' opinion for a virtuous name / May sin at pleasure, and ne'er think of shame" (1.1.168–69). But this suspected likeness becomes an unimpeachable certainty when, in the fourth act, Follywit decides to disguise himself as his father's mistress—that is, as Frank. It is here that the full role reversal (gallant becomes whore), intended all along by Middleton, is most fully worked out. Follywit turns whore in order to steal from Sir Bounteous. When he discovers a casket filled with jewels given to Frank by the old man, he cannot help but "wonder how the quean 'scaped tempting" (4.3.40). The gallant will steal where the whore would not. Nor should we be surprised. At the very outset of the play we were permitted a glimpse of Frank Gullman's fair dealing. She told Penitent Brothel that if she did not manage his business successfully, he would owe her no money. Even Penitent was constrained to remark that "Honesty is removed to the common place" (1.1.125–26).

The maturity and integrity that Follywit (or Penitent Brothel, or Harebrain) lacks are to be found in Frank. She is indeed something of the scholar (1.1.170) and the artist (1.2.75) that she professes to be. Moreover, the history of city comedy's whores, their passage from deceit to marriage and social acceptance, is at one with comedy's (and the playwright's) desire for a unified community and for stability. Frank's mother sees the betrothal to Follywit in terms of his "youth and strength, and wealth" first; she then arrives at the fact that the marriage will make Frank "honest." For Frank, "that's worth 'em all" (4.5.137–39). All Frank's ingenuity and energy are directed toward survival and marriage. She understands that it is necessary to exploit not only men's vanities, but women's too. Or she is wise enough to use the complaints that men have about women to her own best advantage. When the courtesan tricks Harebrain by feigning illness, she is quite clear that "since we were made for a weak, imperfect creature, we can fit that best that we are made for" (2.5.34–35). Frank has our sympathy not merely for sentimental reasons, but because we find virtues in the whore—the stock evil character—that we miss in the citizens and gallants. When Follywit's man boasts that "There's none here but can fight for a whore as well as some Inns o' Court man" (3.3.135–36), the "here" extends to the audience, and the irony is hard to miss. In *A Mad World*, the whore may be the only one worth actually fighting for.

In the main plots of *I* and *II Honest Whore*, the whore

is the only one fought for. But even as Hippolito, Matheo, and Orlando defend or marry Bellafront, she remains throughout a victim. She is caught in an untenable position: she is not entirely acceptable to the community as either a whore or a chaste maid. As a whore, she is denied by her father, disdained by Hippolito, and abandoned by the man who first took her maidenhead—Matheo. As a wife, she is put to the test by Orlando, asked to return to whoring by Hippolito, and abused by her husband. With the only reasonable alternatives denied her, it is no wonder Bellafront considers suicide (*I HW*, 2.1.442 ff.). What might appear to be a melodramatic gesture is in fact an understandable response to despair. (The well-meaning Orlando points specifically to the possibility of Bellafront's falling into despair as his motivation for helping her—*II HW*, 1.2.170 ff.) Bellafront's unacceptable alternatives also explain the concluding scenes in both plays. If she has no place on the edge of society as a whore, and no place within society as a devoted wife, then she must make do in exile—in madness at Bedlam or in prison attire at Bridewell. By the end of each play, the world has been turned upside down.

Bellafront, in *II Honest Whore*, begins where most whores in city comedy leave off. She marries a gentleman and so affords us an opportunity to see what life is like for such a pair. Will marriage bring relief and security, or is it merely a way of bringing another woman under the control of men? Is it true, as the resigned gentlemen of city comedy often argue, that an experienced woman is a better mate than a maid who might yet stray? Dekker's tacit answers to these questions are not pleasant. Matheo turns out to be a murderer, a would-be thief, and an ogre of a husband. Not only is there no security within their marriage, but Bellafront finds that she is still open to the advances of Hippolito. Bellafront's marriage brings with it poverty and the loss of her former beauty (*II HW*, 1.1.96–97). And it does not stop men from thinking of her as the whore that she was. At one and the same moment, the Duke takes note of Bellafront's conversion and accuses her of bewitching Hippolito (4.2.49–

50 and 76). His contradictory response merely echoes his son-in-law's actions. Hippolito first hates Bellafront for being a whore, then spurns her when she offers him her love. In Part II, he seeks her love (and so her downfall) even though he knows that he is acting like a "fool" (4.1.401).

Like the other courtesan plays I have discussed, *I* and *II Honest Whore* tell us less about the titular character than about the men who circle around her. Hippolito sees his attempt to persuade Bellafront to or from whoring as a rhetorical feat. He is merciless in his attack on whores in Part I, and he is specious in his defense in Part II. Hippolito argues that a whore is a beast, a slave, diseased and unhappy—he does not take issue with Bellafront's claim to independence (2.1.258). Nor will he credit her admission that she has not *yet* found "that one man, whose love could fellow [her own]" (2.1.266). Hippolito excites her passion only to dismiss it. In Part II, Hippolito finally acknowledges the whore's claim to freedom ("And who [than whores] with looser wings dare flie?"—4.1.274) and tries to use this argument to his advantage. However, even as he argues that men are whores' slaves, Bellafront retorts that her own experience proves whores to be the slaves of men (ll. 278 and 329). What she must not admit is that marriage too can make slaves of women. As a daughter apparently without a father and as a wife mistreated by her husband, Bellafront is in even worse shape than a whore. She has lost whatever control she might have had and gained little security. In her precarious position, she can only hold onto forms—to marriage and to its expected duties of love and pity (*II HW*, 5.2.468–70). Without these props, she might as well resign herself to Bedlam or Bridewell.

Critics have objected that Bellafront is "a piece of sentimental and cheap idealism" and that "she is nothing more nor less than a successful figure of melodrama . . . the stuff of life is not in her."[65] While there is some truth in such criticism, it misses the important point. At least one of these critics would never claim that city comedy should be measured in terms of realism. Bellafront lacks "the stuff of life" because she, like all characters in city comedy, stages contemporary attitudes. Her significance is contingent upon the visibility of the stereotypes she embodies, not upon some psychological depth of character. If Bellafront calls attention to the contemporary response to whores (honest or otherwise), then she is a successful character in a city comedy. Precisely when she is emptied of individuality, she becomes available as a figure that can exaggerate or condense male notions of a whore. In Bedlam, Bellafront discovers the disguised Hippolito, Infeliche, and Matheo. In Bridewell, the whores denounce gentlemen's fashion (5.2.280) and expose the pander Bots. These confrontations between the dark underbelly of the City and its self-confident masters (the Duke speaks of the Bridewell parade of whores as a "Scene . . . Comicall"—5.2.263) mirror the conjunction of city comedy and its audience. Vice is exposed; but more important still, the social economy and the biases that determine what is and is not a vice are worked out in a conventionalized urban environment. London (or "Milan" with a Bedlam and a Bridewell) is not mirrored in *I* and *II Honest Whore*—it is reconstituted in the terms and figures of the language Londoners used to express their will and desires.

While Bellafront was suffering as an honest whore at the Fortune, the boys of the Queen's Revels were playing *The Dutch Courtesan* at the Blackfriars theater. In the play at the open-air theater, the heroine was rejected and victimized both as a whore and as a wife. In Marston's anatomy of a whore, both courtesan and wife are tolerated as long as each keeps to her place. The wife (Beatrice is about to marry Freevill) is set off in a world of purity and romance, and the whore (Franceschina) is located within a contradictory world of comedy and ridicule on the one hand, realism and revenge on the other.[66] Indeed, Franceschina presents a female instance of the poles of foolishness and menace that I have attributed to city comedy's typical greedy merchant-citizen. We are expected to laugh at her Dutch accent and to understand that she, like Malheureux, is something of a fool for taking herself too seriously.[67] However, we must also find a way to accommodate the sudden and vicious revenge sought by this otherwise "pretty, nimble-ey'd Dutch Tanakin ... that has beauty enough for her virtue, virtue enough for a woman" (1.1.140–43). The best solution offered by Marston/Freevill is to maintain a bifurcated philosophy: apply Montaigne to whores and men's incontinencies, and save Plato for the woman you plan to marry. A man could deal with a whore or a virgin (or, as it is set out in the "Fabulae Argumentum," "a courtesan [or] a wife"), but do not expect him to deal with a woman.

While Freevill's advice to Malheureux is meant to be reasonable and humane, it is based on the already-centuries-old distinction between love and marriage. Marston turned to Montaigne's "Upon Some Verses of Virgil" as translated by Florio: "Wedlocke hath for his share honour, justice, profit and constancie: a plaine, and more generall delight. Love melts in onely pleasure; and truly it hath it more ticklish; more lively, more quaint, and more sharpe: ... there must be a kinde of stinging, tingling and smarting."[68] Thus *men* save their lust for whores and their name for their wives. *Women* must choose, since they are not permitted fully to express both their sexuality and their humanity. The contemporary woman was manageable as a Beatrice and, eventually, as a Franceschina; she was a threat as a Hermione or a Cleopatra. There was to be no ambiguity about a woman. A whore who shows affection is a confusing figure; if "they sell but only flesh" (2.1.37), a man knows where he stands. Even a vicious whore is tolerable, for then she is "a punk rampant," and snares may be set to trip her up. But above all else, and at whatever cost, wives (or maids) and whores must be kept entirely separate.

The irony in this particular play lies in the fact that Freevill's pronouncements do not describe his way of life. The man of reason, the man who argues that "Nothing extremely best with us endures," can know his women only in the extreme. Beatrice corresponds to his soul, Franceschina to his flesh. The cruel revenge plot initiated by the courtesan serves merely to confirm Freevill's view of women. Franceschina cannot understand Freevill's love for Beatrice, or she envies it, or she cannot accept the idea that he is abandoning her; and so, Freevill would have it, she strikes out. Needless to say, this is all that can be expected from "a creature made of blood and hell" (5.1.77). Freevill moves on, without guilt, to Beatrice. The courtesan, however, will meet "the extremest whip and jail" (5.3.59). Thus, the prostitute who misses out on marriage ends, as in *II Honest Whore,* in Bridewell. She can exclaim against men ("O unfaithful men—tyrants! betrayers! De very enjoying us loseth us; and, when you only ha' made us hateful, you only hate us"—2.2.115–17); but she cannot get the upper hand of them. So long as Franceschina, or any whore, represents an independent woman, a woman with a will (cf. 5.3.58), or a woman who is neither wife nor daughter, she must be either dismissed or defeated.

A Trio of Widows

In *Ram Alley,* the widow Taffata is first defeated and then married. Lording Barry introduces all the contemporary stereotypes and clichés about widows because, it would seem, he accepts them. He composes self-consciously but not critically. Taffata is offered as a representative widow, not as an exaggerated embodiment of men's ideas about widows. She enters into various farcical (but never parodic) scenes in which she is mocked and then "rewarded" for her conventional widow's lust and wealth. Barry insures that we will not identify with her by subverting her integrity—even when she is most obviously victimized. However, unlike more accomplished playwrights of city comedy, he does not take advantage of the distance between character and spectator as a space for critical thinking. Offering us what he takes to be the truth, Barry never considers what or who it is that constitutes truth. His gratuitous asides directed at the Inns of Court men in his audience are little more than an attempt to flatter them for their reputed sexual prowess.

Of a piece with this is his defense of young Will Small-shanks at the expense of Sir Oliver, the counterfeit lawyer Throat, and the blundering Captain. Availing himself of ready-to-hand prejudices, Barry plays to his audience's worst instincts. If this means threatening to "gar [a] whyniard through [the widow's] weombe" (l. 2225), so much the better for the theater, and for the "lusty lad" (l. 2248).

If the widow were merely a victim, we might argue that Barry understood her special social position. However, it is Taffata who, after the wooing by sword, calls Smallshanks a "lusty lad." It is a toss-up, for Barry, whether the widow will seem uglier if she decides for Sir Oliver's money or William's vigor. Since widows were notorious for their sexual appetite, and since Taffata has money of her own, Barry can best reveal her in her true colors by having her plump for the "best part of a man" (l. 2478). Surely this is the logical choice for a woman whom we first encounter appraising the eligible men who pass along the street before her house. She complains "how scarce is the world of propper men / And gallants; sure wee neuer more shall see / A good legge worne in a long silke stocking, / With a long codpeece . . ." (ll. 219–22). And she boasts that a "witty woman" can distinguish men "by their noses" (ll. 232 ff.). Within a minute, she has taken a fancy for Boutcher; but it remains one of the play's unspoken ironies that Boutcher has what certainly must be the least active "nose" in *Ram Alley*. First and last, the widow Taffata and her saucy maid Adriana are interested in men's parts: "The rest of the body is not worth a rush, / Though it be nere so handsome" (ll. 2479–80). Taffata dallies with Boutcher, the Captain, and Sir Oliver and his son, and she speaks of gulling "some dozen" more. If there is a subtext to Barry's conventional handling of the widow, then it must be the fear men have of such "plumpe drabe[s]." Here is a woman who is at last free to choose her mate on her own terms. And if this is the unspoken fear, then the staged response is to be found in the fifth-act forced wooing (call it rape). The woman who thinks she is free to choose a husband has a surprise coming to her. Smallshanks' assault/

espousal is a vengeful response to a nightmare widow who toys with men.

This understanding is far from Barry's intention, as is made clear when he takes every opportunity to make the widow look like the monster that moralists made widows out to be. Taffata revels in commonplace insults directed at widows:

> For though the Pye bee broken vp before,
> Yet sayes the prouerbe, the deeper is the sweeter.
> And though a capons wings and legges be caru'd,
> The flesh left with the rumpe I hope is sweet.
>
> (ll. 353–56)

"Widdowes," she reminds Sir Oliver, "are sildome slow to put men to it" (l. 1197). When it comes to setting the terms for her marriage with the knight, she runs through a list of predictable demands:

> shall I keepe
> My chambers by the moneth, if I be pleas'd
> To take Physick, to send for Visitants,
> To haue my maide read *Amadis de Gaule,*
> Or *Donzel del Phoebe* to me? shall I haue
> A Carotch of the last edition . . .
>
> (ll. 1217–22)

> shall we haue two chambers?
> And will you not presume vnto my bed,
> Till I shall call you by my waiting maide.
>
> (ll. 1226–28)

For all her demands and self-confidence, Widow Taffata is rewarded with marriage to the arrogant scoundrel William Smallshanks. She can pay off his debts, satisfy his longings, and help him with what has suddenly become a serious project—besting his father. Except for the Inns of Court men who identified with William, there were probably few who would have argued that Taffata was properly compensated. But even where amends were made to a city widow, her independence was forfeited. In Nathan Field's *Amends for Ladies*, for example, another bold youth secures a widow for himself.[69] The widow—Lady Bright—is everything that Taffata is not; indeed, *she* is the one who wields a sword in the crucial scene. But young Bould has a stratagem to trick her into marriage anyway.

Lady Bright is content with her status as a widow. "I am mine own commander," she tells her maid and married friends, and she appreciates not having a brother "to dice away my patrimony" or a "husbands death [to] / Stand . . . in doubt on" (1.1.40–45). Bould's plot, like that of the wife in *Amends for Ladies*, puts Lady Bright's integrity to the test. Bould, disguised as her waiting woman, gains access to her bed and attempts to seduce her. Lady Bright admits her affection for Bould but will have nothing to do with his trickery. In a wonderful scene, the aroused gallant makes no less than a half dozen sallies at the widow's fortress. He asks her to marry him because she loves him; because if she doesn't marry him, people will talk about their relationship; because if she refuses, he'll be mocked for lack of virility; because a "natural act" like lovemaking cannot taint her soul; because if she refuses, he will rape her; and finally, he suggests that if she will not consent to a marriage, she could at least let him remain her maid to "doe [her] service" at night (4.1.13–123). To all this the widow turns a deaf ear, sure only that Bould has "trusted to that fond opinion, / This is the way to haue a widdow-hood, / By getting to her bed . . ." (4.1.32–34). Beaten and frustrated, Bould is forced to retire, and to plot a new path to the widow's bed.

Field, in his address to the women readers of his earlier play (*A Woman's a Weather-cock*), promised amends for ladies in his next play. Ostensibly, the new play makes the promised reparations. Lady Bright is not wanton, she does not paint, she is frank and advocates a humane sexuality that is free of hypocrisy ("a pox of these nise mouth'd creatures"—3.3.41), and she maintains her honor even though she loves Bould. However, this is not enough for Field. An unmarried woman of such value is not a prize to be left unclaimed. Bould must scheme to make the widow bind herself, her goods, and her lands that she will not hinder his choice in marriage. She goes through with the vow because she has been led to believe that Bould means to marry another woman; but of course, he says, he meant her all along. Threatened with the loss of her property, the widow capitulates and they marry. Field mitigates the underhandedness by reminding us that the widow does love Bould. The comedy's hymeneal conclusion is meant to make us forget that she had not planned on the marriage, and that she knows that "Your widdow (without goods) sels scuruilie" (5.2.249). Yet we wonder still about the amends that have been made: is a widow's honor upheld if she is matched with a man who twice tries to trick her into marriage? The answer must remain uncertain. The Whitefriars audience may admire what the widow stands for, but it is easier to accept her strong will and her forthrightness when they are contained within the legitimizing bands of marriage. Lady Bright, like all city widows on stage, though not "Still made [one of] the disgrac't subjects, in these plaies" (2.2.106-7), is tamed.

The qualified "amends" made to widows in Field's play resemble the uncertain treatment of the widow, Lady Goldenfleece, in Middleton's *No Wit, No Help like a Woman's*. Middleton seems to be struggling with the stereotype of the sex-craved widow—one moment he stages the type uncritically, but in the next moment he uncovers the very human needs and desires which are traditionally distorted by the stereotyped monster. Lady Goldenfleece starts with several strikes against her. She is the widow of the extortionist Sir Avarice Goldenfleece. She entertains as suitors crass gallants like Sir Gilbert Lambstone. And she teases the play's romantic heroine, withholding from her a secret about her past for no apparent reason (beyond extending Middleton's plot). Lady Goldenfleece is also a slave to appearances. The gallant she falls in love with is Kate in disguise. When these two begin to kiss one another (2.3.159 and 186), and when finally they marry, the effect is not merely comic: since we know that Sir Avarice made his fortune at Master Low-water's expense, this lesbian marriage serves to rejoin Mistress Low-water with the money that was once her husband's, but is now Lady Goldenfleece's. The wit of a woman might, theoretically, make do without men altogether.

Of course, Kate Low-water has no affection for Lady Goldenfleece. She wants to chastise her and to recover the Low-water estate. Once she has accomplished these goals, she will arrange for her brother, Beveril, to marry the widow. However, for a few moments, in Act 5, Middleton pauses to enjoy the crisis that his ever-turning plot has reached. Lady Goldenfleece and the disguised Mistress Low-water are alone and supposedly heading for the marriage bed. As is usual in such cases, we are eager to see how the reluctant "husband" is going to keep the eager widow out of bed. The scene should offer excellent proof that widows are in fact hungry only for sex, especially since the righteous person here is the deceiving Mistress Low-water, the compromised figure, Lady Goldenfleece. And it is in this vein that Lady Goldenfleece begins Act 5: "Now, like a greedy usurer alone, / I sum up all the wealth this day has brought me / And thus I hug it" (5.1.1–3). The widow is not only overeager in her embrace of suddenly prudish Kate; she also damns herself by associating her desire with her former husband's profession and the wealth he extorted from Master Low-water. Mistress Low-water puts off the widow, asking whether she thinks she has "married only a cock-sparrow" (l. 10). The two then go back and forth, offering and refusing. But the widow's desire turns out to be more complex than her stereotype would lead us to expect. When Kate protests that marriage is too "serious divine" for love's follies, Lady Goldenfleece responds that she chose "him" for "love, / Youth, and content of heart, and not for troubles" (ll. 37–38).

Suddenly there is something poignant about the wi-

dow's desire to fill her bed. Her concern that her husband
be not yet ripe for "troubles" resonates with memories of
her first marriage. Her desire for "content of heart"—Low-
water's as well as her own—momentarily evokes a loneliness that seems never to have characterized the stereotypical Jacobean widow. Mistress Low-water, who is herself married to an ineffectual husband, may hear some of this. So
she next reasserts her higher morality by reminding the
widow that the Goldenfleece wealth was "wrongfully got"
(l. 43). When their conversation again turns to the bed which
the widow will go to only with her husband, Mistress Low-
water retreats to a tired cliché: "You high-fed widows are
too cunning people / For a poor gentleman to come simply
to" (ll. 59–60). Lady Goldenfleece thinks that "he" must be
"Jealous of that which thought yet never acted" (l. 72) and
goes down on her knees before Low-water. She is refused,
and laments that she has "miss'd love . . . That's all I crav'd,
/ And that lies now a-dying" (ll. 77–79). Middleton undercuts the very stereotype he has staged. In a play in which a
charivari-like wedding masque is acted by discredited, re-
venge-seeking gallants who slander widows because they
have failed in their wooing, and in a play in which Lady
Goldenfleece is damned by her name from the outset, Middleton gives full force to the contemporary character of "the
widow," but then reveals a widow's precariousness, her dependence, and her all-too-human desires. It has been objected that we cannot "easily accept the sudden friendship
[at the end of the play] of Lady Goldenfleece and Mistress
Low-water."[70] Yet Mistress Low-water has worked hard to
marry her own brother to the widow. This undertaking may
stem from her desire to see Beveril's love for the widow
satisfied; however, it may also be Kate Low-water's way of
making up to Lady Goldenfleece for having exploited her
loneliness and desire for "content of heart." Middleton's
treatment of his play's widow is still another example of
city comedy's unsteady critical project. The stereotype that
is exploited is also the stereotype that is tentatively examined.[71]

Chaste Maids

The wives, whores, and widows of city comedy are presented in terms of the threats and the advantages that they offer men. This is also true of the chaste maid. Her character and her actions are meant to reveal what sort of wife the maid will make. Conversely, an eligible maid (like city comedy's whores) may be the figure who tests the mettle of her suitor. Not only do young gallants get what they deserve, they are rewarded frequently with a good deal more than they merit. Mildred, in *Eastward Ho*, is suited perfectly to Golding; however, Livia (in *The Woman's Prize*) may be more than Rowland can handle, and Constantia (in *Ram Alley*) is surely more than Boutcher deserves. A review of the maids presented in the city comedies we are examining suggests that there is no universal type. Some of these women (these girls—they must have been young) are almost entirely effaced from the action of the play. Although Joyce Hoard (in *A Trick to Catch the Old One*) is the gold at the end of the rainbow, she barely attracts our (or the characters') attention. Mary Fitz-allard (in *The Roaring Girl*) and Katherine (in *Your Five Gallants*) set plots in motion and then disappear. When they return in the fifth act, we know no more about them than at the outset. They were and they remain sweet, vulnerable objects of desire. Even Moll (in *A Chaste Maid in Cheapside*), who is actually on and off stage throughout the play, is little more than a silent, and presumably desirable, object of attention. Other maids are witty (Crispinella, in *The Dutch Courtesan*), patient (Constantia, in *Ram Alley*), foolish (Gertrude, in *Eastward Ho*), or coy (Livia, in *The Woman's Prize*). Although there is no unique configuration for city comedy's virgin, the treatment of these characters suggests what I have noted before: when women are at issue, city comedy is no respecter of social class. Assuming that the maid comes well endowed, it is of little consequence that Joyce Hoard is the daughter of a city usurer, that Katherine is the orphaned daughter of a knight, or that Moll is the daughter of a goldsmith. One knight may father reticent and sharp-tongued daughters (Beatrice and Crispinella), and one citizen may have a foolish daughter and a dull one (Gertrude and Mildred). As long as a maid can be made to figure in the urban marriage economy, there is a place for her in city comedy.

The most-sought-after maid, like the most-prized wife, is patient, modest, and virtuous. She is a comic agent to the extent that she can be distressed and then, finally, offered relief. She is the creation of men's fantasies and can exist only on the stage, in romance, and in the lives of saints. Were she not of superhuman patience and meekness, she would cashier the type of man she is inevitably linked with. Hence it is altogether fitting that when we encounter such a creature in the person of Beatrice, in *The Dutch Courtesan*, she should dazzle her lover but exasperate her sister. As a passive, loving maid, Beatrice is everything that delights a gallant and makes more independent women look bad by comparison. If there is irony in Beatrice's declaration of innocence, it arises from the fact that she is proclaiming her virtue to a man who has just left his whore. All that Freevill would keep separate from his whoring, all that is most chaste and pure, is figured in Beatrice's speech:

> I cannot with a mistress' compliment,
> Forced discourses, or nice art of wit
> Give entertain to your dear wished presence;
> But safely thus, what hearty gratefulness,
> Unsullen silence, unaffected modesty,
> And an unignorant shamefastness can express,
> Receive as your protested due. Faith, my heart,
> I am your servant.
> Oh, let not my secure simplicity
> Breed your mislike, as one quite void of skill,
> 'Tis grace enough in us not to be ill.
> I can some good, and, faith, I mean no hurt;
> Do not, then, sweet, wrong sober innocence.
> I judge you all of virtue, and our vows
> Should kill all fears that base distrust can move.
>
> (2.1.12–26)

How does Freevill receive his "protested due" and refuse to "wrong sober innocence"? He will not reveal himself as soon as he might (4.4.78) because he delights not alone in Beatrice's sweetness, but in her "suff'ring sweetness" (4.4.86). Not unlike Quomodo, Freevill is impressed with the "deep affection [with which] she receiv'd [his] death" and with the "kindness" which characterizes her response to his "lewdly intimated wrongs" (4.4.87–89). Having found a maid who believes that it is "grace enough in [women] not to be ill," Freevill can go off to watch Cocledemoy and Malheureux in the gutters of the City.

Crispinella is considerably less tame than her sister. When Beatrice breaks out in lamentation over Freevill's death ("O passion! O my grief! which way wilt break, think, and consume?"—4.4.53–54), Crispinella can cry only "Peace!" When Beatrice begins to languish, her sister pretends that she cannot understand what Beatrice is talking about (4.4.67–69). Crispinella has no patience with "bashfulness" (3.1.29). Beatrice argues that "severe modesty is women's virtue," and Crispinella responds that "Virtue is a free, pleasant, buxom quality" (3.1.46–48). One sister is preoccupied with "virtuous marriage"; the other finds "no more affinity betwixt virtue and marriage than betwixt a man and his horse" (3.1.81–83). And Crispinella's distaste for "ignorant coyness, sour, austere, lumpish, uncivil privateness, that promises nothing but rough skins and hard stools" (3.1.49–51), is just short of an open attack on her sister's modesty. The saucy sister is not ashamed to speak what she is not ashamed to think (3.1.25–26). We can well imagine what she would have to say were Freevill's vows addressed to her.

In a play that mixes the extreme modesty of Beatrice, the extreme viciousness of Franceschina, the philosophy of Freevill, and the precepts of Malheureux, it is something of a relief to come upon Crispinella and Tysefew. Their banter-filled courtship is light and without pretension. Crispinella teases Tysefew, and he responds in kind. She is his "proud ape" and his "tart monkey"; he is her "brother" and her "servant." They share a recognition that their destination is marriage; but Crispinella protests that what wives "must," husbands "may." She knows that a "husband generally is a careless, domineering thing" (3.1.69–70), and she tells Beatrice that she prefers to "live my own woman," rather proving "a wag than a fool" (3.1.79–80). Still, for all the good fun that Marston has with, and invests in, Crispinella, she is no solution to the problem faced by the woman of her day. Tysefew lets her prate, but his purse, his heart, and his body are not Crispinella's until she promises silence in his house, modesty at his table, and wantonness in his bed (4.1.76–78). Indeed, even her frank speech is problematic. It is more attractive than Beatrice's devotions, but it is equally unrealistic. Crispinella speaks as if the Logos were hers to command: "I give thought words, and words truth, and truth boldness" (3.1.36–37). She believes that because "nature [is] without apparel," she can speak in a transparent tongue. Of course, such naturalness is as extreme and as artificial as Beatrice's conventional declarations. It would take a mixture of the one sister's pertness and defensive prattle, the other's modesty, and a good bit more (perhaps some of Franceschina's passion) to fashion a maid who could stand up to men's prejudices. A Rosalind or a Viola might meet the requirements; but then they would fail to dramatize the very assumptions and attitudes that the characters in city comedy act out.

The analytic impulse behind city comedy and the attempt to parody contemporary versions of the chaste maid are best served by characters like Beatrice and Crispinella, or Gertrude and Mildred. The latter two, the goldsmith Touchstone's daughters in *Eastward Ho*, are, like Marston's sisters, opposite sides of the same coin. Both Mildred and Gertrude tell us something about how men characterized citizens' daughters. We have seen already that Gertrude is a fool. She aspires blindly to marriage with a knight—any knight—and ends up the lady of a castle in the air. She insults her father's citizenship, and she expects her life to duplicate the careers of the romantic heroines she has read about. Gertrude is the gallant's idea of a wife who will bring easy money and no bother. She envisions a life of animated clichés, and, wonderfully enough, her fate is ruled by maxims. Unfortunately, the maxims are Mildred's, not Gertrude's: "Where titles presume to thrust before fit means to second them, wealth and respect often grow sullen and will not follow. . . . Where ambition of place goes before fitness of birth, contempt and disgrace follow" (1.2.37–42). Mildred quotes scholars, and Gertrude sings snatches from obscene ballads. Taken together, as representative citizen's daughters, or individually, as eligible maids, there is nothing that an audience could find appealing in these sisters. One stages the moralist's version of a "good girl," the other stages "bad girl" material. Yet the two are at once such accurate presentations of this literature and such fools that we must question the value of all the conventional wisdom about how a daughter ought to behave herself.

Certainly there is little to recommend the example set by modest, obedient Mildred. Mildred is one of those daughters who are perfectly willing to give themselves up entirely to their fathers' will. She is what she should be, and she is dull, boring, even unnerving in her correctness. Whereas we have Crispinella to assure us that Marston is not naively championing Beatrice, Chapman, Jonson, and Marston build parodic elements right into their characterization of Mildred. Her stale propriety is a lesson for those men who demand a meek and obedient wife. She catches up her audience in an old contradiction: they laugh at her, but they laugh at precisely what they write and say that they require in a wife, a daughter, or a maid. Responsible, even more than the authors of *Eastward Ho*, for Mildred are the men in the audience who desire such women without ever considering what total docility might mean in a relationship.

Lording Barry, with no sign of self-consciousness or skill, seems almost in spite of himself to present yet another version of the patient-maid/undeserving-gallant paradigm. In *Ram Alley*, for reasons that are never clear, Constantia is in love with Boutcher. In order to keep an eye on him, and at times, in order to coach him, Constantia disguises herself as a page and enters Boutcher's service. Her only role in the play is to remain constant while Boutcher fumbles in his attempt to win the widow Taffata. And Constantia saves Boutcher's life when he tries to hang himself. It is hard to know whom we should wonder at more—the gallant who makes a fool of himself, or the maid who remains faithful to him. Barry gave no thought to the figure cut by Boutcher, and he implies that Constantia's fidelity is not merely exemplary, but expectable too. Only for a moment do we glimpse an awareness on Barry's part that Boutcher is crazy to go after the widow. In his usual coarse fashion, Smallshanks asks Boutcher, "Does not the faire *Constantia Sommerfield* / Doate on thy filthy face; and wilt thou wed / A wanton widdow?" (ll. 1891–93). However, this question is not raised again.

Constant Beatrice, constant Mildred, and constant Constantia. Perhaps some would argue that these are merely conventional figures and that we ought not to make much of them. But then why are there so many of them, and why do we feel their presence even when they are merely suggested by women who are their opposites? In raising these figures, city comedy puts before its audiences images of their desires. Constancy, meekness, and obedience in and of themselves are not questioned; rather the motivations and interests which lead to or advocate these "virtues" are exposed. Morose wants a silent wife not because meekness is a Christian virtue, but because he would maintain his power; Freevill wants a woman he can idolize; Rowland cannot bear a woman who teases him; and Follywit wants a wife who will not remind him of his mistresses. The city merchant is held to be greedy because this will overshadow the gentry's profligacy. So too, the city maid is said to be a fool, or is advised to be meek, because this will make room for a gentleman's wantonness, or it will guarantee the reputation of his home and family. It is probably too much to say that these plays "advocate" sexual equality. However, it is clear that the women on the public and private stages, in their relations with their fathers, their husbands, and their suitors, reveal men's shortcomings. And they point to men, in all roles and of all classes, as the origin of the codes that restrict and define a woman's activities. It is the happy marriages that conclude these comedies that are conventional, not the women's patience or frustration. And we discover that the difference betwixt a courtesan and a wife is just as great as men make it.

Notes
Bibliography
Index

Notes

Chapter 1

1 Samuel Calvert, *Winwood Memorials,* ed. Edmund Sawyer (London: T. Ward, 1725), 2:54.
2 Jeffrey L. Sammons, *Literary Sociology and Practical Criticism* (Bloomington: Indiana Univ. Press, 1977), p. 38.
3 Elizabeth Burns, *Theatricality: A Study of Convention in the Theatre and in Social Life* (London: Longman, 1972), p. 144.
4 Cf. Kenneth Burke, *Attitudes toward History* (Boston: Beacon Press, 1961), p. 57: "poetic forms are symbolic structures designed to equip us for confronting given historical and personal situations."
5 Richard Levin, *New Readings vs. Old Plays: Recent Trends in the Reinterpretation of English Renaissance Drama* (Chicago: Univ. of Chicago Press, 1979), p. 147.
6 R. C. Bald wrote about Middleton's "city comedy" in 1934, in the *Journal of English and Germanic Philology,* 33 (1934), 373–87. Brian Gibbons mapped out the territory with the first book-length discussion of city comedy (*Jacobean City Comedy* [Cambridge: Harvard Univ. Press, 1968]). Alexander Leggatt defines city comedy as "comedy set in a predominantly middle-class social milieu." See his *Citizen Comedy in the Age of Shakespeare* (Toronto: Univ of Toronto Press, 1973), pp. 3–5, for important qualifications to this brief definition.
7 David Bevington, *Tudor Drama and Politics: A Critical Approach to Topical Meaning* (Cambridge: Harvard Univ. Press., 1968), passim.
8 Jean Jacquot ("Le répertoire des compagnes d'enfants à Londres, 1600–1610," in Jean Jacquot, ed., *Dramaturgie et société, XVIe*

et XVIIe siècles [Paris: Editions du Centre National de la Recherche Scientifique, 1968], 2:766) and Michael Shapiro (*Children of the Revels: The Boy Companies of Shakespeare's Time and Their Plays* [New York: Columbia Univ. Press, 1977], p. 211) have argued that city comedy refracts (as opposed to reflects) social reality. E. M. Waith discusses the "comic mirror" which unmasks as well as it reflects in "The Comic Mirror and the World of Glass," *Research Opportunities in Renaissance Drama*, 9 (1966), 16–23. Of course, the relationship between art and history is a chief concern among Marxist critics. See, for example, the work of Walter Benjamin, Terry Eagleton, Lucien Goldmann, and Raymond Williams.

9 Peter L. Berger and Thomas Luckmann, *The Social Construction of Reality* (New York: Doubleday, 1966), p. 84, cite the historical example of "the Jew."

10 Ben Jonson, *Timber: or, Discoveries* in *Ben Jonson,* ed. C. H. Herford and Percy and Evelyn Simpson (Oxford: Clarendon Press, 1947), 8:597. Having completed this book, I discovered that Lawrence Danson recently examined the limits of Jonson's faith in our ability to "returne to our selves." Danson cites these lines from *Discoveries* in the same article in which he quotes from Berger and Luckmann. See "Jonsonian Comedy and the Discovery of the Social Self," *PMLA*, 99 (1984), 179–93; and see my discussion of *Eastward Ho* and *Every Man in His Humor,* in Chapter 4.

11 Perez Zagorin, *The Court and the Country: The Beginnings of the English Revolution* (London: Routledge & Kegan Paul, 1969), p. 23.

12 Ibid., p. 122.

13 Ibid., p. 124.

14 I have taken these words from an article by Michael Wood. They were written in the context of a discussion of Brecht's "principle of the epic theater." See *New York Review of Books*, 15 May 1980, p. 17.

15 Thomas Hobbes, *Leviathan* (London: J. M. Dent, 1914), p. 44 (1.10). Cf. Ulysses and Achilles in *Troilus and Cressida*, 3.2.

16 Harry Berger, Jr., "Text against Performance in Shakespeare: The Example of *Macbeth*," in Stephen Greenblatt, ed., *The Power of Forms in the English Renaissance* (Norman: Pilgrim Books, 1982), p. 59.

17 Erving Goffman, *The Presentation of Self in Everyday Life* (New

York: Doubleday Anchor Books, 1959), pp. 16 and 13; also Berger and Luckmann, *Social Construction of Reality*, pp. 29–30 and passim. For a discussion of the relationship between self-presentation and self-dramatization (as exhibitionism and theatricalism), see Jonas Barish, "Exhibitionism and the Antitheatrical Prejudice," *English Literary History*, 36 (1969), 1–29. And see Stephen Greenblatt's *Renaissance Self-Fashioning: From More to Shakespeare* (Chicago: Univ. of Chicago Press, 1980).

18 Berger, "Text against Performance in Shakespeare," p. 77.

19 Sammons, *Literary Sociology and Practical Criticism*, p. 5.

20 Louis A. Montrose, "The Purpose of Playing: Reflections on a Shakespearean Anthropology," *Helios*, n.s. 7 (1979–80), 68.

21 *Hamlet*, ed. Willard Farnham (Baltimore: Penguin Books, 1970), 2.2.512 and 3.2.20–23.

22 Madeleine Doran, *Endeavors of Art: A Study of Form in Elizabethan Drama* (Madison: Univ. of Wisconsin Press, 1964), pp. 70–84.

23 Montrose ("Purpose of Playing") cites Hildred Geertz's relevant observation that "in complexly differentiated societies, the traditional frameworks are constantly being challenged, in part by the lack of fit between actual experience and the ready-made concepts at hand for dealing with it, and in part by the presence of contrary frameworks" (p. 54).

24 Cf. George Meredith: "The comic poet is in the narrow field, or enclosed square, of the society he depicts; and he addresses the still narrower enclosure of men's intellects, with reference to the operation of the social world upon their characters" (*An Essay on Comedy*, ed. Wylie Sypher [Baltimore, Md.: Johns Hopkins Univ. Press, 1980], p. 46).

25 L. C. Knights, *Drama and Society in the Age of Jonson* (1936; rpt. London: George W. Stewart, 1951), pp. 5–6.

26 Anthony Covatta, *Thomas Middleton's City Comedies* (Lewisburg, Pa.: Bucknell Univ. Press, 1973), p. 32.

27 Frank Freeman Foster, *The Politics of Stability* (London: Royal Historical Society, 1977); R. G. Lang, "London's Aldermen in Business, 1600–1625," *Guildhall Miscellany*, 3 (1971), 242–64. Lawrence Stone and Jeanne C. Fawtier Stone have recently argued that "Only a small handful of very rich merchants succeeded in buying their way into the elite," and most of these men sold their countryseats in their lifetime or at death. "The

mere existence in considerable numbers of numerous bourgeois purchaser-sellers of seats suggests that there were many successful business men who had no desire to become assimilated with the landed classes." *An Open Elite? England, 1540–1880* (Oxford: Clarendon Press, 1984), pp. 402–3 and 287.

28 Gibbons, *Jacobean City Comedy*, p. 29. Cf. Richard Horwich, "Wives, Courtesans, and the Economics of Love in Jacobean City Comedy," *Comparative Drama*, 7 (1973), 291–92.

29 The notion of an "interrogative text" is developed by Catherine Belsey in *Critical Practice* (London: Methuen, 1980), pp. 91–92.

30 Leggatt, *Citizen Comedy in the Age of Shakespeare*.

31 Anne Barton, "London Comedy and the Ethos of the City," *London Journal*, 4 (1978), 158–60.

32 Margot Heinemann, *Puritanism and Theatre: Thomas Middleton and Opposition Drama under the Early Stuarts* (Cambridge: Cambridge Univ. Press, 1980), pp. 21, 29, and 35.

Chapter 2

1 F. J. Fisher, "Some Experiments in Company Organization in the Early Seventeenth Century," *Economic History Review*, 4 (1932), 177; Richard Grassby, "The Personal Wealth of the Business Community in Seventeenth-Century England," *Economic History Review*, 2d Series, 23 (1970), 222; David Cressy, "Describing the Social Order of Elizabethan and Stuart England," *Literature and History*, 3 (1976), 37. See also R. G. Lang, "London's Aldermen in Business, 1600–1625," *Guildhall Miscellany*, 3 (1971), 243; and see Roy Bert Westerfield, "Middlemen in English Business," *Transactions of the Connecticut Academy of Arts and Sciences*, 19 (1915), 329–33.

2 John Browne, *The Marchants Avizo* (London, 1589), "To the Reader."

3 Cressy, "Describing the Social Order of Elizabethan and Stuart England," p. 33.

4 A prominent exception in the years between 1603 and 1613 is Thomas Heywood's *If You Know Not Me, You Know Nobody*, Part II (1605). Like Dekker's *The Shoemaker's Holiday*, Heywood's play is not what I would call a city comedy. His version of Thomas Gresham is pure fantasy: unlike the clever and prudent financial agent who enriched himself as he served Cecil, Heywood's Gresham will "daunce all my care away" (l. 1532)

when he loses £60,000. Equally fantastic is the haberdasher Hobson—in gown and slippers, he loses himself in the early-morning mist on the Bankside. Heywood's merchants spend, they do not get; they give away money or they lose it, but they do not make profits. Their "care how to get, and fore-cast to encrease," are unseen but guaranteed "especiall vertues, being cleare / From avarice and base extortion" (ll. 15 and 17–18). Hobson and Gresham are patriots who think of the common-wealth at least as much as of the City. Like Simon Eyre, they disregard social boundaries that are uniformly observed in city comedy so that they may treat with their sovereign. They are unthreatened by the genre's typically aggressive gallants, and they have no daughters to be robbed of. It is the occasion for no lasting disappointment when the Queen fails to recognize Hobson. The entanglements and social tensions specific to the City have disappeared from the fantasy world depicted in *If You Know Not Me*. Only a hint of defensiveness remains, assuring us that "fore-cast to encrease" is not avarice, that Thomas Gresham is no prodigal (ll. 1559–61), and that Jack Gresham, who is a prodigal, is entirely harmless. *If You Know Not Me, You Know Nobody*, Part II, ed. Madeleine Doran, for the Malone Society (Oxford: Oxford Univ. Press, 1934–35).

5 R. H. Tawney, Intro., *A Discourse upon Usury*, by Thomas Wilson (New York: Harcourt, Brace, n.d.), p. 91; B. E. Supple, *Commercial Crisis and Change in England, 1600–1642* (Cambridge: Cambridge Univ. Press, 1959), p. 4.

6 Laura Stevenson O'Connell, "The Elizabethan Bourgeois Hero-Tale: Aspects of an Adolescent Social Consciousness," in Barbara C. Malament, ed., *After the Reformation: Essays in Honor of J. H. Hexter* (Philadelphia: Univ. of Pennsylvania Press, 1980), pp. 285 and 272.

7 John Wheeler, *A Treatise of Commerce* (1601), ed. George B. Hotchkiss (New York: Columbia Univ. Press, 1931), pp. 6–7. This tactic should be borne in mind when we consider that in *Michaelmas Term*, the representative of the gentry, Easy, is an Everyman figure, and the merchant-citizen Quomodo is something of a devil (see Brian Gibbons, *Jacobean City Comedy* [Cambridge: Harvard Univ. Press, 1968], p. 129; also Rubi Chatterji, "Unity and Disparity in *Michaelmas Term*," *Studies in English Literature* 8 [1968], 350).

8 Edmund Bolton, *The Cities Advocate* (London, 1629).

9 Louis B. Wright, *Middle-Class Culture in Elizabethan England* (Chapel Hill: Univ. of North Carolina Press, 1935), p. 22.

10 Cressy, "Describing the Social Order of Elizabethan and Stuart England," p. 30; see also Margot Heinemann, *Puritanism and Theatre: Thomas Middleton and Opposition Drama under the Early Stuarts* (Cambridge: Cambridge Univ. Press, 1980), p. 3, and Joyce Oldham Appleby, *Economic Thought and Ideology in Seventeenth-Century England* (Princeton: Princeton Univ. Press, 1978), p. 114.

11 Richard Grassby, "Social Mobility and Business Enterprise in Seventeenth-Century England," in Donald Pennington and Keith Thomas, eds., *Puritans and Revolutionaries* (Oxford: Clarendon Press, 1978), pp. 359, 361, and 362.

12 Henry Brinklow, "Complaint," cited in R. H. Gretton, *The English Middle Class* (London: G. Bell, 1917), p. 98.

13 Robert Crowley, cited in Gretton, *English Middle Class*, p. 93. We may appreciate just how old comment about socially ambitious merchants is when we read from a sermon by Friar Bromyard, composed sometime between the late 1320s and 1390: "Merchants and moneyed men recken themselves 'ennobled' and on the road to enrichment, when they are seen to have friendships with the nobility, when they can wear their robes and are summoned to their banquets, and when they can go a-hunting with them." Three hundred years of debate was not to do away with this complaint. Sylvia L. Thrupp, *The Merchant Class of Medieval London, 1300–1500* (Chicago: Univ. of Chicago Press, 1948), p. 259.

14 *The Selected Works of Robert Crowley*, ed. J. M. Cowper (London: EETS, 1972).

15 Philip Stubbes, *The Anatomie of Abuses* (1583), L3ᵛ–L4.

16 Sylvia L. Thrupp, Intro., *An Essay of Drapery*, by William Scott (Cambridge: Harvard Univ. Printing Office, 1953), p. 1.

17 R. H. Tawney, *Religion and the Rise of Capitalism* (1926; rpt. New York: Mentor Books, 1960), p. 194.

18 C. L. Barber, *Shakespeare's Festive Comedy* (Princeton: Princeton Univ. Press, 1959), p. 257.

19 See also Appleby, *Economic Thought and Ideology in Seventeenth-Century England*, pp. 107–8.

20 *Dictionary of National Biography*, 8:1183–86.

21 Thomas Mun, *England's Treasure by Forraign Trade* (London, 1664); pages are unnumbered (all citations are from the first

chapter). See also Appleby, *Economic Thought and Ideology in Seventeenth-Century England*, pp. 37–41.

22 Thomas Nashe, *Christs Tears ouer Ierusalem* (1593), in *The Works of Thomas Nashe*, ed. R. B. McKerrow (Oxford: Basil Blackwell, 1958), 2:93–95. For a thoughtful comparison of Nashe, "the consistent upholder of the Elizabethan establishment," and Middleton, see Heinemann, *Puritanism and Theatre*, pp. 52–57.

23 Caroline M. Barron, "Richard Whittington: the Man behind the Myth," in A. E. J. Hollaender and William Kellaway, eds., *Studies in London History presented to Philip E. Jones* (London: Hodder & Stoughton, 1969), pp. 198, 204, and 221. It is worth noting that the Whittington legend dates from 1605.

24 The reader may compare my reading of *The Rich Cabinet* with that of Louis B. Wright. Wright describes Gainsford as an unequivocally staunch "believer in the virtues of mercantile ideals." "Although he disarms criticism by taking cognizance of some of the conventional faults of merchants, he hastens to offset these faults with greater virtues." I would argue that Gainsford hastens to offset citizen virtues with reminders of their faults. See Wright, *Middle-Class Culture in Elizabethan England*, pp. 31–32.

25 Thomas Gainsford, *The Rich Cabinet* (1616); facsimile rpt. in *The English Experience*, no. 458 (New York: Da Capo Press, 1972), sig. 89^{r-v}. Here and in the following citations from this pamphlet, the emphasis is my own.

26 Thrupp, *Merchant Class of Medieval London*, p. 293.

27 Lawrence Stone, "Social Mobility in England, 1500–1700," *Past & Present*, 33 (1966), 27.

28 Erving Goffman, *The Presentation of Self in Everyday Life* (New York: Doubleday Anchor Books, 1958), p. 36.

29 Lawrence Stone, *The Crisis of the Aristocracy, 1558–1641* (Oxford: Oxford Univ. Press, 1965), p. 63; Charles Wilson, *England's Apprenticeship, 1603–1763* (New York: St. Martin's Press, 1965), pp. 18–19. J. H. Hexter, while denying the category of a Renaissance "middle class," has argued that the Tudor merchants reinforced the hierarchy model; see *Reappraisals in History: New Views on History and Society in Early Modern Europe*, 2d ed. (Chicago: Univ. of Chicago Press, 1979), pp. 95 and 114.

30 Stone, *Crisis of the Aristocracy*, p. 157; "Social Mobility in England," p. 33.
31 Wilson, *England's Apprenticeship*, p. 51.
32 Stone, "Social Mobility in England," p. 31.
33 Ibid., p. 23.
34 Wilson, *England's Apprenticeship*, p. 38
35 Tawney, *Discourse upon Usury*, p. 31.
36 Lang, "London's Aldermen in Business," p. 259.
37 *SPD* Eliz. 75, #54, cited in Tawney, *Discourse upon Usury*, p. 123.
38 Tawney, *Discourse upon Usury*, pp. 115 and 155–61.
39 Lang, "London's Aldermen in Business, pp. 261–62.
40 Stone, *Crisis of the Aristocracy*, p. 532.
41 Sir Thomas Culpepper, *A Tract against Usury* (1621); cited in Stone, *Crisis of the Aristocracy*, p. 532.
42 Lang, "London's Aldermen in Business," p. 247. John Stow was content to point out that "Sir *Baptist* kept his Shop, after he was knighted; which was looked upon as some Disparagement to him . . ." (*A Survey of London*, 1603 ed., ed. Charles L. Kingsford [Oxford, 1908], 2: 486).
43 Stone, *Crisis of the Aristocracy*, pp. 534–35.
44 Ibid., p. 533.
45 Ibid., p. 538.
46 Supple, *Commercial Crisis and Change in England*, pp. 23 and 28.
47 Stow, *Survey of London*, cited in Lewis Mumford, *The City in History* (New York: Harcourt, Brace & World, 1961), p. 117. Mumford's remarks are pertinent: "only in a city can a full cast of characters for the human drama be assembled: hence only in the city is there sufficient diversity and competition to enliven the plot and bring the performers up to the highest pitch of skilled, *intensely conscious* participation" (p. 116, my emphasis). It is only fair to compare Stow's London with Robert Crowley's:

> . . . this is a Citye in name, but, in dede,
> It is a packe of people that seke after meede;
>
> . . . .
> But for the wealth of the commons not one taketh pain.
> And Hell with out order,
> I may it well call

Where every man is for him selfe,
And no manne for all.
                Selected Works of Robert Crowley, p. 132.
48 Thomas Milles, cited in L. C. Knights, *Drama and Society in the Age of Jonson* (1936; rpt. London: George W. Stewart, 1951), p. 138.

Chapter 3

1 See Ann Jennalie Cook, *The Privileged Playgoers of Shakespeare's London, 1576–1642* (Princeton, N.J.: Princeton Univ. Press, 1981), pp. 142, 16, and passim. Michael Shapiro (*Children of the Revels: The Boy Companies of Shakespeare's Time and Their Plays* [New York: Columbia Univ. Press, 1977]) makes the sensible suggestion that "the private-theater audience was made up of actual, potential, or *self-styled* figures of power and responsibility" (p. 68, my emphasis). The discussion concerning the audience and repertory of the Elizabethan and Jacobean companies is extensive. The reader may consult William Armstrong, "The Audience of the Elizabethan Private Theatre," *Review of English Studies*, n.s. 10 (1959), 243–49; J. Leeds Barroll et al., *The Revels History of Drama in English*, Vol. 3: 1576–1613 (London: Methuen, 1975); M. C. Bradbrook, *The Living Monument: Shakespeare and the Theatre of His Time* (Cambridge: Cambridge Univ. Press, 1976); Philip J. Finkelpearl, *John Marston of the Middle Temple: An Elizabethan Dramatist in His Social Setting* (Cambridge: Harvard Univ. Press, 1969); Alfred Harbage, *Shakespeare and the Rival Traditions* (1952; rpt. New York: Barnes & Noble, 1968) and *Shakespeare's Audience* (New York: Columbia Univ. Press, 1961); as well as E. K. Chambers (*The Elizabethan Stage* [1923; rpt. Oxford: Clarendon Press, 1951]) and G. E. Bentley (*The Jacobean and Caroline Stage* [Oxford: Clarendon Press, 1968]), and the many prologues, inductions, and epilogues cited by these writers.
2 George R. Price, *Thomas Dekker* (New York: Twayne, 1969), p. 173; and David J. Lake, *The Canon of Thomas Middleton's Plays* (Cambridge: Cambridge Univ. Press, 1975), p. 47 (Lake is in agreement with Chambers [*Elizabethan Stage*]). Citations from *Westward Ho* and *Northward Ho* are from *The Dramatic Works of Thomas Dekker*, ed. Fredson Bowers (Cambridge: Cambridge Univ. Press, 1955), Vol. 2.

3 Susan Wells, "Jacobean City Comedy and the Ideology of the City," *English Literary History*, 48 (1981), pp. 42–43.
4 Harbage, *Shakespeare and the Rival Traditions*, p. 97; see also pp. 108–12.
5 Thomas Dekker, *The Gull's Horn-Book*, in *Thomas Dekker*, ed. E. D. Pendry (London: Edward Arnold, 1967), p. 98. In a prefatory note to the 1609 quarto of *Troilus and Cressida*, we read, "were but the vaine names of commedies changde for the titles of Commodities, or of Playes for Pleas," they would be sought for "the maine grace of their gravities." Arthur Kirsch notes that Middleton's satirical commentators are "stage directors . . . who help create and control the response to their respective plays." *Jacobean Dramatic Perspectives* (Charlottesville: Univ. Press of Virginia, 1972), p. 81.
6 Clifford Leech, "Three Times *Ho* and a Brace of Widows: Some Plays for the Private Theater," in David Galloway, ed., *The Elizabethan Theatre III* (Hamden, Ct.: Shoestring Press, 1973), p. 18.
7 Brian Gibbons (*Jacobean City Comedy* [Cambridge: Harvard Univ. Press, 1968], p. 138) is of the contrary opinion; he sees a "symmetry of design" and "sure control" in plotting in *Northward Ho*.
8 Alexander Leggatt, *Citizen Comedy in the Age of Shakespeare* (Toronto: Univ. of Toronto Press, 1973), pp. 133–34.
9 I rely on Lake's (*Canon of Middleton's Plays*) dating, one which Levin, it would seem, agrees with. Harbage and Schoenbaum (*Annals of English Drama, 975–1700* [London: Methuen, 1964]) and the *Revels History*, place *Michaelmas Term* in 1606. My citations are from Levin's edition (Lincoln: Univ. of Nebraska Press, 1966).
10 George E. Rowe, Jr., *Thomas Middleton and the New Comedy Tradition* (Lincoln: Univ. of Nebraska Press, 1979), p. 64.
11 In her unpublished paper "Quomodo, Sir Giles, and Triangular Desire: Social Aspiration in Middleton and Massinger," Gail Kern Paster notes that Middleton would have us "regard critically" the socially determined conventionality of his characters. Paster concludes that "Middleton refuses to allow us comfortably to identify with anyone in his play" (pp. 7 and 23).
12 Harbage and Schoenbaum (*Annals of English Drama*) date both plays between 1604 and 1607; Lake (*Canon of Middleton's Plays*) dates them between 1605 and 1606; the *Revels History*

dates *A Trick* to 1605, *A Mad World* to 1606. *A Trick* seems to have been performed at Blackfriars soon after it was presented at the song school. My citations are from Standish Henning's edition of *A Mad World, My Masters* (Lincoln: Univ. of Nebraska Press, 1965) and George R. Price's edition of *A Trick to Catch the Old One* (The Hague: Mouton, 1976).

13 See Charles A. Hallett, "Penitent Brothel, the Succubus and Parsons' *Resolution:* A Reappraisal of Penitent's Position in Middleton's Canon" *Studies in Philology,* 69 (1972), 72–86; Arthur Marotti, "Middleton's Mature Drama, 1611–1623," Diss. Johns Hopkins Univ. 1965, p. 65; and Rowe, *Thomas Middleton and the New Comedy Tradition,* pp. 110–14.

14 Cited in Jeffrey L. Sammons, *Literary Sociology and Practical Criticism* (Bloomington: Indiana Univ. Press, 1977), p. 112.

15 G. J. Watson, Intro., *A Trick to Catch the Old One* (London: Ernest Benn, 1968), p. xi.

16 M. L. Wine (*The Dutch Courtesan* [Lincoln: Univ. of Nebraska Press, 1965]) favors Chambers' dating (1603–4)—see p. xii. Finkelpearl (*John Marston of the Middle Temple*), following Anthony Caputi (*John Marston, Satirist* [Ithaca, N.Y.: Cornell Univ. Press, 1961]), makes a strong case for 1605 (see pp. 196–97). Citations are from Wine's edition.

17 Wine, *Dutch Courtesan,* p. xx.

18 Brian Gibbons (*Jacobean City Comedy,* p. 155), Clifford Leech ("Three Times *Ho* and a Brace of Widows"), Alexander Leggatt (*Citizen Comedy in the Age of Shakespeare,* pp. 47–53), and R. W. Van Fossen (the editor of the Revels edition: Manchester and Baltimore: Manchester Univ. Press and Johns Hopkins Univ. Press, 1979) all call our attention to the parodic nature of *Eastward Ho.* None of them sees this as an instance of what other city comedies were already doing and would continue to do. All citations from *Eastward Ho* are from Van Fossen's edition.

19 Leggatt, *Citizen Comedy in the Age of Shakespeare,* pp. 51 and 52.

20 Cf. M. C. Bradbrook's definition of city comedy: "first, the artificial plotting, with symmetrically grouped characters, based on the old learned moral play as modified by Jonson's theory of social humours: second, the vigorous and direct recording of the London scene, its language, habits and sometimes its features: third, the constant rousing of the spectator's judgement by lit-

erary parody, comment and discussion." *The Growth and Structure of Elizabethan Comedy* (London: Chatto & Windus, 1955), p. 141.

21 Francis Beaumont, *The Knight of the Burning Pestle*, ed. Michael Hattaway (N.Y.: W. W. Norton, 1981). Citations are from this edition.

22 Ronald F. Miller, "Dramatic Form and Dramatic Imagination in Beaumont's *The Knight of the Burning Pestle*," *English Literary Renaissance*, 8 (1978), 67–84; and Hattaway, Intro., *Knight of the Burning Pestle*, pp. xi–xii. Miller's brilliant interpretation of this play has greatly influenced my reading of it.

23 Lake (*Canon of Middleton's Plays*) has argued that Middleton's original version, probably written for the Paul's boys, dates from 1602–3. He believes that Dekker tampered with it in 1605 and that Barry had a hand in the 1607 version—the one we have today (pp. 91–108). My citations are from *The Works of Thomas Middleton*, ed. A. H. Bullen (1885; rpt. New York: AMS Press, 1964), Vol. 3.

24 Most scholars accept the 1609 date given on the title page in the folio of 1616, but the Children of the Chapel were not called the Queen's Revels until 4 January 1610. See Edward Partridge, ed., *Epicoene* (New Haven: Yale Univ. Press, 1971), pp. 199–200.

25 Margot Heinemann, *Puritanism and Theatre: Thomas Middleton and Opposition Drama under the Early Stuarts* (Cambridge: Cambridge Univ. Press, 1980), pp. 82–83. In his book *The Family of Love* (Cambridge: James Clarke, 1981), Alastair Hamilton comments on the mercantile character of Family sectaries.

26 See Arthur Marotti, "The Purgations of Middleton's *The Family of Love*," *Papers on Language and Literature*, 7 (1971), pp. 80–84.

27 Lording Barry, *Ram Alley or Merrie-Trickes*, ed. Claude E. Jones (Louvain: Librairie Universitaire, 1952).

28 Alfred Harbage, *Shakespeare and the Rival Traditions*, pp. 77 and 277.

29 Prince Henry's Men were using the Fortune in 1604. Peter Ure ("Patient Madman and Honest Whore: The Middleton-Dekker Oxymoron," *Essays and Studies*, n.s. 19 [1966], p. 19) also presumes that the play was staged at this theater. Citations from *I* and *II Honest Whore* are from the Bowers edition, Vol. 2.

30 Chambers, *Elizabethan Stage*, 2:435.

31 Bentley, *Jacobean and Caroline Stage*, 6:146–48.

32 Price (*Thomas Dekker*, p. 30) and Ure ("Patient Madman and Honest Whore," p. 164) believe that Middleton was responsible for Candido in *I Honest Whore.*

33 Lake (*Canon of Middleton Plays*, p. 53) and R. C. Bald ("The Chronology of Middleton's Plays," *Modern Language Review*, 32 [1937], 37–39) date the play 1607–8. A more convincing argument has been made for late April or early May 1611. See P. A. Mulholland, "The Date of *The Roaring Girl*," *Review of English Studies*, 28 (1977), 18–31. All citations are from the Bowers edition, vol. 3.

34 Peter Laslett, *The World We Have Lost* (New York: Charles Scribner's Sons, 1965), p. 3.

35 The play was first produced in 1613, by Lady Elizabeth's Men, at the Swan. As R. B. Parker notes, Middleton may have "designed the play originally for the Queen's Revels and handed it over to Lady Elizabeth's Men only when the two companies amalgamated in March 1613" (Intro., *A Chaste Maid in Cheapside* [London: Methuen, 1969], p. lxi). All citations are from Parker's edition. For issues concerning the dating of the play, see Bald, "Chronology of Middleton's Plays."

36 Several readers have discussed the problematic families in this play. See Ruby Chatterji, "Theme, Imagery and Unity in *A Chaste Maid in Cheapside*," *Renaissance Drama*, 8 (1965), 106–16; Parker, *Chaste Maid in Cheapside*, pp. l–li; and Samuel Schoenbaum, "*A Chaste Maid in Cheapside* and Middleton's City Comedy," in J. W. Bennett et al., eds, *Studies in the English Renaissance Drama . . . in Memory of Karl J. Holzknecht* (New York: New York Univ. Press, 1959), pp. 292–93.

37 Chatterji, "Theme, Imagery and Unity in *A Chaste Maid in Cheapside*," p. 125.

38 Parker, *Chaste Maid in Cheapside*, p. 87.

39 Richard Levin, *The Multiple Plot in English Renaissance Drama* (Chicago: Univ. of Chicago Press, 1971), p. 200.

40 Leggatt, *Citizen Comedy in the Age of Shakespeare*, p. 140.

41 Don Graham, "Situation Esthetics: Impermanent Art and the Seventies Audience," *Artforum*, 18 (1980), 25.

Chapter 4

1 F. P. Wilson, *The Plague in Shakespeare's England* (Oxford: Oxford Univ. Press, 1927), p. 215; Alfred Harbage, *Shakespeare's*

Audience (New York: Columbia Univ. Press, 1961), pp. 39–41; and Lawrence Stone, *The Crisis of the Aristocracy, 1558–1641* (Oxford: Oxford Univ. Press, 1965), p. 386.

2 Ann Jennalie Cook, *The Privileged Playgoers in Shakespeare's London, 1576–1642* (Princeton: Princeton Univ. Press, 1981), p. 93.

3 Stone, *Crisis of the Aristocracy*, p. 185.

4 Ruth Kelso, *The Doctrine of the English Gentleman in the Sixteenth Century*, University of Illinois Studies in Language and Literature, no. 14 (Urbana: Univ. of Illinois Press, 1929), p. 29.

5 Richard Brathwait, "To the Knowing Reader," in *The English Gentleman* (London, 1630).

6 F. J. Fisher, "The Development of London as a Centre of Conspicuous Consumption in the 16th and 17th Centuries," *Transactions of the Royal Historical Society*, 4th Series, 30 (1948), 37–50.

7 Thomas Wright, *The Passions of the Minde* (London, 1604), sig. A4^v.

8 Fisher, "Development of London as a Centre of Conspicuous Consumption in the 16th and 17th Centuries," p. 37.

9 Cited in ibid., p. 46.

10 Cited in G. E. Mingay, *The Gentry* (London: Longman, 1976), p. 2.

11 Brathwait, *English Gentleman*, pp. 451–52.

12 Henry Peacham, *The Complete Gentleman* (London, 1634) in *The Complete Gentleman, The Truth of Our Times, and The Art of Living in London*, ed. Virgil B. Heltzel (Ithaca: Cornell Univ. Press, 1962), p. 144.

13 Peacham, *Complete Gentleman*, p. 12.

14 James Cleland, *Pro-Paideia; or, The Institution of a Young Noble Man* (Oxford, 1607), sigs. A^v–A2.

15 Cleland, *Pro-Paideia*, sig. B1^v.

16 Stephen J. Greenblatt, *Sir Walter Ralegh: The Renaissance Man and his Roles* (New Haven: Yale Univ. Press, 1973), p. 23.

17 Jonas A. Barish, "Exhibitionism and the Antitheatrical Prejudice," *English Literary History*, 36 (1969), 11.

18 Brathwait, *English Gentleman*, p. 305.

19 Peacham, *Complete Gentleman*, p. 144.

20 Brathwait, *English Gentleman*, p. 454.

21 The full epigram is cited in Greenblatt's *Sir Walter Ralegh*, p. 26.

22 Thomas Dekker, *The Gull's Horn-Book*, in Thomas Dekker, ed. E. D. Pendry (London: Edward Arnold, 1967), p. 89.

23 Mingay, *Gentry*, pp. 15–16.

24 Ibid., pp. 40–44.

25 Lawrence Stone, "Social Mobility in England, 1500–1700," *Past & Present*, 33 (1966), 26; Mingay, *Gentry*, p. 45.

26 Mingay, *Gentry*, p. 48.

27 Thomas Middleton, *No Wit, No Help like a Woman's*, ed. Lowell E. Johnson (Lincoln: Univ. of Nebraska Press, 1976), 2.2.182–89. The date of composition is not easily determined—Johnson makes a plausible case for 1611.

28 Gabriele Bernhard Jackson, "Structural Interplay in Ben Jonson's Drama," in Alvin Kernan, ed., *Two Renaissance Mythmakers: Christopher Marlowe and Ben Jonson* (Baltimore, Md.: Johns Hopkins Univ. Press, 1977). We may substitute self or identity for Jackson's "reality." Compare Elizabeth Burns: "Perhaps there seems to the observer to be nothing left [after all roles are subtracted], but to the individual sanity may depend on the belief in this residual reality against which all his false selves and false actions can be tested." See *Theatricality: A Study of Convention in the Theatre and in Social Life* (London: Longman, 1972), pp. 17–18.

29 Alexander Leggatt, *Citizen Comedy in the Age of Shakespeare* (Toronto: Univ. of Toronto Press, 1973), p. 133.

30 George E. Rowe, Jr., discusses prodigal sons in and out of *Michaelmas Term* in *Thomas Middleton and the New Comedy Tradition* (Lincoln: Univ. of Nebraska Press, 1979), Chap. 3.

31 Richard Levin, *The Multiple Plot in English Renaissance Drama*, (Chicago: Univ of Chicago Press, 1971), p. 182.

32 George R. Price, ed. *A Trick to Catch the Old One* (The Hague: Mouton, 1976), p. 215.

33 All quotations are taken from the AMS Press (New York, 1964) reprint of A. H. Bullen's *The Works of Thomas Middleton*, Vol. 3. Harbage and Schoenbaum (*Annals of English Drama, 975–1700* [London: Methuen, 1964]) list the play under 1605, but set limits between 1604 and 1607. Lake (*The Canon of Thomas Middleton's Plays* [Cambridge: Cambridge Univ. Press, 1975]) argues for 1605–7 (p. 20).

34 On Middleton's association of gallantry with roguery, see C. Lee Colegrove, *A Critical Edition of Thomas Middleton's Your Five Gallants* (New York: Garland, 1979), pp. 26–27.

35 Cf. Philip J. Finkelpearl, *John Marston of the Middle Temple* (Cambridge: Harvard Univ. Press, 1969), p. 198.

36 For this distinction, see Lawrence Danson, "Jonsonian Comedy and the Discovery of the Social Self," *PMLA*, 99 (1974).

37 Cf. ibid.: "Jonson disallows the possibility for a stable self to emerge" (p. 189).

38 All quotations from *Every Man in His Humor* are drawn from Gabriele Bernhard Jackson's edition of the play (New Haven: Yale Univ. Press, 1969). Jackson (pp. 221–39) indicates that she is least taken with the possibility that Jonson revised *Every Man in His Humor* in 1604; she favors 1607–8 or 1612–13, but admits to considerable uncertainty. Revision during any of these years would have been influenced by the many city comedies on the boards during the decade spanning 1603–13.

39 Danson, "Jonsonian Comedy and the Discovery of the Social Self," p. 190.

40 *The Puritan* (1606), in *The Shakespeare Apocrypha*, ed. C. F. Tucker Brooke (Oxford: Clarendon Press, 1918), 219–48.

41 Tucker Brooke, Intro., *Shakespeare Apocrypha*, pp. xxxi–xxxii, argues inconclusively that Marston wrote *The Puritan*. In both this play and *The Dutch Courtesan*, the gentry are endorsed, citizens are bested, and city Puritans are gulled. Wilbur D. Dunkel, in "The Authorship of *The Puritan*," *PMLA*, 45 (1930), 804–8, and Marilyn L. Williamson, in "Middleton's Workmanship and the Authorship of *The Puritan*," *Notes & Queries*, 202 (1957), 50–51, argue without much force for Middleton.

42 A 1607 entry in the Stationer's Register notes that the play was "lately acted" by the King's Revels, a company that began its performances in 1607. It remains possible that an earlier version of this play was performed, perhaps by the Paul's boys (cf. Lake, *Canon of Middleton's Plays*, p. 91 ff.).

43 See Arthur Marotti, "The Purgations of Thomas Middleton's *The Family of Love*," *Papers on Language and Literature*, 7 (1971), 82.

44 Anthony Covatta, *Thomas Middleton's City Comedies* (Lewisburg, Pa.: Bucknell Univ. Press, 1973), pp. 59–60.

45 Ben Jonson, *Epicoene*, ed. Edward Partridge (New Haven: Yale Univ. Press, 1971). All citations are drawn from this excellent edition.

46 W. David Kay, "Jonson's Urbane Gallants: Humanistic Contexts for *Epicoene*," *Huntington Library Quarterly*, 39 (1976), 255.

47 Jonas Barish, *Ben Jonson and the Language of Prose Comedy* (1960; rpt. New York: W. W. Norton, 1970), pp. 145–86.

48 Kay, "Jonson's Urbane Gallants," p. 258.

49 Michael Shapiro, *Children of the Revels: The Boy Companies of Shakespeare's Time and Their Plays* (New York: Columbia Univ. Press, 1977), pp. 86–88.

50 Cited in Kay, "Jonson's Urbane Gallants," p. 258.

51 Barish, *Ben Jonson and the Language of Prose Comedy*, pp. 156–57.

52 Shapiro, *Children of the Revels*, pp. 83 and 50.

53 Barish, *Ben Jonson and the Language of Prose Comedy*, p. 152; Partridge, *Epicoene*, p. 5; and L. G. Salingar, "Farce and Fashion in *The Silent Woman*," *Essays & Studies*, 20 (1967), 38. My emphasis in each citation.

54 Ben Jonson, *Timber: or, Discoveries*, in *Ben Jonson*, ed. C. H. Herford and Percy and Evelyn Simpson (Oxford: Clarendon Press, 1947), 8:586.

55 "To the memory of my beloved The AVTHOR Mr. William Shakespeare: And what he hath left vs," l. 59. See *Ben Jonson*, 8:390–92.

56 All citations are from Alvin B. Kernan's edition of *The Alchemist* (New Haven: Yale Univ. Press, 1974).

57 William Hazlitt, *The Complete Works*, ed. P. P. Howe (London, 1931), 6: 235.

58 Cf. Charles Barber, in his Introduction to *A Chaste Maid in Cheapside* (Fountainwell Drama Texts; Berkeley: Univ. of California Press, 1969): "What is striking in our play is that the gentry and the citizens are so much alike" (p. 3). All citations are from R. B. Parker's edition (London: Methuen, 1969), as in the previous chapter.

59 See Parker, ed., Introduction, *A Chaste Maid in Cheapside* (London: Methuen, 1969), pp. lvi–lix.

60 *A Woman's a Weather-cocke*, 4.1.69, in *The Plays of Nathan Field*, ed. William Perry (Austin: Univ. of Texas Press, 1950).

Chapter 5

1 Ester Sowernam (pseud.) *Ester hath hang'd Haman* (1617), sig. B2ᵛ; *The Winter's Tale*, 1.2.91–92 (Arden Edition, ed. J. H. P. Pafford [1963; rpt. London: Methuen, 1971]).

2 Joseph Swetnam, *The Araignment of Lewde, idle, froward, and*

vnconstant women . . . (London, 1615), sig. A4; Sir Thomas Overbury, *The Overburian Characters*, ed. W. J. Paylor, (Oxford: Basil Blackwell, 1936), pp. 4–5; Nicholas Breton, *The Good and the Badde* (1616), "A Wanton Woman," pp. 27–28; and Thomas Gainsford, *The Rich Cabinet* (London, 1616), p. 162.

3 Sixteenth-century adage and Frederick, duke of Wirtemberg, quoted in Violet A. Wilson, *Society Women in Shakespeare's Time* (London, 1924), p. 7; Constantia Munda, *The Worming of a Woman* (1617), p.3.

4 Roger Thompson, *Women in Stuart England and America* (London: Routledge & Kegan Paul, 1974), p. 8.

5 Ruth Kelso, *Doctrine for the Lady of the Renaissance* (1956; rpt. Urbana: Univ. of Illinois Press, 1978), p. 18.

6 Louis B. Wright, *Middle-Class Culture in Elizabethan England* (Chapel Hill: Univ. of North Carolina Press, 1935), p. 506.

7 James Turner Johnson, *A Society Ordained by God: English Puritan Marriage in the First Half of the Seventeenth Century* (Nashville: Abingdon Press, 1970), passim; and William and Mallewille Haller, "The Puritan Art of Love," *Huntington Library Quarterly*, 5 (1942), 235–72. For a persuasive, revisionary argument, see Kathleen M. Davies, "The Sacred Condition of Equality—How Original Were Puritan Doctrines of Marriage?" *Social History*, 5 (1977), 563–80.

8 Alice Clark, *Working Life of Women in the Seventeenth Century* (London, 1919; rpt. New York: A. M. Kelley, 1968), pp. 286, 290, and 301.

9 Linda T. Fitz [Woodbridge], "'What Says the Married Woman?': Marriage Theory and Feminism in the English Renaissance," *Mosaic*, 13 (1980), 18; Linda Woodbridge, *Women and the English Renaissance: Literature and the Nature of Womankind, 1540–1620* (Urbana: Univ. of Illinois Press, 1984), p. 326.

10 Katherine M. Rogers ("Forward," in the 1978 reprint of Kelso, *Doctrine for the Lady of the Renaissance*, pp. viii–ix) argues that Renaissance women were thought of as "fillers of various functions rather than as independent human beings . . . the lady existed primarily in relationship to others, each of whom defined her in terms of his own requirements." Juliet Dusinberre writes that "In late Elizabethan drama the struggle for women is to be human in a world which declares them only female." *Shakespeare and the Nature of Women* (New York: Harper & Row, 1975), p. 93. See also Sherry B. Ortner and Harriet White-

head's Introduction to *Sexual Meanings: The Cultural Construction of Gender and Sexuality* (Cambridge: Cambridge Univ. Press, 1981), p. 8.

11 James A. Brundage, "Prostitution in the Medieval Canon Law," *Signs*, 1 (1976), passim.

12 D. G. Berger and M. G. Wenger, "The Ideology of Virginity," *Journal of Marriage and the Family*, 35 (1973), 667.

13 Robert Greene, *Works*, ed. Alexander B. Grosart (London, 1881–83), 7:258.

14 Swetnam, *Araignment of Lewde, idle, froward and vnconstant women*, sig. A2ᵛ.

15 *The Court of good Counsell*, sig. D4ᵛ, quoted in Carroll Camden, *The Elizbethan Woman* (1952; rpt. New York: Paul P. Appel, 1975), p. 130.

16 Thompson, *Women in Stuart England and America*, p. 22.

17 Swetnam, *Araignment of Lewde, idle, froward and vnconstant women*, sig. C4.

18 Nicholas Breton, *The Praise of vertuous Ladies* (1599), pp. 12–13.

19 Sowernam, *Ester hath hang'd Haman*, sig. A4.

20 John Marston, "Fabulae Argumentum," *The Dutch Courtesan*.

21 Gainsford, *Rich Cabinet*, p. 165.

22 Richard Brathwait, *A Strappado of the Diuell* (London, 1615), p. 151.

23 Brundage, "Prostitution in the Medieval Canon Law," p. 835.

24 Ibid., pp. 841–43. See also Anne M. Haselkorn, *Prostitution in Elizabethan and Jacobean Comedy* (New York: Whitston, 1983), pp. 144–46.

25 Caroline Cherry, *The Most Unvaluedst Purchase: Women in the Plays of Thomas Middleton*, Salzburg Studies in English Literature (Salzburg: Universität Salzburg, 1973), p. 30.

26 Overbury, *Overburian Characters*, p. 29.

27 Ibid., p. 28.

28 See, for example, the works cited in note 7, above.

29 Johnson, *Society Ordained by God*, p. 93.

30 William Heale, *An Apologie for Women* (1609), p. 11.

31 William Whately, *A Bride-Bush* (1619), sig. A3.

32 Cf. Fitz, "'What Says the Married Woman?,'" p. 6: "The Woman who wanted to eat had little choice but marriage."

33 Davies, "Sacred Condition of Equality," p. 567.

34 Haller, "Puritan Art of Love," p. 250.

35 Davies, "Sacred Condition of Equality," p. 572.
36 Cited in Thompson, *Women in Stuart England and America*, p. 117.
37 Haller, "Puritan Art of Love," pp. 253 ff.
38 Whately, *Bride-Bush*, sig. Bb3.
39 Cited in Camden, *Elizabethan Woman*, p. 82.
40 Linda Woodbridge's chapter "The Gossips' Meeting" includes an examination of several not entirely successful satirical portraits of independent women. *Women and the English Renaissance*, pp. 224–43. Much of Part 2 and Part 3 discusses the threat to men posed by women who rejected the role of "obedient wife."
41 Overbury, *Overburian Characters*, p. 70.
42 Ibid., p. 71.
43 Robert Brustein, "The Monstrous Regiment of Women," in G. R. Hibbard, ed., *Renaissance and Modern Essays* (New York: Barnes & Noble, 1966), p. 40.
44 Cf. Linda Woodbridge, who notes that widows who remarried were said to be guilty of "posthumous cuckoldry." Woodbridge also writes of men's concern that their widows will waste their wealth on young men (*Women and the English Renaissance*, pp. 177–78). Lisa Jardine also calls attention to the threat posed by unbalanced relations between widows and young spouses; but Jardine goes on to insist that this is actually a very small threat to social order. Lisa Jardine, *Still Harping on Daughters: Women and Drama in the Age of Shakespeare* (Sussex: Harvester Press, 1983), pp. 128–30.
45 John Taylor, *A Iuniper Lecture* (London, 1639), Epigram III, p. 233.
46 Cited in Lawrence Stone, *The Family, Sex and Marriage in England, 1500–1800* (New York: Harper & Row, 1977), p. 610.
47 Woodbridge, *Women and the English Renaissance*, pp. 139–44.
48 Ibid., p. 327.
49 Alfred Harbage, *Shakespeare and the Rival Traditions* (1952; rpt. New York: Barnes & Noble, 1968), pp. 71 and 86.
50 Ibid., p. 101.
51 Cf. ibid., p. 283: "Among the coterie dramatists, only Jonson and Chapman give evidence of any political thinking at all."
52 I stress the social and economic aspects because the wives do: Mistress Openwork insults the gallants, refers to the women as "we shop-keepers," and concludes on a note of citizen pride

("Oh if it were the good Lords wil, there were a law made, no Cittizen should trust any of 'em all"—4.2.57–58).

53 Historical background pertinent to Mary Frith may be found in A. H. Bullen (*The Works of Thomas Middleton* [1885; rpt. New York: AMS Press, 1964], 4:3–5) and Margaret Dowling, "A note on Moll Cutpurse—'The Roaring Girl,'" *Review of English Studies*, 10 (1934), 67–71. Most of Bullen's information is based on the 1662 pamphlet *The Life and Death of Mrs. Mary Frith, Commonly called Mal Cutpurse*. For a recently published reading of this play, see Mary Beth Rose, "Women in Men's Clothing: Apparel and Social Stability in *The Roaring Girl*," *English Literary Renaissance*, 14 (1984), 367–91. Rose's reading agrees with my own; she stresses Moll's "ambiguous, marginal, and problematic . . . social identity" (p. 390).

54 Cherry, *Most Unvaluedst Purchase*, p. 102.

55 Andor Gomme, Introduction, *The Roaring Girl* (New York: W. W. Norton, 1976), p. xxiii.

56 Cherry, *Most Unvaluedst Purchase*, p. 105.

57 Celeste T. Wright presents a survey of Elizabethan Amazons in "The Amazons in Elizabethan Literature," *Studies in Philology*, 37 (1940), 433–56.

58 Cherry, *Most Unvaluedst Purchase*, p. 105.

59 All citations from *The Woman's Prize* are drawn from George B. Ferguson's edition (The Hague: Mouton, 1966). The play was first performed in 1611; the auspices are unknown.

60 Cf. Alexander Leggatt, *Citizen Comedy in the Age of Shakespeare* (Toronto: Univ. of Toronto Press, 1973), p. 94.

61 Thomas Middleton, *No Wit, No Help like a Woman's*, ed. Lowell E. Johnson (Lincoln: Univ. of Nebraska Press, 1976). All citations are drawn from this edition.

62 See, for example, Richard Levin, Intro., *Michaelmas Term* (Lincoln: Univ. of Nebraska Press, 1966), p. xviii.

63 Tony Tanner has commented on the relationship between puns and adultery: "puns and ambiguities are to common language what adultery and perversion are to 'chaste' (i.e. socially orthodox) sexual relations. They both bring together entities (meanings/people) that have 'conventionally' been differentiated and kept apart; and they bring them together in deviant ways, bypassing the orthodox rules governing communications and relationships." *Adultery and the Novel* (Baltimore: Johns Hopkins Univ. Press, 1979), p. 53.

64 R. W. Van Fossen, Intro., *Eastward Ho* (Baltimore: Johns Hopkins Univ. Press, 1979), p. 37; Richard Levin, *The Multiple Plot in English Renaissance Drama* (Chicago: Univ. of Chicago Press, 1971), p. 89; "while it [the Security/Winifred plot] can scarcely be claimed as a norm for the play, it does provide a very familiar and unambiguous base."

65 Una Ellis-Fermor, quoted in Leggatt (*Citizen Comedy in the Age of Shakespeare*), and Leggatt himself, p. 115.

66 Michael Scott discusses Marston's contradictory worlds based on Montaigne and realism, Neoplatonism and romance, in *John Marston's Plays* (New York: Barnes & Noble, 1978), pp. 38–47; see especially p. 45.

67 Cf. R. W. Ingram, *John Marston* (Boston: Twayne, 1978), p. 120.

68 Scott, *John Marston's Plays,* cites this passage from *The Essayes;* see p. 39. Freud follows upon Montaigne when he draws the connection between degradation of the sexual object and masculine desire. See "The Most Prevalent Form of Degradation in Erotic Life," trans. Joan Riviere, in *Sexuality and the Psychology of Love,* ed. Philip Rieff (New York: Collier Books, 1963).

69 All citations are from William Perry's edition, *The Plays of Nathan Field* (Austin: Univ. of Texas Press, 1950). The play dates from 1611, and was performed under the auspices of the Queen's Revels at the Whitefriars theater (see Perry, p. 144). It is interesting to note that Field played female parts.

70 George E. Rowe, Jr., *Thomas Middleton and the New Comedy Tradition* (Lincoln: Univ. of Nebraska Press, 1979), p. 129.

71 Cf. Renu Juneja, "The Widow as Paradox and Paradigm in Middleton's Plays," *Journal of General Education,* 34 (1982), 17: Middleton's "comprehension of social realities sustains [his] portraits [of widows] and forces the audience to question its assumptions about the traditional vices and virtues attributed to women."

Bibliography

Primary Sources

Barry, Lording. *Ram Alley; or, Merrie-Trickes.* Ed. Claude E. Jones. Louvain: Librairie Universitaire, 1952.

Beaumont, Francis. *The Knight of the Burning Pestle.* Ed. Michael Hattaway. New York: W. W. Norton, 1981.

Bolton, Edmund. *The Cities Advocate.* London, 1629.

Botero, Giovanni. *A Treatise, Concerning the Causes of the Magnificencie and Greatnes of Cities.* Trans. Robert Peterson. London, 1606.

Brathwait, Richard. *The English Gentleman.* London, 1630.

Brathwait, Richard. *A Strappado of the diuell.* London, 1615.

Breton, Nicholas. *The Good and the Badde . . .* London, 1616. Rpt. London: Longman, Hurst, Rees, Orme, and Brown, 1815. Vol 1.

Breton, Nicholas. *The Praise of vertuous Ladies.* London, 1599.

Browne, John. *The Marchants Avizo.* London, 1589.

Cleaver, Robert. *A Godlie Forme of Household Government.* London, 1598.

Cleland, James. *Pro-Paideia; or, The Institution of a Young Noble Man.* Oxford, 1607.

Crowley, Robert. *The Selected Works of Robert Crowley.* Ed. J. M. Cowper. London: EETS, 1972.

Dekker, Thomas. *The Dramatic Works of Thomas Dekker.* Ed. Fredson Bowers. Cambridge: Cambridge Univ. Press, 1955 and 1958. Vols. 2 and 3.

Field, Nathan. *The Plays of Nathan Field.* Ed. William Perry. Austin: Univ. of Texas Press, 1950.

Fletcher, John. *The Woman's Prize; or, The Tamer Tamed.* Ed. George B. Ferguson. The Hague: Mouton, 1966.

Gainsford, Thomas. *The Rich Cabinet* (1616). Facsimile rpt. in *The*

English Experience, no. 458. New York: Da Capo Press, 1972.

Greene, Robert. *Works.* Ed. Alexander B. Grosart. London, 1881–83. Vol. 7.

Heale, William. *An Apologie for Women.* London, 1609.

Heywood, Thomas. *If You Know Not Me, You Know Nobody.* Ed. Madeleine Doran. Malone Society Reprints. Oxford: Oxford Univ. Press, 1934–35.

Hobbes, Thomas. *Leviathan.* London: J. M. Dent, 1914.

Jonson, Ben. *The Alchemist.* Ed. Alvin Kernan. New Haven: Yale Univ. Press, 1974.

Jonson, Ben. *Ben Jonson.* Ed. C. H. Herford and Percy and Evelyn Simpson. Oxford: Clarendon Press, 1925–52.

Jonson, Ben. *Epicoene.* Ed. Edward Partridge. New Haven: Yale Univ. Press, 1971.

Jonson, Ben. *Every Man in His Humor.* Ed. G. B. Jackson. New Haven: Yale Univ. Press, 1969.

Marston, John. *The Dutch Courtesan.* Ed. M. L. Wine. Lincoln: Univ. of Nebraska Press, 1965.

Middleton, Thomas. *A Chaste Maid in Cheapside.* Ed. R. B. Parker. London: Methuen, 1969.

Middleton, Thomas. *A Mad World, My Masters.* Ed. Standish Henning. Lincoln: Univ. of Nebraska Press, 1965.

Middleton, Thomas. *Michaelmas Term.* Ed. Richard Levin. Lincoln: Univ. of Nebraska Press, 1966.

Middleton, Thomas. *A Trick to Catch the Old One.* Ed. George R. Price. The Hague: Mouton, 1976.

Middleton, Thomas. *No Wit, No Help like a Woman's.* Ed. Lowell E. Johnson. Lincoln: Univ. of Nebraska Press, 1976.

Middleton, Thomas. *The Works of Thomas Middleton.* Ed. A. H. Bullen. 1885. Rpt. New York: AMS Press, 1964. Vols. 4 and 7.

Mun, Thomas. *England's Treasure by Forraign Trade.* C. 1630. Rpt. London, 1664.

Munda, Constantia [pseud.]. *The Worming of a Woman.* London, 1617.

Nashe, Thomas. *Christs Tears ouer Ierusalem.* 1593. In *The Works of Thomas Nashe.* Ed. R. B. McKerrow. Oxford: Basil Blackwell, 1958. Vol. 2.

Overbury, Sir Thomas. *The Overburian Characters.* Ed. W. J. Paylor. Oxford: Blackwell, 1936.

Peacham, Henry. *The Complete Gentleman.* 1634. In *The Complete Gentleman, The Truth of Our Times, and The Art of Living*

Bibliography

in London. Ed. Virgil B. Heltzel. Ithaca: Cornell Univ. Press, 1962.

The Puritan. In *The Shakespeare Apocrypha*. Ed. C. F. Tucker Brooke. Oxford: Clarendon Press, 1918.

Scott, William. *An Essay of Drapery*. Ed. Sylvia L. Thrupp. Cambridge: Harvard Univ. Printing Office, 1953.

Sowernam, Ester [pseud.]. *Ester hath hang'd Haman*. London, 1617.

Stubbes, Philip. *The Anatomie of Abuses*. London, 1583.

Swetnam, Joseph. *The Araignment of Lewde, idle, froward, and vnconstant women* . . . London, 1615.

Taylor, John. *A Iuniper Lecture*. London, 1639.

Whately, William. *A Bride-Bush* . . . London, 1619.

Wheeler, John. *A Treatise of Commerce*. 1601. Ed. George B. Hotchkiss. New York: Columbia Univ. Press, 1931.

Wilson, Thomas. *A Discourse upon Usury*. Ed. R. H. Tawney. New York: Harcourt, Brace, n.d.

Winwood Memorials. Ed. Edmund Sawyer. London: T. Ward, 1925. Vol 2.

Wright, Thomas. *The Passions of the Minde*. London, 1604.

Secondary Sources

Appleby, Joyce Oldham. *Economic Thought and Ideology in Seventeenth-Century England*. Princeton: Princeton Univ. Press, 1978.

Armstrong, William. "The Audience of the Elizabethan Private Theatre." *Review of English Studies*, n.s. 10 (1959), 243–49.

Ashton, Robert. *The City and the Court, 1603–1643*. Cambridge: Cambridge Univ. Press, 1979.

Bald, R. C. "The Chronology of Middleton's Plays." *Modern Language Review*, 32 (1937), 33–43.

Bald, R. C. "Middleton's Civic Employments." *Modern Philology*, 31 (1933–34), 65–78.

Barber, C. L. *Shakespeare's Festive Comedy*. Princeton: Princeton Univ. Press, 1959.

Barish, Jonas A. *Ben Jonson and the Language of Prose Comedy*. 1960. Rpt. New York: W. W. Norton, 1970.

Barish, Jonas A. "Exhibitionism and the Antitheatrical Prejudice." *English Literary History*, 36 (1969), 1–29.

Bibliography

Barroll, J. Leeds, et al. *The Revels History of Drama in English.* Vol. 3: 1576–1613. London: Methuen, 1975.

Barron, Caroline M. "Richard Whittington: The Man behind the Myth." In *Studies in London History Presented to Philip E. Jones.* Ed. A. E. J. Hollaender and William Kellaway. London: Hodder & Stoughton, 1969. Pp. 197–248.

Barton, Anne. "London Comedy and the Ethos of the City." *London Journal,* 4 (1978), 158–80.

Beier, A. L. "Vagrants and the Social Order in Elizabethan England." *Past & Present,* 64 (1974), 3–29.

Belsey, Catherine. *Critical Practice.* London: Methuen, 1980.

Bentley, G. E. *The Jacobean and Caroline Stage.* Oxford: Clarendon Press, 1968. Vol. 6.

Berger, D. G., and M. G. Wenger. "The Ideology of Virginity." *Journal of Marriage and the Family,* 35 (1973), 666–76.

Berger, Harry, Jr. "Text against Performance in Shakespeare: The Example of *Macbeth.*" In *The Power of Forms in the English Renaissance.* Ed. Stephen Greenblatt. Norman: Pilgrim Books, 1982. Pp. 49–79.

Berger, Peter L., and Thomas Luckmann. *The Social Construction of Reality.* New York: Doubleday, 1966.

Bergeron, David. *English Civic Pageantry, 1558–1642.* Columbia: Univ. of South Carolina Press, 1971.

Bevington, David. *Tudor Drama and Politics: A Critical Approach to Topical Meaning.* Cambridge: Harvard Univ. Press, 1968.

Bradbrook, M. C. *The Growth and Structure of Elizabethan Comedy.* London: Chatto & Windus, 1955.

Bradbrook, M. C. *The Living Monument: Shakespeare and the Theatre of His Time.* Cambridge: Cambridge Univ. Press, 1976.

Brundage, James. "Prostitution in the Medieval Canon Law." *Signs,* 1 (1976), 825–45.

Brustein, Robert. "The Monstrous Regiment of Women." In *Renaissance and Modern Essays.* Ed. G. R. Hibbard. New York: Barnes & Noble, 1966. Pp. 35–50.

Burke, Kenneth. *Attitudes toward History.* Boston: Beacon Press, 1961.

Burns, Elizabeth. *Theatricality: A Study of Convention in the Theater and in Social Life.* London: Longman, 1972.

Calendar of State Papers and Manuscripts . . . of Venice. Ed. Horatio Brown. London: Her Majesty's Stationery Office, 1900. Vol. 15.

Bibliography

Camden, Carroll. *The Elizabethan Woman.* 1952. Rpt. New York: Paul P. Appel, 1975.

Caputi, Anthony. *John Marston, Satirist.* Ithaca: Cornell Univ. Press, 1961.

Chambers, E. K. *The Elizabethan Stage.* 1923. Rpt. Oxford: Clarendon Press, 1951. Vol. 2.

Chambers, E. K. *The Medieval Stage.* Oxford: Oxford Univ. Press, 1903. Vol. 2.

Champion, Larry S. "From Melodrama to Comedy: A Study of the Dramatic Perspective in Dekker's *The Honest Whore, Parts I and II.*" *Studies in Philology,* 69 (1972), 192–209.

Chatterji, Ruby. "Theme, Imagery and Unity in *A Chaste Maid in Cheapside.*" *Renaissance Drama,* 8 (1965), 106–16.

Chatterji, Ruby. "Unity and Disparity in *Michaelmas Term.*" *Studies in English Literature,* 8 (1968), 349–63.

Cherry, Caroline. *The Most Unvaluedst Purchase: Women in the Plays of Thomas Middleton.* Salzburg Studies in English Literature. Salzburg, Austria: Universität Salzburg, 1973.

Clark, Alice. *Working Life of Women in the Seventeenth Century.* London, 1919. Rpt. New York: A. M. Kelley, 1968.

Cook, Ann Jennalie. *The Privileged Playgoers of Shakespeare's London, 1576–1642.* Princeton: Princeton Univ. Press, 1981.

Cope, Jackson I. "*Bartholomew Fair* as Blasphemy." *Renaissance Drama,* 8 (1965), 127–52.

Covatta, Anthony. *Thomas Middleton's City Comedies.* Lewisburg, Pa.: Bucknell Univ. Press, 1973.

Danson, Lawrence. "Jonsonian Comedy and the Discovery of the Social Self." *PMLA,* 99 (1984), 179–93.

Davies, Kathleen. "The Sacred Condition of Equality—How Original Were Puritan Doctrines of Marriage?" *Social History,* 5 (1977), 563–80.

Donaldson, Ian, ed. *Ben Jonson: Poems.* Oxford: Oxford Univ. Press, 1975.

Doran, Madeleine. *Endeavors of Art: A Study of Form in Elizabethan Drama.* Madison: Univ. of Wisconsin Press, 1964.

Dowling, Margaret. "A Note on Moll Cutpurse—'The Roaring Girl.'" *Review of English Studies,* 10 (1934), 67–71.

Dusinberre, Juliet. *Shakespeare and the Nature of Women.* New York: Harper & Row, 1975.

Eliot, T. S. *Selected Essays.* London: Faber & Faber, 1944.

Bibliography

Fairholt, Frederick W. *Lord Mayors' Pageants*. London: Percy Society, 1843–44.

Finkelpearl, Philip J. *John Marston of the Middle Temple: An Elizabethan Dramatist in His Social Setting*. Cambridge: Harvard Univ. Press, 1969.

Fisher, F. J. "The Development of London as a Centre of Conspicuous Consumption in the 16th and 17th Centuries." *Transactions of the Royal Historical Society*, 4th Series, 30 (1948), 37–50.

Fisher, F. J. "Some Experiments in Company Organization in the Early Seventeenth Century." *Economic History Review*, 4 (1932), 177–94.

Fitz, Linda T. "'What Says the Married Woman?': Marriage Theory and Feminism in the English Renaissance." *Mosaic*, 13 (1980), 1–22.

Foster, Frank Freeman. "Merchants and Bureaucrats in Elizabethan London." *Guildhall Miscellany*, 4 (1972), 149–60.

Foster, Frank Freeman. *The Politics of Stability: A Portrait of the Rulers of Elizabethan London*. London: Royal Historical Society, 1977.

Gibbons, Brian. *Jacobean City Comedy: A Study of Satiric Plays by Jonson, Marston and Middleton*. Cambridge: Harvard Univ. Press, 1968.

Goffman, Erving. *The Presentation of Self in Everyday Life*. New York: Doubleday Anchor, 1959.

Gomme, Andor. Introduction. *The Roaring Girl*. New York: W. W. Norton, 1976.

Gomme, Sir Laurence. *London*. Philadelphia: J. B. Lippincott, 1914.

Graham, Don. "Situation Esthetics: Impermanent Art and the Seventies Audience." *Artforum*, 18 (1980), 24–26.

Grassby, Richard. "The Personal Wealth of the Business Community in Seventeenth-Century England." *Economic History Review*, 2d Series, 23 (1970), 220–34.

Grassby, Richard. "Social Mobility and Business Enterprise in Seventeenth-century England." In *Puritans and Revolutionaries: Essays in Seventeenth-Century History Presented to Christopher Hill*. Ed. Donald Pennington and Keith Thomas. Oxford: Clarendon Press, 1978.

Greenblatt, Stephen J. *Sir Walter Ralegh: The Renaissance Man and His Roles*. New Haven: Yale Univ. Press, 1973.

Haller, William and Mallewille. "The Puritan Art of Love." *Huntington Library Quarterly*, 5 (1942), 235–72.

Hallett, Charles A. "Penitent Brothel, the Succubus and Parsons' *Resolution*: A Reappraisal of Penitent's Position in Middleton's Canon." *Studies in Philology*, 69 (1972), 72–86.

Hamilton, Alastair. *The Family of Love*. Cambridge: James Clarke, 1981.

Harbage, Alfred. *Annals of English Drama, 975–1700*. Revised by S. Schoenbaum. London: Methuen, 1964.

Harbage, Alfred. *Shakespeare and the Rival Traditions*. 1952. Rpt. New York: Barnes & Noble, 1968.

Harbage, Alfred. *Shakespeare's Audience*. New York: Columbia Univ. Press, 1961.

Haselkorn, Anne M. *Prostitution in Elizabethan and Jacobean Comedy*. New York: Whitston, 1983.

Hazlitt, William. *The Complete Works*. Ed. P. P. Howe. London, 1931. Vol. 6.

Heinemann, Margot. *Puritanism and Theatre: Thomas Middleton and Opposition Drama under the Early Stuarts*. Cambridge: Cambridge Univ. Press, 1980.

Hentzner, Paul. *Travels in England during the Reign of Queen Elizabeth*. Trans. Horace Walpole. London, 1797.

Hexter, J. H. *Reappraisals in History*. 2d ed. Chicago: Univ. of Chicago Press, 1979.

Horwich, Richard. "Wives, Courtesans, and the Economics of Love in Jacobean City Comedy." *Comparative Drama*, 7 (1973), 291–309.

Ingram, R. W. *John Marston*. Boston: Twayne, 1978.

Jackson, Gabriele B. "Structural Interplay in Ben Jonson's Drama." In *Two Renaissance Mythmakers: Christopher Marlowe and Ben Jonson*. Ed. Alvin Kernan. Baltimore: Johns Hopkins Univ. Press, 1977. Pp. 113–45.

Jacquot, Jean. "Le répertoire des compagnes d'enfants à Londres, 1600–1610." In *Dramaturgie et société, XVIᶜ et XVIIᶜ siècles*. Ed. Jean Jacquot. Paris: Editions du Centre National de la Recherche Scientifique, 1968. 2:729–82.

James, Mervyn. *Family, Lineage, and Civil Society*. Oxford: Clarendon Press, 1974.

Jardine, Lisa. *Still Harping on Daughters: Women and Drama in the Age of Shakespeare*. Sussex: Harvester Press, 1983.

Johnson, James Turner. *A Society Ordained by God: English Puri-*

tan Marriage in the First Half of the Seventeenth Century. Nashville: Abingdon Press, 1970.

Johnson, Paula. "Jacobean Ephemera and the Immortal World." *Renaissance Drama,* 8 (1977), 151–71.

Jones-Davies, Marie-Thérèse. "La glorification de Londres, ou les triomphes de Troia-Nova." In *Les cités au temps de la Renaissance.* Ed. M. T. Jones-Davies. Paris: Université de Paris-Sorbonne, 1977. Pp. 77–101.

Jordon, W. K. *The Charities of London, 1480–1660.* London: George Allen & Unwin, 1960.

Juneja, Renu. "The Widow as Paradox and Paradigm in Middleton's Plays." *Journal of General Education,* 34 (1982), 3–19.

Kay, W. David. "Jonson's Urbane Gallants: Humanistic Contexts for *Epicoene.*" *Huntington Library Quarterly,* 39 (1976), 251–66.

Kelso, Ruth. *Doctrine for the Lady of the Renaissance.* 1956. Rpt. Urbana: Univ. of Illinois Press, 1978.

Kelso, Ruth. *The Doctrine of the English Gentleman in the Sixteenth Century.* University of Illinois Studies in Language and Literature, no. 14. Urbana: Univ. of Illinois Press, 1929.

Kipling, Gordan. "Triumphal Drama: Form in English Civic Pageantry." *Renaissance Drama,* 8 (1977), 37–56.

Kirsch, Arthur. *Jacobean Dramatic Perspectives.* Charlottesville: Univ. Press of Virginia, 1972.

Knights, L. C. *Drama and Society in the Age of Jonson.* 1936. Rpt. London: George W. Stewart, 1951.

Lake, David J. *The Canon of Thomas Middleton's Plays.* Cambridge: Cambridge Univ. Press, 1975.

Lang, R. G. "London's Aldermen in Business, 1600–1625." *Guildhall Miscellany,* 3 (1971), 242–64.

Lang, R. G. "Social Origins and Social Aspirations of Jacobean London Merchants." *Economic History Review,* 2d Ser. 27 (1974), 28–47.

Laslett, Peter. *The World We Have Lost.* New York: Charles Scribner's Sons, 1965.

Leech, Clifford. "Three Times *Ho* and a Brace of Widows: Some Plays for the Private Theater." In *The Elizabethan Theatre III.* Ed. David Galloway. Hamden, Ct.: Shoestring Press, 1973. Pp. 14–32.

Leggatt, Alexander. *Citizen Comedy in the Age of Shakespeare.* Toronto: Univ. of Toronto Press, 1973.

Levin, Richard. *The Multiple Plot in English Renaissance Drama.* Chicago: Univ. of Chicago Press, 1971.

Levin, Richard. *New Readings vs. Old Plays: Recent Trends in the Reinterpretation of English Renaissance Drama.* Chicago: Univ. of Chicago Press, 1979.

Mack, Maynard. "The Jacobean Shakespeare: Some Observations on the Construction of the Tragedies." In *Jacobean Theatre.* Ed. John Russell Brown and Bernard Harris. Stratford-upon-Avon Studies, I. New York: St. Martin's Press, 1960. Pp. 11–41.

McVeagh, John. *Tradefull Merchants: The Portrayal of the Capitalist in Literature.* London: Routledge & Kegan Paul, 1981.

Manheim, Michael. "The Thematic Structure of Dekker's 2 *Honest Whore.*" *Studies in English Literature,* 5 (1965), 363–81.

Marotti, Arthur. "Middleton's Mature Drama, 1611–1623." Diss. Johns Hopkins Univ. 1965.

Marotti, Arthur. "The Purgations of Middleton's *The Family of Love.*" *Papers on Language and Literature,* 7 (1971), 80–84.

Meredith, George. *An Essay on Comedy.* In *Comedy.* Ed. Wylie Sypher. Baltimore: Johns Hopkins Univ. Press, 1980.

Miller, Ronald F. "Dramatic Form and Dramatic Imagination in Beaumont's *The Knight of the Burning Pestle.*" *English Literary Renaissance,* 8 (1978), 67–84.

Mingay, G. E. *The Gentry.* London: Longman, 1976.

Montrose, Louis A. "The Purpose of Playing: Reflections on a Shakespearean Anthropology." *Helios,* n.s. 7 (1979–80), 51–74.

Mulholland, P. A. "The Date of *The Roaring Girl.*" *Review of English Studies,* 28 (1977), 18–31.

Mumford, Lewis. *The City in History.* New York: Harcourt, Brace & World, 1961.

Notestein, Wallace. "The English Woman, 1580–1650." In *Studies in Social History.* Ed. J. H. Plumb. London: Longman, Green, 1955. Pp. 69–107.

O'Connell, Laura Stevenson. "The Elizabethan Bourgeois Hero-Tale: Aspects of an Adolescent Social Consciousness." In *After the Reformation: Essays in Honor of J. H. Hexter.* Ed. Barbara C. Malament. Philadelphia: Univ. of Pennsylvania Press, 1980.

Parker, R. B. Introduction. *A Chaste Maid in Cheapside,* by Thomas Middleton. London: Methuen, 1969.

Parker, R. B. "Middleton's Experiments with Comedy and Judgement." In *Jacobean Theatre.* Ed. John Russell Brown and Bernard

Harris. Stratford-upon-Avon Studies, I. New York: St. Martin's Press, 1960. Pp. 179–99.

Pearl, Valerie. *London and the Outbreak of the Puritan Revolution: City Government and National Politics, 1625–43.* London: Oxford Univ. Press, 1961.

Pocock, J. G. A. *The Machiavellian Moment: Florentine Political Thought and the Atlantic Republican Tradition.* Princeton: Princeton Univ. Press, 1975.

Price, George R. *Thomas Dekker.* New York: Twayne, 1969.

Rowe, George E., Jr. *Thomas Middleton and the New Comedy Tradition.* Lincoln: Univ. of Nebraska Press, 1979.

Rye, William B. *England as Seen by Foreigners in the Days of Elizabeth and James the First.* 1865. Rpt. London: Benjamin Bloom, 1967.

Salingar, L. G. "Farce and Fashion in *The Silent Woman*." *Essays & Studies,* 20 (1967), 29–46.

Sammons, Jeffrey L. *Literary Sociology and Practical Criticism.* Bloomington: Indiana Univ. Press, 1977.

Schoenbaum, Samuel. "*A Chaste Maid in Cheapside* and Middleton's City Comedy." In *Studies in the English Renaissance Drama . . . in Memory of Karl J. Holzknecht.* Ed. J. W. Bennett et al. New York: New York Univ. Press, 1959. Pp. 287–309.

Scott, Michael. *John Marston's Plays.* New York: Barnes & Noble, 1978.

Shapiro, Michael. *Children of the Revels: The Boy Companies of Shakespeare's Time and Their Plays.* New York: Columbia Univ. Press, 1977.

Simmel, George. "On the Theory of Theatrical Performance." Trans. Tom Burns. In *Sociology of Literature and Drama.* Ed. Elizabeth and Tom Burns. Baltimore: Penguin Books, 1973. Pp. 304–10.

Slights, William W. E. "The Trickster Hero and Middleton's *A Mad World, My Masters*." *Comparative Drama,* 3 (1969), 87–98.

Spivack, Charlotte. "Bedlam and Bridewell: Ironic Design in *The Honest Whore*." *Komos,* 3 (1973), 107–16.

Stone, Lawrence. *The Crisis of the Aristocracy, 1558–1641.* Oxford: Oxford University Press, 1965.

Stone, Lawrence. *The Family, Sex and Marriage in England, 1500–1800.* New York: Harper and Row, 1977.

Stone, Lawrence. "Social Mobility in England, 1500–1700." *Past & Present,* 33 (1966), 16–55.

Stone, Lawrence, and Jeanne C. Fawtier. *An Open Elite? England, 1540–1880.* Oxford: Clarendon Press, 1984.

Supple, B. E. *Commercial Crisis and Change in England, 1600–1642.* Cambridge: Cambridge Univ. Press. 1959.

Tanner, Tony. *Adultery and the Novel.* Baltimore: Johns Hopkins Univ. Press, 1979.

Tawney, R. H. *Religion and the Rise of Capitalism.* 1926. Rpt. New York: Mentor Books, 1960.

Thompson, Roger. *Women in Stuart England and America.* London and Boston: Routledge & Kegan Paul, 1974.

Thrupp, Sylvia L. *The Merchant Class of Medieval London, 1300–1500.* Chicago: Univ. of Chicago Press, 1948.

Unwin, George. *Industrial Organization in the Sixteenth and Seventeenth Centuries.* Oxford: Clarendon Press, 1904.

Ure, Peter. "Patient Madman and Honest Whore: The Middleton-Dekker Oxymoron." *Essays & Studies,* n.s. 19 (1966), 18–40.

Van Fossen, R. W. Introduction. *Eastward Ho,* by Chapman, Jonson, and Marston. Manchester and Baltimore: Manchester Univ. Press and Johns Hopkins Univ. Press, 1979.

Waage, Frederick O. *Thomas Dekker's Pamphlets, 1603–1609, and Jacobean Popular Literature.* Salzburg Studies in English Literature. Salzburg, Austria: Universität Salzburg, 1977.

Waith, E. M. "The Comic Mirror and the World of Glass." *Research Opportunities in Renaissance Drama,* 9 (1966), 16–23.

Watson, G. J. Introduction. *A Trick to Catch the Old One,* by Thomas Middleton. London: Ernest Benn, 1968.

Weimann, Robert. *Shakespeare and the Popular Tradition in the Theater.* Baltimore: Johns Hopkins Univ. Press, 1978.

Weimann, Robert. *Structure and Society in Literary History.* Charlottesville: Univ. Press of Virginia, 1976.

Wells, Susan. "Jacobean City Comedy and the Ideology of the City." *English Literary History,* 48 (1981), 37–60.

Wickham, Glynne. *Early English Stages, 1300–1600.* New York: Columbia Univ. Press, 1963. Vol. 2.

Wiener, Carol Z. "Sex Roles and Crime in Late Elizabethan Hertfordshire." *Journal of Social History,* 8 (1975), 38–60.

Williams, Clare, ed. *Thomas Platter's Travels in England, 1589.* London: Jonathan Cape, 1937.

Williams, Sheila. "The Lord Mayor's Show in Tudor and Stuart Times." *Guildhall Miscellany,* 1 (1959), 3–18.

Williams, Sheila. "Two Seventeenth Century Semi-Dramatic Allegories of Truth the Daughter of Time." *Guildhall Miscellany*, 2 (1963), 207–20.

Wilson, Charles. *England's Apprenticeship, 1603–1763.* New York: St. Martin's Press, 1965.

Wilson, F. P. *The Plague in Shakespeare's London.* Oxford: Oxford Univ. Press, 1927.

Wilson, Violet A. *Society Women in Shakespeare's Time.* London, 1924.

Woodbridge, Linda. *Women and the English Renaissance: Literature and the Nature of Womankind, 1540–1620.* Urbana: Univ. of Illinois Press, 1984.

Wright, Celeste T. "The Amazons in Elizabethan Literature." *Studies in Philology*, 37 (1940), 433–56.

Wright, Louis Booker. *Middle-Class Culture in Elizabethan England.* Chapel Hill: Univ. of North Carolina Press, 1935.

Zagorin, Perez. *The Court and the Country: The Beginnings of the English Revolution.* London: Routledge & Kegan Paul, 1969.

Index

Index

Foster, Frank Freeman, 17
Freud, Sigmund, 218n68
Frith, Moll, 73, 142, 157, 217n53

Gainsford, Thomas, 36–37, 86, 151
Geertz, Hildred, 199n23
Gibbons, Brian, 17–18, 19
Goffman, Erving, 13
Gosson, Stephen, 19
Gouge, William, 144, 145
Grassby, Richard, 21
Gulling, 52–53, 57

Haller, William, and Mallewille
  Haller, 145
Harbage, Alfred, 69–70, 130
Haughton, William, 7–8
Hazlitt, William, 132
Heale, William, 144
Heinemann, Margot, 19, 68
Henslowe, Philip, 143
Hexter, J. H., 17, 203n29
Heywood, Thomas: *If You Know
  Not Me, You Know Nobody*, Part
  II, 200n4
Hicks, Sir Baptist, 41–42
Hobbes, Thomas, 12–13
Hoskyns, John, 10

Jackson, G. B., 91, 212n38
Jardine, Lisa, 216n44
Jonson, Ben, 16, 83, 130. *See also*
  Chapman, George, Ben Jonson,
  and John Marston
—*The Alchemist*, 11, 44, 128–30
—*Bartholomew Fair*, 9
—*Discoveries*, 11
—*Epicoene*, 9, 45, 67, 68, 74, 118,
  121, 124–28
—*Every Man In His Humor*, 115–
  19
—*Volpone*, 11
Juneja, Renu, 218n71

Kay, W. David, 125

Kelso, Ruth, 82, 85, 138, 140–41,
  145, 147, 150
King, Gregory, 22
Kirsch, Arthur, 206n5
Knights, L. C., 15–16, 17, 19

Lang, R. G., 17, 41–42
Laslett, Peter, 74
Leggatt, Alexander, 18–19, 63, 79
Levin, Richard, 5–6, 78
The London Prodigal, 8
Lord Mayors: shows of, 26, 37;
  country born, 39

Marston, John: *The Dutch Courtesan*, 9, 33, 61–63, 110–13, 178–
  80, 187–90; *The Phoenix*, 58. *See
  also* Chapman, George, Ben Jonson, and John Marston
Meredith, George, 199n24
Middleton, Thomas, 16, 19, 46,
  129. *See also* Dekker, Thomas,
  and Thomas Middleton
—*A Chaste Maid in Cheapside*, 35,
  44, 55, 67, 76–79, 131, 133–36,
  139, 168–69, 187
—*The Family of Love*, 58, 67–68,
  121–23, 169–70
—*A Mad World, My Masters*, 9,
  56–59, 103–7, 132, 139, 174–75
—*Michaelmas Term*, 7, 9, 23, 24,
  35, 48, 51–56, 99–103, 123, 139,
  164–65, 171
—*No Wit, No Help like a Woman's*, 89, 162–64, 184–86
—*A Trick to Catch the Old One*,
  38, 56, 59–61, 68, 91, 103, 107–9,
  124, 134, 139, 174, 187
—*Your Five Gallants*, 9, 61, 109–
  10, 187
Milles, Thomas, 43
Montaigne, Michel de, 111, 179
Montrose, Louis Adrian, 14
Mumford, Lewis, 204n47
Mun, Thomas, 34–35

Index

COMPOSED BY GRAPHIC COMPOSITION, INC., ATHENS GEORGIA
MANUFACTURED BY THOMSON-SHORE, INC., DEXTER, MICHIGAN
TEXT AND DISPLAY LINES ARE SET IN TRUMP MEDIAEVAL

Library of Congress Cataloging-in-Publication Data
Leinwand, Theodore B.
The city staged.
Bibliography: pp. 219–230.
Includes index.
1. English drama—17th century—History and criticism.
2. English drama (Comedy)—History and criticism.
3. City and town life in literature. 4. Theater and
society—Great Britain. 5. Theater—Great Britain—
History—17th century. I. Title. II. Title: Jacobean
comedy, 1603–1613.
PR658.C6L44   1986   822'.0523'09355   86–1683
ISBN 0-299-10670-5